W9-BYA-579

Spanish Comedies
and
Historical Contexts
in the 1620s

PENN STATE STUDIES
in ROMANCE LITERATURES

Editors
Frederick A. de Armas
Alan E. Knight

Refiguring the Hero:
From Peasant to Noble in Lope de Vega and Calderón
by Dian Fox

Don Juan and the Point of Honor:
Seduction, Patriarchal Society, and Literary Tradition
by James Mandrell

Narratives of Desire:
Nineteenth-Century Spanish Fiction by Women
by Lou Charnon-Deutsch

Garcilaso de la Vega and the Italian Renaissance
by Daniel L. Heiple

Allegories of Kingship:
Calderón and the Anti-Machiavellian Tradition
by Stephen Rupp

Acts of Fiction:
Resistance and Resolution from Sade to Baudelaire
by Scott Carpenter

Grotesque Purgatory:
A Study of Cervantes's *Don Quixote*, Part II
by Henry W. Sullivan

Spanish Comedies and Historical Contexts in the 1620s
by William R. Blue

Spanish Comedies
and
Historical Contexts
in the 1620s

William R. Blue

The Pennsylvania State University Press
University Park, Pennsylvania

Publication of this book has been aided by a grant from the Program for Cultural Cooperation Between Spain's Ministry of Culture and United States' Universities.

Library of Congress Cataloging-in-Publication Data

Blue, William R.
    Spanish comedies and historical contexts in the 1620s / William R. Blue.

        p.   cm. — (Penn State studies in Romance literatures)
    Includes bibliographical references and index.
    ISBN 0-271-01546-2 (alk. paper)
    1. Spanish drama—Classical period, 1500–1700—History and criticism.   2. Spanish drama (Comedy)—Themes, motives.
    3. Literature and society—Spain.   4. Madrid (Spain)—Social life and customs.   I. Title.   II. Series.
    PQ6105.B59   1996
    862'.052309—dc20   95-31053
                                                                                  CIP

Copyright © 1996 The Pennsylvania State University
All rights reserved
Printed in the United States of America
Published by The Pennsylvania State University Press,
University Park, PA 16802-1003

It is the policy of The Pennsylvania State University Press to use acid-free paper for the first printing of all clothbound books. Publications on uncoated stock satisfy the minimum requirements of American National Standard for Information Sciences—Permanence of Paper for Printed Library Materials, ANSI Z39.48-1992.

Contents

Preface

This study grew from a series of seminars that I gave at the University of Kansas from 1990 to 1993. The seminars, in turn and in part, attempted to address my growing disatisfaction with the theories I had been reading and using, particularly deconstruction and its crumbling of meaning into balanced positive and negative bits, one cancelling the other in a frustrating game wherein, as Terry Eagleton (1983) puts it, "the winner is the one who has managed to get rid of all his cards and sit with empty hands" (147).[1] I was sure that the comedies meant something to somebody, though not necessarily the same thing to everyone. I felt that the comedies were grounded in their "historical" context, in contexts that the local audience could grasp immediately. As I began to read plays by decade, it seemed to me that the comedies written in the 1620s were different from those done in the 1630s or 1640s and beyond, even though the basic comic situations did not change all that much from one decade to the next. After all, if a character hides where he or she should not be and then makes his or her escape in the nick of time or in the flimsiest of

---

1. I pick on deconstruction here but I could have just as easily cited speech-act theory with its ahistorical generalities or reader response criticism with its hubris. That is not to say, however, that I did not learn new and often exciting ways of looking at texts from those theories and others, because I did. The seminars were not intended to trash these theories but rather to follow them as far as we could and then to look at the plays from other angles.

disguises leaving the irate guardian flabbergasted and fuming, any audience will laugh with relief. The differences seemed more contextual and tonal than anything.

A comedy can be appreciated on many levels. A reader or viewer need not ever have heard of Lacan or Derrida, need not be a specialist in reception theory or New Historicism nor even a specialist in Golden Age *comedia* to enjoy the comedies included in this study. I have been to the Chamizal Festival often enough to know that the mixed audience there has little difficulty understanding the plays' basic set-up, knowing when to hold their breath, knowing when to laugh, or recognizing a good performance when they see it. In Madrid, I attended a performance of Alarcón's *La verdad sospechosa* with some friends who were not academics and who had never read Alarcón's play, but they had no trouble laughing at the right places and even carrying on a lively discussion about the play and the characters, even if they could not list the images in detail or dissertate extensively on structure.

It is not the basic comedic set-up, not the gags that fix a comedy in its period; rather its relations to the historical moment, to the cultural, social, and economic, among other, contexts. References to people, places, events, styles, usages, situations, and particular words often appear in footnotes to editions and have been used to help establish dates for plays. In several comedies from the 1620s, we can find mentioned Mantua, the duke of Feria, the Spanish victory in Cadiz, the Seville flood of 1626, and the 1628 deflationary measures that, were they to appear in works from the 1630s or 1640s, would be anachronistic or potentially meaningless. But that is not so strange. Since the fundamental gags and situations, comedy's tried and true devices, are constant, an author needs to make the situations and characters "real" and meaningful for the audience. One of the ways to encourage a relation between the audience and the character is to have the character talk about what the audience might be talking about, mention people, places, styles, whatever.

It might sound odd, but I see some parallels between Spanish Golden Age comedy and U.S. television sitcoms. Both are part of "popular culture" intended for mass, mixed audiences; both feature stock characters, situations, and gags. Sitcoms offer a new show each week, and a week was about an average run for a *comedia*. Both strive to capture the audience's imagination, get them to relate to the characters as they set up a conflictive situation and resolve it comically. Both contextualize, and both reflect the decade in which they were written.

In the 1970s in *All in the Family,* Archie was working-class, conservative, Mike a college student, liberal. In a recent rerun, Mike appeared with long, greasy-looking hair, wearing bell-bottoms while Archie wore khaki work clothes and his plaid wool coat. The two argued about the Vietnam War, race relations, clothes and styles, and Nixon. In the 1960s in the *Dick Van Dyke Show,* Rob commuted into the city to his white-collar television writing job while Laura stayed in their suburban, middle-class tract home to care and cook for her husband and their child. Their only arguments seemed to revolve around the neighbors, Richie's friends, or whether to attend this or that party. Rob wore close-cropped, always combed hair, a thin tie, and a suit everywhere but in bed. In *Love and War,* a sitcom from a few years ago, the female lead was divorced and trying to make a go of it as the chef/part owner of a bar and restaurant. She and her new love interest not only kissed onscreen but directly addressed the audience recounting their first, hesitant attempts at lovemaking. Rob and Laura had been married for years, had a child, but slept in separate beds, Laura fully garbed in a nightgown, Rob in pajamas buttoned up to the collar. In the 1980s in a *Cheers* episode, Rebecca worried about Robin's going to jail because of his financial dealings involving leveraged buy-outs and junk bonds while Norm, an unemployed white-collar worker, sat at the bar making snide comments and drinking beer after beer. Meanwhile, Fraser, a pompous psychiatrist, looked the fool when confronted by the earthy, experienced Carla.

When I checked the dates of these and other sitcoms, I found that the good ones, the ones that held the public's attention, lasted about ten years and that they began their run near the start of the decade they would come to represent: *I Love Lucy,* 1951–60; the *Dick Van Dyke Show,* 1961–66; *All in the Family,* 1971–83; *M*A*S*H*,* 1972–83; the *Mary Tyler Moore Show,* 1970–77; *Cheers,* 1982–93. These shows seemed to capture and reproduce something essential and relevant about their time, just as did the Beatles (1962–70) in music; when the decade was over, the run ended because the contexts had changed and so had the times.

The situations the characters from the sitcoms and from the Spanish comedies get into are funny and similar because they employ time-tested gags: misunderstandings, misinterpretations, secrets, disguises, etc., but they are different from each other because they are rooted in their time. One does not have to know anything about the United States in the 1950s to enjoy *I Love Lucy.* But, if one is going to study that comedy as part of the history of U.S. television, one needs to know about the cultural, political, social, and economic contexts;

about what could be said and shown in that forum and what could
not; about styles and customs; about big band leaders and show business; about attitudes toward Latin men and North American women;[2]
about housing and family values; about the first use of multiple cam-
eras and the ins and outs of live television. And, it might be a good
idea to be familiar with Derrida, Lacan, New Historicism, reception
theory, speech-act theory, images, and structure among other inter-
pretative tools and models.

But it is precisely at the level of context that comparisons between
Spanish Golden Age comedy and U.S. sitcoms must stop. While particular references to Nixon or to Philip IV signal historical peri-
odicity, other more profound engagements are even more important.
Spanish *comedia* was written and staged in a monarchical, imperialist,
semifeudal, semimercantilist, protocapitalist, heterosexual, male-dominated, sexist, racist, socially stratified country. It may be disheartening
for some to admit that, but better to admit it than to pretend to overlay
seventeenth- and twentieth-century phenomena and suggest that they
are essentially the same.

A decade approach seemed reasonable to me, but only after I tried a
more global approach to comedy during the entire reign of Philip IV. I
soon found that I was overwhelmed by the material at hand and unable to dedicate more that a few pages to a play. I found that I was
lapsing into sweeping generalizations and moving farther and farther
away from the problems that were bothering me in the first place. A
year-by-year, play-by-play approach seemed tedious and repetitive, so
I chose what I have done here as an appropriate and manageable
measure. The period I study corresponds to the last fifteen months of
Philip III's reign (d. 31 March 1621) and the first nine years, in round
numbers, of Philip IV's. The comedies written in that period, I hope to
show, have much in common.

The study is divided into six parts. The introduction offers a brief
"topography" of comedy, setting *comedia* between two poles of secular
entertainment—royal pageant and Carnival—noting its debts to
both. In addition, I comment on moralists' attacks against theater in
general, and comedy in particular, to show where the plays stood in
some writers' opinions and to show the fears that the plays raised in
their minds. The first chapter deals with the plays' main topic: love.
After a discussion of Northrop Frye on comedy in general and of
Bruce Wardropper on Spanish comedy, I argue for a change in per-

---

2. For a fascinating look at these and other topics in *I Love Lucy* and particularly the
show's role in Cuban-American culture, see Pérez Firmat (1991; 1994).

spective moving away from the stock endings and focusing more on the paths that lead the characters there. The next three chapters deal with specific contexts: the Madrid setting, economic conditions, and legal situations. The final chapter draws on all of the foregoing to see how these matters and others affect the concept of self in the plays.

This study could not have been carried out without the help and encouragement of many colleagues and friends. I thank my students at the University of Kansas for challenging some of the ideas in this study. I express my deep gratitude to those who read and commented on parts of this study: Danny J. Anderson, John S. Brushwood, Margaret Greer, Roberta Johnson, Patricia Kenworthy, James Parr, and Robert ter Horst. Thanks also to those who talked with me face to face, in letters, or by e-mail about ideas and questions I had: Renato Barahona, Frederick de Armas, José Ruano de la Haza, Robert Spires, Henry Sullivan, and Shirley Whitaker. My appreciation goes out to those who sent me materials: Paz Bueno, Frank Casa, José del Corral, Margaret Greer, Daniel Heiple, Teresa Kirschner, Thomas Middleton, Valerie Oakey, and José Simón Díaz. Many thanks to friends and colleagues who provided a warm reception, advice, and aid during my stay in Madrid: Paz Bueno, José del Corral, Miguel Angel Coso, Luciano García Lorenzo, Juan Guerrero Roiz de la Parra, Thomas Middleton, Juan Sanz, and José Simón Díaz. My sincere thanks to Paula Malone, Pam LeRow, and Lynn Porter at the Wescoe Word Processing Center. I thank the University of Kansas for a one-month summer grant in 1992 and for a fall sabbatical in the same year. Thanks also go to the Hall Center for the Humanities for a travel grant, and I offer deep appreciation to the Program for Cultural Cooperation Between Spain's Ministry of Culture and United States' Universities for a research grant.

I thank my wife, Peggy, for all her support, questions, and critiques throughout this entire project, and thank her and my children for understanding when I had to go "up to the office."

Finally, I offer backhand, grudging thanks to the unknown S.O.B. who stole my computer and all of my backup disks when I was about halfway through this work. The wrenching theft forced me to rewrite and thus to rethink what I had done up to then. I find compensation in the thought that the final product was made better as a result.

INTRODUCTION

Public entertainment took many forms in seventeenth-century Spain but for the topological purposes I have in mind, I posit two extremes of secular celebration: the royal pageant and Carnival. The former presents for all to see, and to some degree to participate in, official society vertically arranged. Social and political structures join in such parades to objectify what many considered real and necessary. Each segment of society, each rank, has its place exquisitely mapped out in the orderly procession. The parade expresses difference, degree, and control, social, religious, and political harmony; that is to say, what is "natural" within the reigning ideology.

León Pinelo (1931a) recounts one such pageant, "Entrada que hizo en Madrid . . . la Serenísima Princesa de España, nuestra Señora Madama Isabel de Borbón" (Entrance that the Serene Princess of Spain, our Lady Madame Isabel of Bourbon made into Madrid) wherein Madrid becomes a huge stage on which Philip (IV) and Isabel are the principal actors. The procession begins:

Iban primero veinticuatro atabaleros a caballo y veinticuatro
trompetas y ministriles con la librea de la Villa; tras ellos ci-
ento cincuenta alguaciles de Villa y Corte, y las dos naciones de
las Guardias Española y Tudesca, con la librea del Rey nuestro
Señor, carmesí y amarilla en cuerpo con cadenas de oro y es-
paldas doradas, con sus Capitanes: el marqués de Camarasa, de
la Guardia Española, y el marqués de Siete Iglesias, de la
Tudesca, y sus Tenientes en medio de las guardias; y todos los
caballeros de hábito y sin él que en la corte se hallaron, que no
refiero, y quince grandes: los unos y los otros vestidos de camino con costosísimos y muy lucidos vestidos y con botas y es-
puelas; todo era bordados y gran suma de joyas y de diamantes.
Seguían luego los maceros de Su Majestad con sus mazas de
plata doradas al hombro, y detrás de ellos los Reyes de Armas,
vestidas sus cotas con las armas reales en ellas; seguían tras
ellos los mayordomos de Rey y Reina, y luego los grandes, y los
últimos el duque de Lerma y duque del Infantado; después iba
el palio, debajo del cual iba Su Alteza, rodeada de cabellerizas.
Su Alteza iba vestida a lo francesa . . . iba con mucho donaire y
garbo y muy grande alegría, rostro aguileño, hermosos ojos
mirando a todas partes con general contento del pueblo. (466)

(First came twenty-four mounted kettledrummers and twenty-
four trumpets and wind instruments dressed in the city's livery; behind them one hundred and fifty city and court bailiffs,
and the two corps of the Spanish and German Guards wearing
the King our Lord's livery, crimson and yellow with golden
chains and epaulets, with their Captains: the Marquis of Car-
marasa of the Spanish Guards, and the Marquis of Siete Iglesias of the German, and their Lieutenants in the midst of the
Guards; and [then] all the Knights of the Orders and those
without the livery that I do not specify that could be found in
the court, and fifteen grandees: all dressed in very costly trav-
eling clothes with boots and spurs; everything was embroidery
and great sums of jewels and diamonds. His Majesty's mace-
bearers followed with their gilded silver maces on their shoul-
ders, and behind them the Earl Marshals, wearing the royal
coat of arms; the King and Queen's majordomos followed them,
and then the Grandees, the last of whom were the Duke of
Lerma and the Duke of the Infantado; afterwards came the
canopy under which came Her Highness, surrounded by masters of the horse. Her Highness was dressed in the French style

. . . she went very gracefully, elegantly and joyously, an ac-
quiline face, beautiful eyes looking all around to the general
contentment of the people.)[1]

In this lineup, we see first the costumed drummers and trum-
peteers from the city announcing the celebration and the homage the
city pays to the court. There follow the representatives of local, national, and international law and control, each group dressed accord-
ingly and accompanied by, in the case of the royal guards, the nobleman, and his lieutenants, who oversee them. Then come those men
honored by king and country for services rendered, *hábitos* (livery of
particular knights' orders), and fifteen *grandes* (grandees). Again, the
narrator stresses their luxuriously appropriate costumes emblematic
of their position. Then, the king's own men with their signs of office
followed by the king and queen's majordomos and the upper levels of
the social and political structure. Next come the two most important
men in the kingdom, save the royals, the duke of Lerma and the duke
of the Infantado, their importance stressed by their proximity to Isabel. Finally, focusing on Her Majesty, the narrator emphasizes both
her dress and her reactions to what she sees as well as the positions
and reactions of the less high lining the streets who see her and her
entourage.

There is an ascending hierarchy in those who parade in order before the king and prince who watch from a window in the house of D.
Juan de Acuña, the president of Castile. All of the necessary links
between city and court, among local, national, and international,
among high, low, and in-between, the powerful and powerless are put
on display for all to see, to marvel at, to participate in. All rejoice in
the order, contagious pomp, and harmonious mutual love expressed
by the future queen and her husband toward all the citizens of Madrid, and by implication, of the nation who return her love equally.

Everyone wanted to or was required to participate in this loving
show either as marchers in the parade, as onlookers, or as decorators
along the route:

A los plateros se les mandó sacasen todo lo mejor que tuviesen,
así de joyas de oro y diamantes y otras piedras preciosas, como
de plata dorada del servicio de mesa . . . para lo cual se hicieron
aparadores en la platería, consagradas que llegaban desde el
suelo hasta los primeros balcones . . . que sólo ver la platería se

1. Unless otherwise stated, all translations are my own.

podía caminar diez leguas. De manera que desde San Jerónimo
hasta Palacio . . . tuvo bien Su Alteza en qué extender y entretener la vista, así en las ricas y vistosas colgaduras, como en
las danzas, comedias, arcos triunfales, platería, y en los balcones toda la bizarría de damas de la corte. (463–64)

(The silversmiths were ordered to get out the best they had
whether of gold, diamonds and other precious stones, as well as
the gilded silver table service . . . for which they made show-
cases set up in such a way that they reached from the ground
to the first balcony level . . . so that just to see the silverwork
one could walk for ten leagues. So, from San Jerónimo to the
Palace . . . Her Highness had a lot to look at and be charmed
by, whether the rich, showy hangings, or the dances, plays, triumphal arches, silverwork, or the balconies whereupon were
the gallant ladies of the court.)

In this mutual exhibition, royal, local, national, and international
allegory reaches its heights. Such pageantry is a political tool by
means of which any conflict, any disorder—social, economic, or political—is expunged from the supposedly harmonious and mutually reinforcing vertical organization that is the sociopolitical structure. More
specifically, in the continuing celebrations where a series of *carros*
(carts) passed before the crowd, iconographic or emblematic codes
come into play making metaphorical connections plain for all to see:

El primer carro significaba la Paz. . . . Tenía este carro en lo
alto de él la Iglesia . . . que como a su querida esposa [Cristo]
dio el primer lugar, así le tenga de las divinas paces de España
y Francia. (468)

(The first cart signified Peace. . . . At the highest point was the
Church . . . which like unto his beloved wife [Christ] gave the
first position, may thus stand the divine peace between Spain
and France.)

The couple stand in direct relation to God and Church, to Christ and
Man:

Lleva en la delantera este carro la Fama con su trompeta, en
significación de que la fama de la junta de dos coronas volará
por todo el mundo y dice la letra:

La fama de entre los dos
sube a los ojos de Dios.
(468)

(This cart carries Fame with her trumpet in the fore, signifying
that the fame of the joining of the two crowns will fly around
the world, and the writing says:

The fame between these two
will rise up to God's eyes.)

Philip and Isabel participate in the here and now in the orderly nature of the parade but they participate as well as in the timeless by
their identification with allegorical figures on the *carro*, as well as in
their literally spelled-out relation with God. Thus it is in royal processions where the search for "propaganda," for a doctrine of right
order, for an ideology, is most rewarding.

If such processions promote rule, Carnival celebrates misrule.
While in the procession costume is a marker of one's relation to order,
in Carnival, travesty, cross-dressing, reigns. In the raucous atmosphere of Carnival, the links between insignia and order invert: "costumes, insignia of rank and identity, and all other symbolic manifestations are mimicked or misappropriated for purposes of aggressive
mockery and laughter. In the pageantry of popular festivals, no fixed
order may be set forth, because travesty subverts the possibility of
orderly setting forth through the monstrous proliferation of differences and identities" (Bristol 1989, 64).

In Carnival, moreover, no one was exempt from satirical attack.
For example, in 1637:

Martes de Carnestolendas salió la mogiganga de la villa que en
diversidad de trajes y de personas, emblemas y hierglíficos
sobrepujó mucho á la otra, aunque no en el gasto. Estaba divid-
ida en diferentes cuadrillas, y como en la procesión de Semana
Santa hay pasos, habíalos también en esta, mezclándose lo di-
vino con lo humano, si bien todo lo permitía el tiempo. Trayan
todos sus máscaras encubriendo con ellas su borrachera. Sus
motes y divisas fueron agudas y algunas con gran donaire sa-
tírico. El letrero de la cuadrilla de los escribanos decía

Todos los de esta cuadrilla
Son los gatos de la villa.

(On Shrove Tuesday the city's masque came forth in the form
of a diversity of costumes and of people, emblems and hiero-
glyphs and excelled the other [parade], though not in costli-
ness. It was divided into squads, and like in the Holy Week
procession there are skits, so also there were in this one, mixing the divine and the secular, since the time of year permitted
it. Everyone wears their mask to cover their drunkeness. Their
emblems and mottos were pointed and some were cleverly satirical. The scribes' squad's placard said:

> All those in this squad
> Are the thieves of the city.)

Las demás cuadrillas traían letreros. . . . Entre las demás fig-
uras había uno vestido de pieles de carnero, el pelo adentro, y
decía su letrero

> Sisas, alcabalas y papel sellado
> Me tienen desollado.

(The rest of the squads also had placards. . . . Among the other
figures was one man dressed in sheep skins, fleece side in, and
his placard said:

Local sales taxes, general sales taxes, and stamped paper
have skinned [fleeced] me.)

Otra traía muchos hábitos y cruces de las Ordenes y decía el
letrero: "Estas se venden." . . . A muchos ha parecido de-
masiada libertad la de un borrachon que teniendo en la mano
un cuerno, el mayor que he visto en mi vida, y un cántaro de
agua en la otra, que iba echando en el cuerno, la bebía diciendo
á voces: "Nadie diga, de este agua no beberé"; y lo repitió delante de S.M. y de las damas. (*La corte y monarquía de España
en los años 1636 y 37,* 107–9)

(Another wore many uniforms and crosses of the Orders and
his placards read: "These are for sale." . . . To many the liberty
taken by one drunk was too much, for he had in one hand a
[animal's] horn, the biggest one I have ever seen, in the other a
jug of water which he went along pouring into the horn; he
drank from it shouting: "Let no one say that I will not drink of

this water"; and he repeated it before Her Majesty and the ladies of the court.)

Even religious symbols did not come away unscathed:

> Desnudóse en carnes un hombre y púsose una corona de papel a la cabeza, y un cetro o bastón en la mano . . . y dos pajes con hachas encendidas [iban] delante y otros pocos con gran copia de chirimías tocando delante por las calles principales, y los que oían el sonido salían a sus ventanas entendiendo que era el Santísimo Sacramento para adorarle, y como la figura veía las mujeres a las ventanas, volvíase a ellas, y así él como los acompañantes les decían muchas desvergüenzas. (Caro Baroja 1965, 99)

> (A man stripped naked and put a paper crown on his head, and had a scepter or staff in his hand . . . and two pages with lighted torches went before him along with some others playing a lot of flageolets down the main streets, and those who heard the sounds came to their windows thinking to worship the Holy Sacrament as it passed, and when the man saw women at the windows, he turned to them and he and his cohorts said many brazen things.)

The sound of the instruments announcing the passage of the sacramental bread draws the women to the windows where not only are they insulted by the participants but treated as well to the sight of a naked man wearing a paper crown. In Carnival, a crown is a ridiculous hat and any ridiculous hat can be a crown, as Bristol suggests (65). But, as opposed to Bristol's contention that there is no order in Carnival, these examples show plainly that there is order, but order parodied.

Between the two poles of royal procession and carnival procession stands public theater. Theater must bow in the direction of the power structure because that authority legitimates its role and existence, because local, state, and religious authorities physically police the theater through the presence of *alguaciles* (bailiffs), and ethically through censorship; theater depends literally, economically on such legitimation. Yet theater bows equally toward popular, Carnival culture not only in its often self-conscious, satirical role-playing, but also because it includes elements of festival, imitation, representation, role-playing, costume, raucous language, popular sentiment, and the symbolic orders in its performance.

As public theater flourishes in Spain, as elsewhere, so too does antitheatrical sentiment. When the theater becomes a potent force in community life, its values seem to run headlong into the received ideas promulgated by church and state (see Barish 1981, 5–220). Cotarelo (1904) lists twelve antitheatrical writers in his *Controversias* prior to 1589, from 1589 to 1630, forty-three. As the *corrales* (playhouses) and the *comedia* (plays) grew in popularity, 1589–1630, so too did they become the object of much scrutiny.

In the next few pages, I focus on P. Juan de Mariana's *Tratado de los espectáculos* (Treatise on public shows) (1609) because he says what others will to varying degrees repeat, because he was an important and influential writer, because his is a thoughtful and relatively full treatise, and because he is less vitriolic than some other critics, some of whom I shall cite from time to time. His writing covers most of the ground that others will take up only partially and thus can serve as a fairly complete model of the attacks on theater.[2] I shall present his concerns in the order he does, then categorize his accusations, and finally suggest the broader implications of his critique.

He begins by saying that the world has changed in recent years and people have veered away from older customs. Whereas in olden times the people pronounced with one voice the clear distinction between right and wrong, in recent years customs have been sliding toward the worse. Nowhere is this more visible than in the theater and in the plots of the plays most commonly presented. Theater is "una oficina de deshonestidad y desverguenza" (laboratory of dishonesty and shame) (413a) that has a corrosive effect on everyone, "de toda edad, sexo y calidad" (of every age, sex, and state) (413a), but the effects are most devastating on "doncellas en primer lugar y mozos" (first, unmarried young women and then young men) (413a). There, in the theater, young and impressionable people learn "antes de tiempo" (before their time) (413a) sexual impropriety since the plays most commonly represented deal with "caidas de doncellas, amores de

---

2. Alan Soons (1982), 84–92, offers a brief summary of Mariana's arguments but resists the treatise throughout defending *comedia* and challenging Mariana, "bacchanalian shows are not the standard by which the highly ethical and poetical plays of (frequently clerical) dramatists, and even their studies of the intrigues in love and adventure of high-born ladies and men, ought ever to be judged" (88). Nonetheless, Soons correctly judges that *comedia* is, in part, an excuse for Mariana's displaced vehemence (92).

rameras, artes de rufianes y alcahuetas, engaños de criados y criadas"
(the fall of young women, whores' loves, the arts of pimps and
madams, servants' deceits) (413a). Worse yet, the plays sugarcoat
these evils "con versos numerosos y elegantes y de hermosas y claras
sentencias esmaltado por donde mas tenazmente á la memoria se
pega" (with many elegant verses and beautiful, clear maxims enam-
eled in where they most tenaciously stick to memory) (413a). Add to
this the lascivious movements of the actresses, and lust ignites in the
hearts of men. So powerful is this combination of elegant poetry and
live action that when the play ends, all the spectators "se refieren y
cuentan con risa [what they witnessed] y poco después se cometen sin
verguenza" (relate and recount laughingly to each other [what they
witnessed], and shortly afterward they shamelessly commit the same
sins) (413b). Laughter, he says, is particularly dangerous "porque las
cosas torpes en dicho y en obra cuando se ríen juntamente se
aprueban" (because misguided acts spoken about or carried out are
approved when everyone laughs at them) (413b).

If in the remote past, non-Christians would not suffer theaters in
their midst, why, he wonders, should we today since "el teatro es una
peste gravísima de las costumbres cristianas" (theater is a grave
plague on Christian customs) (414a). Mariana then offers a short history of public entertainment in which theater is a "juego escénico"
(scenic game) that has its roots in celebrations dedicated to Bacchus
and Venus, "y no es maravilla por andar juntos el uno y el otro deleite" (and it is no surprise to see one pleasure in the company of the
other) (415b). Men, even "los hombres de gran corazón" (valorous
men) (418a), are susceptible to the lure of pleasure since of all the
animals "en el hombre tiene mayores aguijones, y esto, ó por ser
mayor el conocimiento que el hombre tiene y la carne mas blanda, ó
para que la virtud, de la cual solo el hombre es capaz, pelease con mas
fuerza deleite como con enemigo doméstico" (in man [pleasure] has
the greatest spurs, and this is because, either man has the greatest
knowledge and the weakest flesh or so that virtue, of which only man
is capable, might battle fiercely against pleasure as against a domes-
tic enemy) (418b). And pleasure enters powerfully through the ears
and eyes (419b) particularly in the theater: "La causa es que estos
hombres [the players] han juntado en uno todas las maneras é inven-
ciones, para deleitar el pueblo, que se pueden pensar" (Because these
men [the players] have brought together in one all manners of inven-
tions that can be imagined to delight the public) (419b). Plays appeal
to our curiosity, our sense of awe, to our love of eloquence, music, and
song, to our sense of humor, to our prurient interests by positioning

us as eavesdroppers or Peeping Toms (420a), to lust, and to our love of finery, "cuan gran deleite traen consigo para atraer y entretener la muchedumbre el raso, la púrpura el brocado, las guarniciones y bordaduras de recamados" (what great delight the purple, brocade, adornments, and embrodiery bring with them to attract and entertain the masses) (420a).

In the past, not all plays were evil, but those good ones have been replaced by "la nueva, en la cual se trataba de caidas de doncellas, matrimonios de mancebos, engaños de rameras" (the new, which deal with young women's falls, young marriages, and whores' deceptions) (421a), he repeats. Today even plays about saints' lives are improper because of the vile reputation of actors and actresses who play the roles, thus "el borracho no es bueno para enseñar la templanza" (the drunkard is a poor choice to teach temperance) (422b). "¿Sufriremos," he wonders, "que una mujer deshonesta represente á la virgen María ó sancta Catalina, y un hombre infame se vista de las personas de san Augustin y san Antonio? (Must we suffer a dishonest woman to represent the Virgin Mary or Saint Catherine or an infamous man to dress as Saint Augustine or Saint Anthony?) (423a).

Theatrical representations should be kept out of and away from churches because they disturb those who have come to pray. And women should be forbidden to act because today "mujeres de excelente hermosura, de singular gracia, de meneos y posturas, salen en el teatro á representar diversos personajes en forma y traje y hábito de mujeres, y aun de hombres, cosa que grandemente despierta á la lujuria, y tiene muy gran fuerza para corromper los hombres, porque como sea así que esta gente ponga todo su cuidado en allegar dinero y todo lo refieran a ganancia, inventan mil embustes, sin ningún cuidado de honestidad para atraer la muchedumbre, la cual saben con la vista y oido de las mujeres mas que con otra cosa se mueve" (very beautiful women of singular grace, movements and postures come out on the stage to play many different characters in the shape and dress of women and even of men, something that quickly awakens lust and has a corrupting effect on men because since these people put all their efforts toward earning money and make all depend on monetary gain, they invent a thousand tricks, with no care for honesty, to attract the masses, whom they [the actresses] know are moved more forcefully by the sight and sound of women than anything else) (424b). The sight of a woman's body and the sound of her voice incite desire in men, thus "echa el demonio leña y sopla y enciende los pensamientos torpes, ansí por otras cosas como con la vista y oido de las mujeres" (the devil throws on wood and blows on the flames of vulgar thoughts, like those aroused by the sight and sound of women) (423a). But it would be worse yet if young and lovely boys were to dress as women since "se muevan á mayor torpeza y maldad" (they might inspire even greater vulgarity and evil) (423b).

Men are naturally attracted to women, but women are attracted to men as well, "á las mujeres se les para peligro mirar los varones, principalmente desnudos" (it is dangerous for women to look at men, especially naked men) (426a). Now if attraction is simply natural, in the theater it becomes dangerous because "las tales mujeres que andan con los representantes y los acompañan son ordinariamente deshonestas y que se venden por dinero, ¿cómo es posible estando rodeados de tantos hombres lujuriosos y ociosos de día y de noche vivir honestamente?" (such women as live with and accompany actors are usually dishonest and sell themselves for money, for how it is possible for a woman to be surrounded by so many lustful and continually slothful men and live honestly?) (426a). He then wonders what "mozos ociosos y perdidos, de los cuales hay gran número en todas partes" (slothful and purposeless men, of which there are a great number everywhere) would do when they see such women (426b), and he answers his question by reference to contemporary stories of kidnappings of actresses, fights, and murders. He tells of actors who pimp for their actress wives who suck the economic lifeblood from the starry-eyed young men who fall for them. He bemoans the "hijos de padres honrados, que perdida la verguenza y el respeto, se andan abiertas las bocas tras estas mujeres" (sons of honorable parents/fathers, who with respect and shame lost, follow these women with their mouths hanging open [tongues hanging out]) (426b). He ends this section calling for the extirpation of actresses defending this step as "necesaria en nuestro tiempo la severidad y recato cuando hay tanta corrupción de costumbres y tantos por todas partes que las estraguen" (a severe and cautious necessity in our time when there is so much corruption of customs and so many people everywhere who destroy them) (427a).

In the next section he declares himself against building any theater or setting aside any site for theatrical representations. He attacks the notion that theaters are necessary for the charitable contributions they provide (427a–29b). Since men and women alike go to the theaters, the place becomes a site for assignations, for indecent liberties, and concludes that "el teatro se mudará en burdel" (the theater will become a whorehouse) (427b). Women particularly are at risk because such is the pleasure theater arouses that women "se venciese[n] fácilmente con el aparejo del teatro" (are easily conquered by theater's tools) (428a). There is nothing so difficult to guard, "No hay muralla ni riqueza ni otra cosa alguna tan mala de guardar como la mujer" (There is no wall, no riches, nothing so difficult to guard as woman) (428a) especially in the theatrical environment with its incitement to pleasure and the ease it offers of "trato y conversación con los hombres" (intercourse and conversation with men) (428a).

Since theater rental is expensive, many plays must be performed and thus young men "despreciado el mandamiento de sus padres y cuidado de la hacienda, por ninguna manera los podrán apartar" (rejecting their fathers' commands and the care of their wealth can in no way be turned [from the theater]) (428a). In addition, "Oficiales y labradores . . . dejando los ejercicios de cada día, correrán á aquellos lugares. . . . Los criados se distraerán del servicio que deben á sus señores . . . por el apetito de oír hurtarán en casa y sisarán con que poder pagar lo que se acostumbra en estos juegos. Las mujeres, quitada la verguenza y menospreciado el cuidado de la casa, concurrirán sin poder tenerlas . . . que muchas veces antes de mediodía dejan las casas para tomar lugar á próposito para ver la comedia que á la tarde se representa" (Officials and workers . . . abandoning their daily tasks, will run to those places. . . . Servants become distracted from the duties they owe their masters . . . hungry for more [plays] they will steal at home and skim [on the road] to get money to pay for what usually happens in these games. Women, abandoning shame and debasing their care for the home, will attend with no one able to hold them back . . . for often before noon they leave their homes to get a good seat to see the play to be put on that afternoon) (428a/b). Such women put him in mind of representations of the whore who was "parlera y andariega" (a chatterer and a gadabout) (428b), by contrast, Juno, the goddess of marriage, was painted emblematically seated on a tortoise because the tortoise moved slowly and had no voice.

Furthermore, such has the wealth and fame of some performers grown that today many men "de voz y fuerzas corporales" (with deep voices and strong bodies) (428b) are attracted to that dirty and soft profession (428b) and away from dutiful service to the country as soldiers or officials. So vitiated are customs that widows marry before mourning ends; men and women marry against the wishes of their guardians; soldiers prove cowardly; and wretched comedians "aspiran á cosas mejores" (aspire to things above their station) (430b). So vile are players that they must be refused the sacraments (429b–31a).

In sections 11 and 12, Mariana condemns music in the theaters and rails against dance, especially the *zarabanda* (zaraband). Spain, he says, has enjoyed a time of plenty during the last few years of peace, but the people have become lazy and dissolute enjoying "juegos, disoluciones, trajes, comidas y banquetes muy fuera de lo que antiguamente se acostumbraba y muy fuera de aquello á que la naturaleza de nuestra nación inclina" (games, clothing, meals, and banquets out of line with what one was accustomed to in older days and completely out of line with what our nation's nature inclines us to) (433a).

In section 13 he marshals opinions of the church fathers against public entertainment, opinions that generally connect theater to diabolic invention and design (434a–39b). I cite only one example, "sobre el cap 4 de san Mateo donde dice: De los demonios son, no de los hombres, los espectáculos seglares" ("from Matthew 4 where it says: from the demons and not from man come secular spectacles") (435b).[3] In section 15 he enlists philosophers against theater, among them Plato, "manda que los poetas, y el mismo Homero, sean desterrados de la ciudad" (who orders that poets, even Homer himself, be exiled from the city) (442b). And, in section 16, he briefly restates his arguments. Then, with barely a breath after "Harto se ha dicho de los juegos escénicos y representaciones" (We've said enough about theatrical games and representations) he moves directly to a consideration of prostitution, "á las casas públicas" (houses of prostitution) (445a). In his discussion of houses of prostitution, prostitutes, and pimps, he uses the same set of images, the same rhetorical devices he did when speaking of the theater. He writes of prostitutes' liberties, their selling themselves, their monetary gain versus citizens' losses; he decries prostitution as a plague, as an *afrenta, torpeza, deshonestidad* (affront, lewdness, dishonesty) as a danger to youth, to customs, to virtue, and to the nation (446). He stands against the building, setting aside, or rental of houses for prostitution. He demands restrictions on the clothing prostitutes may wear, "Las rameras no usen de mantos largos ni traigan guantes, sombreros ó chapines, sino para diferenciarse de las mujeres honestas, traigan mantillas amarillas" (Whores should not wear long cloaks nor gloves, hats, or platform shoes, but rather to differentiate themselves from honest women, they should wear short yellow cloaks) (449a). And he recalls the 1575 *prágmatica*, "que ninguna mala mujer, ramera pública traiga hábito de alguna

3. I do not find this in Matthew 4. The first part of that chapter deals with Christ's temptations in the wilderness. It may be, then, that Mariana is reading that section metaphorically. Verses 8 and 9 say, "Again, the devil took him to a very high mountain, and showed him all the kingdoms of the world and the glory of them; and he said to him, 'All these I will give you, if you will fall down and worship me.'" Could Mariana be interpreting this vision as diabolic secular spectacles?

religión; que no lleven escuderos que las aconpañan; que en los templos no usen de almohadas ó de estrados como las otras mujeres honestas" (that no prostitute or public whore may wear a habit of any order; that they may not be accompanied by squires; that in church they may not use (kneel on) pillows or platforms like honest women do) (449a). In the next section, he condemns bullfighting, partly because of its roots in heathen/diabolic practices (451a), because it is cruel, and because any game "en el cual hay peligro de muerte, es ilícito y se debe desterrar de la república" (in which there is the danger of death, is illicit and should be exiled from the republic) (453b).

In his conclusion, he overtly links his three areas of concern and rehearses his reasons for their condemnation: (1) the corruption of traditional customs and practices, (2) the evil of pleasure for pleasure's sake, (3) the deceit of public entertainment and the bad consequences they bring, (4) sloth, (5) public congregation and mixing that leads to indecencies, gossip, and fights, (6) the decline of the nation, and (7) public entertainment's ability to lead people away from godly worship.

He recounts Spain's past glories and victories but laments its present condition stating that current material losses are a divine punishment for loss of spiritual and cultural ideals:

> La glotonería, lujuria, pereza y deleites de todas maneras nos han enflaquecido y subjetado á las injurias de aquellos que temblaban ante el nombre de España. (460a)

> Las comidas delicadas y el vestido ha estragado las costumbres de tanta manera, que mas se gasta hoy en una ciudad de golosinas, confituras y mas cantidad de azúcar que en toda España en tiempo de nuestros padres. ¡Cuanta seda, Dios poderoso, se gasta! Mas pulidos andan el día de hoy y con vestidos mas arreados y costosos los carniceros, los sastres y zapateros que en otros tiempos las cabezas y principales de las ciudades. (460b)

> . . . en las particulares casas, en los campos, por las calles no oirán otra cosa sino alabanzas de Vénus y sus hazañas. Antigua verguenza y infamia es esta; pero nuevamente se hacen torpes espectáculos con grandes concursos y aplauso del pueblo; invéntanse tonadas deshonestas y malas, ayudándolas con los meneos del cuerpo, con los cuales lo que torpemente se hace en el retrete y aun en el burdel, todo se pone delante de los ojos y orejas de la muchedumbre. ¡Oh afrenta digna de todo castigo! (461b)

(Gluttony, lust, sloth, and pleasures of all kinds have weakened us and subjected us to injuries from those who earlier trembled before Spain's name.)

(Refined food and dress have corrupted customs to such a degree that today in one city more money is spent on sweets, confectionaries, and sugar than in all Spain in our parents' time. How much silk, dear God, is used! Today butchers, tailors, and shoemakers go around wearing more expensive clothing than in other times the most important people in the cities did.)

(. . . in individual homes, in the country, along the streets you will hear nothing but praises of Venus and her works. This is an ancient shame and infamy; but anew appear lewd spectacles applauded and attended by the masses; dishonest and evil melodies are written which, abetted by writhing bodies more appropriate to the private rooms or even to whorehouses, are all placed before the eyes and ears of the masses. Oh, affront worthy of every punishment!)

In Mariana's attack on theater, his topics include actors and actresses, plays' plots, public theaters, the powerful effects of representation (that is to say, the material conditions of the theater); laughter, pleasure, lust (the immediate effects); the disruption of "normalcy" in clothing, customs, responsibilities, and rights; the pernicious effects of theater on gender and rank; the diabolic connection; the connections between theater and other kinds of public entertainments; and the state of Spain today.

Theater, for Mariana, is both a symptom and a cause of the nation's and the people's decline. It is symptomatic of the softness, the lure of pleasure, the waywardness of individuals, and of societal chaos. It is a cause because it teaches in powerful, memorable ways how to deceive, shirk responsibility, and gain illicit rewards. Theater shows to those who can see the evils of "representation," or what Stephen Greenblatt in another context has termed "self-fashioning," of not being true to one's essence: underlying Mariana's complaints lies an essentialist theory of the self.

Theater teaches through imitation and those who imitate, those who see others imitate successfully, may try to "become" what they imitate. Fray Jerónimo de la Cruz, in 1635 lists some of theater's evil lessons in mimesis:

A la doncella la incitan á que piense lo que no sabe y desee lo que no entiende. Danla modo de divertir la severidad del padre y el cuidado de la madre. Enséñanla á recibir billetes, á responder á cartas, . . . á fingir en lo público, á perder los temblores en lo secreto, á hacer llaves falsas, á buscar puertas ocultas, . . . á no temer la oscuridad de la noche, ni los peligros de la casa. A los mozos, libertades, atrevimientos y insolencias; la razón bien dicha, la palabra blanda, el suspiro mentiroso. (203a)

(The young woman is encouraged to think about what she does not yet know and to desire what she does not understand. They [comedies] offer her means to divert her father's strictness and her mother's care. They teach her how to accept secret notes and respond to letters . . . to feign in public, to lose her fear of secrecy, to make pass keys, to seek out hidden entrances . . . not to fear night's darkness nor the house's dangers. Young men learn liberties, daring and insolency; [they learn] clever repartee, sweet words, and lying sighs.) (Cotarelo 1904)

In 1613, P. Juan de Ferrer complains:

Anda podrido el marido de ver inquieta la mujer y de ver en ella algunos malos indicios que le quitan el sueño al triste marido y le traen cabizbajo. ¿Qué maravilla es todo eso si la hija y la mujer no pierden comedias de éstas? Si aquí les enseñan á la una y á la otra á ser malas con artificio, ¿qué han de hacer después sino repetir y practicar la lición que en la comedia aprendieron? (253a) (Cotarelo 1904)

(The husband goes about distraught to see his wife restless and to see in her evil signs that leave the husband sad and crestfallen. Is any of this surprising given that his daughter or his wife never miss any of these comedies? If there they are taught to be evil and crafty, what will they do afterwards but repeat and put into practice the lessons they learned from comedies?)

Imitations should follow suitable models—good men and women from history and especially from the Christian tradition—thus whatever, whoever leads men and women away from what is essential, good, and necessary for the preservation of the state and the people offers a challenge to correct role-modeling by presenting illicit alternatives and thus must be condemned. This is especially damaging if those professional imitators, who are really good at it, who are attractive, who have convincing voices and beguiling bodies, are vile to begin with. Thus even if such people imitate good people, saints, or divinities, their wantonness taints what they portray.

Mariana's critique of the theater, when looked at carefully, is symptomatic of greater fears than just the potential corruption it may provoke. Theater is a threat to gender and rank distinctions that must be preserved in a vertically organized, hierarchized state. He betrays a fear of idleness in terms of cultural, social, and economic practices. Performers produce nothing yet they reap economic benefits for their play. P. Juan de Ferrer (1613) stresses *comedia*'s economic sapping:

> Orto daño es, y no pequeño según están los tiempos de agora estos reinos de España, que estas comedias los ayudan a empobrecer y arruinar, porque los tales representantes llevan mucho dinero á trueque del cual dejan muchos pecados. (254a)

> (Another harm, and no small one given how times are today in Spain, is that these comedies help impoverish and ruin people, because the actors take a lot of money in exchange for which they leave behind many sins.) (Cotarelo 1904)

Mariana stresses what should be the correct management of time and work, a doctrine perfectly suited to the mercantilist, protocapitalist world, wherein the regulation of work as duty is necessary in the lives of the leaders and the workforce alike who inhabit the swelling urban areas.

The attacks on clothing, on luxuries, other writers will relate to concerns about the sapping of the national economy or to the violation of *pragmáticas* (royal decrees). In the anonymous *Diálogos de las comedias* (1620), for example, the Teólogo states:

> entre las pragmáticas que ahora se trazan, alguna de las tocantes á los trajes ordenase que los comediantes y comediantas no trajesen seda ni la pudiesen vestir fuera del tablado, ni vestidos guarnecidos de seda, ni ellos trajesen espadas, ni ellas mantos ni chapines, sino mantellinas como las mugeres perdidas. (230a) (Cotarelo 1904)

> (among the pragmatics now being planned, there is one that orders that actors and actresses not wear silk on- or offstage, nor even costumes adorned with silk, that the actors not carry

swords, nor the actresses long cloaks or platform shoes, but rather short cloaks like loose women.)

One of the *pragmáticas* (1615), in fact states, "Que no traigan [las mujeres que representan en el teatro] vestidos contra las pragmáticas del reino, fuera de los teatros y lugar donde representaren, que para representar se les permite andar con ellos" (That [women who act in the theater] not wear costumes that violate the pragmatics of the kingdom outside of the theaters or places where they act, but they may wear them on stage) (626b). Arguments directed toward controlling what may be worn may bring to mind Foucault's (1979) discussion of the desire of absolutist regimes to inscribe the body with visible marks of subjection (54–57). For Mariana, fine clothes are both lures, and deceptions that blur rank distinction and further destabilize fixed social order. Since actors and actresses on stage wear expensive, gorgeous finery to imitate social superiors, they or others might do so outside the playhouses with, at best, confusing consequences. But even wearing such finery on stage can have debiliting effects on men in the audience. Fr. José de María (1600) writes that after seeing the actress, or "la astutísimsa ramera" (the shrewd whore) as he calls her, "cubierta de seda y oro" (covered with silk and gold) men return home and see "á sus mugeres honestas y con hábito modesto, les parecen feas y desagradables y por eso las desprecian. De aquí nacen las riñas y pendencias, de aquí la discordia y la guerra, y de aquí también la muerte algunas veces" (their honest wives wearing modest clothing, and they seem ugly and disagreeable and therefore they scorn them. From this, arguments and quarrels are born, from this discord and war, from this also death sometimes) (383a) (Cotarelo 1904). Moreover such is the appeal of these high fashions that already outside the theater people dress above their station. Visually, on stage and beyond, fixed hierarchies are no longer reliable. Theatergoing becomes allied with the loss or confusion of identity and potential usurpation of social position.

Women figure prominently in Mariana's treatise and he is particularly angry with actresses. Their enticing beauty, their enchanting voices, their seductive movements, their lovely costumes, their sly representations hide the whore beneath. They use their charms to lure men to economic ruin, to lust and whoring, to fights and death. They cause social disruption since young men heed not the warnings of their fathers and pursue actresses who lead them on to destruction. Not only actresses but also the women who attend plays come under scrutiny. Those women abandon house and home to attend the theater where they meet and converse with men. Moreover, there they learn the art of deception and fall prey to the blandishments of illicit pleasure. They see how to disguise themselves with luxurious clothing, makeup, and even men's costume. Such changeability incites desire and debases those who look upon it. Women seem to have forgotten their places, usurped male prerogative. Mariana's often misogynistic, always policing, rhetoric betrays a powerful gender tension. He attempts throughout to demonize actresses and the women who see them and emulate them as he further marginalizes and vilifies those who participate in (and benefit from), directly or indirectly, the theatrical life. He links these fears with the mixing that goes on in the theaters, a mixing that breeds instability.

Times have changed for the worse, customs have degenerated, soldiers lack the will to fight, wastrel and socially rebellious men and women fall prey to lust, sloth, debauchery. The theater is the institution wherein the threats to traditional social order are most visible. Mariana's "slippage" from theater to the state of the state, to the moral, ethical order, is, I hazard, calculated. And in that calculation is a condemnation of social, spiritual, and national leadership. Priests attend and even defend theater, otherwise good men proclaim theater's necessity, and national leaders, "los prudentes príncipes y los gobernadores" (the prudent princes and governors) (439b), must move to address excesses. There arises here a political/social/ethical subtext about who should be in charge of teaching the modeling, the "fashioning" of the selves. Comedians must not for they are vile, low creatures risen above their state, women cannot for they are subject to inherent weaknesses and to diabolic enticement, young men cannot for they are prisoners of their appetites. Only those who can see how far Spain has fallen, or only those who will heed the warnings issued by those who can see will be able to re-right/re-write the world.

Public theater was a disputed site since public theater was one of the ideological state apparatuses, as defined by Althusser (1972), in late sixteenth- and all of seventeenth-century Spain. Playhouses provided a space both popular and institutional "for the dissemination of images and narratives through which imaginary relations to the real were represented and playgoers were positioned within ideology" (Howard 1994, 164). The theaters not only offered the possibility of the reconfirmation of state and church ideologies but also the possibility of resistance to received notions, or from Mariana's perspective, an active subversion of traditional values. To what degree the theater reinforced received aristocratic values, to what degree the theater and the state are coextensive, has been, and will continue to be, a topic for discussion (see Maravall, Díez Borque, Stern, and others). Plays were subject to state and ecclesiastical censorship and theaters were overseen by city and national bodies. But the fact that such oversight and censorship was deemed necessary, and that it often came down hard on playwrights, acting companies, and individuals, suggests strongly the volatility of plays, performances, and public reception.

From Mariana's and others' perspective, theater has gone entirely too far in the direction of Carnival and is in dire need of policing, of restoration to right order. Theater, they say, is a powerful teaching tool, but it teaches all the wrong things about relations between men and women, and about love. They were right; theater does teach about love and about relations between men and women, and they were right about the marriages at the end being less important, relatively, than the action that precedes. But their reading and mine, while starting from the same premise, will quickly diverge.

1

COMEDY AND LOVE

"Well, if you've read one of these plays, you've read them all," and with those words a graduate student politely returned to me the syllabus for my upcoming seminar on Golden Age comedy and left my office. That sentence sums up many readers' attitudes toward comedies, and not just ones from the Spanish Golden Age. Gary Waller (1991), in his introductory remarks to Terrence Hawkes's essay on Shakespearean comedy says, "Shakespeare, many critics have observed, wrote the same story over and over again" (168). Seen from a certain perspective, all love comedies do seem to tell the same tale, a tale Northrop Frye (1957) summarized extremely well.

The fundamental comic action, Frye says, posits a young man who wants a young woman, but a blocking force, a guardian figure, usually a father, opposes the young man's desires until the end of the play when "some twist in the plot enables the hero to have his will" (163). As the play begins, the blocking character controls the play's society whereas at the end, a new community coalesces around the recently joined couple. Entrance into the new society is celebrated by a festival, in most cases by a wedding. The frequent portrayal of blocking forces as older men moves generational conflict to center stage. Since the older generation usually loses out, society is rejuvenated and the fathers or father-surrogate figures are dismissed as imposters or usurpers. Their "claim to possess the girl must be shown up as somehow fraudulent . . . and the extent to which they have power implies some criticism of the society that allows them their power" (165).

Frye lists the stock comedic types but insists that just because comedy works with stock characters does not mean that particular manifestations of those roles automatically seem less than lifelike: the "stock type," while not the character, "is as necessary to the character as a skeleton is to the actor who plays it" (172). The character types he discusses are *alazons,* imposters; *eirons,* self-deprecators; *bomolochoi,* buffoons; and *agroikos,* literally rustics but often churls. Frye subdivides each group mentioning the *senex iratus* or "heavy father" as central to *alazons;* the hero and the tricky slave as two principal representations of *eirons;* fools, clowns, or pages as proper *bomolochoi;* while gulls, straight-men, or killjoys illustrate the *agroikos* category.

Setting comedy on his genre ring between irony and romance, Frye offers six comedic gradations that move from one side to the other. In the most ironic phase, "a humorous society triumphs or remains undefeated" (177); in the next phase, the hero, unable to change society, escapes "leaving its structure as it was before" (180); in the third case, or what Frye calls the "normal one," the *senex iratus* "gives way to the young man's desire" (180); in the fourth, the characters and society "move out of the world of experience into the ideal world of innocence or romance" (181–82). At this point Frye presents the opposition normal world/green world: "[T]he green world charges the comedies with the symbolism of the victory of summer over winter. . . . The green world has analogies, not only to the fertile world of ritual, but to the dream world that we create out of our own desires" (183). In the fifth phase, comedy becomes "less utopian and more Arcadian, less festive and more pensive" (184); and in the final, sixth phase, there is "the collapse and disintegration of the comic society. . . . In this kind of comedy, we have finally left the world of wit and the awakened critical intelligence for the opposite pole, an oracular solemnity" (185).

Since all *anatomies* are arbitrary, Frye's is as adequate or inadequate as any. Nevertheless, I want to point out some of the problems with Frye's *anatomy* that touch on how I shall approach the plays included here. Frye's system, appearing as it does in the midst of New

Critical flowering on the one hand and in the broader context of the burgeoning North American scientific and managerial modes, as Terry Eagleton (1983) has observed, falls in step with the latter to recast literary criticism as an objective, classificatory system. Literature is now governed by modes, archetypes, myths, and genres, with all works subject to those laws (Eagleton 1983, 91). There are four narrative structures—tragedy, irony or satire, comedy, and romance—corresponding to the four mythoi of autumn, winter, spring, summer.[1] There are, in addition, four hero types and three repeated symbolic patterns. Once the principal parts of the system are understood, the critic may choose a work from any national literature, from any period, and by fitting the work to the pattern, he or she may classify the images, the hero, the narrative structure, and show the myth that the work reproduces in displaced form. Throughout, the taxonomical model works much like the printing press Domingo describes in "Rectificación de línea," José Corrales Egea's short story, "Una palanca que se mueve, un diente que corre, una pieza que gira y, de pronto, todo se pone en movimiento con un ruido rítmico y exacto" (A lever moves, a cog engages, a piece turns and suddenly the whole thing takes off with a rhythmic, precise noise) (Menton 1961, 160).

Frye eliminates the particularities of individual works and uses specific examples only insofar as they conform to the general outline he presents. More important, his Vishnu-like view collapses history or diachrony into sameness, into repetitive synchrony. From Frye's distance, all phenomena look pretty much the same: "de noche todos los gatos son pardos," (at night all cats are brown) as the Spanish proverb has it. The particular elements that helped make the works "real" for their intended audience—references to contemporary events, people, and situations, to economics, to social practices and concerns, to psychology, philosophy, religion, or politics—are surgically removed from consideration. Literature becomes a cleaner, less subjective, more self-referential system than the New Critics, for example, had made it. History is eliminated because history is sticky, accidental. Literature comes to be a "spiritual home" for readers who

1. In some ways, Frye's four mythoi and their associated imagery are parallel to E. M. Wilson's (1936) four elements in Calderón's imagery. There have been many individual studies of comedies in the Golden Age, but fewer more general pieces. Among the general works are Wardropper (1967; 1966); Darst (1974); C. A. Jones (1971); Varey (1972); Wade (1974; 1981); *Rire et société dans le théâtre espagnol du Siècle d'Or* (1981); Nomland (1946); and ter Horst (1981). Some general studies of comedy include Langer (1953); Kern (1980); McFadden (1982); Gurewitch (1975); and Jenkins (1994).

find there "pre-urban images of the natural cycles, nostalgic memories of a history before industrialism" (Eagleton 1983, 93). Frye's powerful formalism anticipates but does not take the final step into structuralism.

In and of itself, there is nothing "wrong" with Frye's system, and the obvious truth of his categories and subcategories stands apparent in the tidy machine he constructed that allows the critic to line up works like so many punch cards and sort them with Univac-like efficiency into their respective slots (the Univac was up and running in 1952 when, for example, it was used to predict the outcome of national elections in the United States; Frye published *Anatomy of Criticism* in 1957). Eagleton (1983) says that for Frye literature becomes a substitute for history:

> Actual history is for Frye bondage and determinism, and literature remains the one place where we can be free. . . . The beauty of the approach is that it deftly combines an extreme aestheticism with an efficiently classifying "scientificity," and so maintains literature as an imaginary alternative to modern society while rendering criticism respectable in that society's terms. It displays an iconoclastic briskness toward literary waffle, . . . but blends this with the most romantic of yearnings. In one sense it is scornfully "anti-humanist," decentering the individual subject and centering all on the collective literary system itself; in another sense it is the work of a committed Christian humanist (Frye is a clergyman), for whom the dynamic which drives literature and civilization—desire—will finally be fulfilled in the kingdom of God. . . . Frye offers literature as a displaced version of religion. Literature becomes an essential palliative for the failure of religious ideology, and supplies us with various myths which are of relevance to social life. (93)

Eleven years after Frye's book appeared, Bruce Wardropper offered what may yet stand as the broadest statement on Spanish Golden Age comedy: his justly acclaimed "La comedia española del siglo de oro" (Spanish comedy of the Golden Age) written in 1968 but published in 1978 along with a Spanish translation of Elder Olson's *The Theory of Comedy*. Wardropper describes and defines three fundamental types of Spanish comedy (and in so doing implies the "uniqueness" of its development): *entremeses, comedias fantásticas,* and *comedias de capa y espada*. The *entremés* is a short piece treating problems from a rebellious, sometimes farcical, stance. It places a stamp of approval on the antisocial as it highlights "el conflicto entre instinto vital y coerción social" (the conflict between natural instinct and social coercion) (208) thereby marking its affinity with Carnival. The *comedia fantástica* is defined by its temporal and/or spatial displacement, "las comedias que no se desarrollan en el 'aquí y ahora' " (comedies that do not take place in the "here and now") (209). These plays investigate "no por vía lógica sino por vía poética . . . la naturaleza de la verdad y cómo se la descubre" (not by logical means but rather by poetic ones . . . the nature of truth and how it is to be discovered) (213). He offers as examples *El perro del hortelano* and *El vergonzoso en palacio,* both of which examine the concept of nobility proposing "la idea más bien revolucionaria de que la nobleza puede ser un rasgo del temperamento antes que una circunstancia geneológica . . . [these plays] afirman la primacía del derecho de los individuos a la felicidad amorosa por encima del valor social del honor familiar" (the essentially revolutionary idea that nobility can be a characteristic of temperament rather than a genealogical happenstance . . . [these plays] affirm the primacy of the individual's right to happiness in love over the social value of familial honor) (214). The final group, cape and sword plays, do take place in the here and now as urban plays often set in Madrid. But, he adds, the young lovers live in the city as though the city did not exist carrying out "la ilógica búsqueda de la Arcadia en el corazón de la capital" (the illogical search for Arcady in the heart of the city) (216). Still, the "city" and its values, particularly money and desire, do invade the lovers' world as impediments to true love.

In the final section, Wardropper offers many penetrating insights into Spanish comedy: Spanish comedy often adopts a "punto de vista femenino" (a feminine point of view) (226) since women win over men.[2] That perspective makes us "conscientes de la imperfección y fosilización de" (conscious of the imperfection and fossilization of) social institutions (226–27). The ends of the plays frequently project not "la restitución de dos jóvenes descarriados a la sociedad, [but rather] una continuación de las travesuras" (the restitution of two errant young people into society [but rather] a continuation of the pranks) (222). Spanish comedy "no refleja la realidad de la sociedad y de sus valores, sino la forma como el público entiende y malentiende los pre-

---

2. One could argue, however, that whatever victories women achieve are pyrrhic; that women are allowed a temporary liberty at best since in the end, through marriage, they resume their place in the male-dominated system. Walter Cohen (1985) notes, "On the one hand, married love could be a progressive step for women and men alike. On the other, the concluding matrimony of many a comedy reintegrates women into a family and a society dominated by men, thereby alleviating male sexual, procreative, and emotional anxieties" (188).

juicios, expectativas y mitos sociales relativos a esa sociedad" (does not reflect society's reality, its values, but rather the way that the public understands and misunderstands the prejudices, expectations, and social myths relative to that society) (230).

Yet in some places, the waters muddy. He says, for example, that in the comedies, "el amor debilita el poder de los imperativos sociales" (love debilitates the power of social imperatives) (231) and that "El mensaje de la comedia es el de que los individuos tienen derechos que exceden a los de la sociedad. Este mensaje era, y es, revolucionario" (Comedy's message is that individuals have rights that excede those of society. This message was, and is, revolutionary) (235). But when he compares comedy and tragedy, he seems to qualify the foregoing noting that "la confrontación de las comedias con las obras graves revela que quien vence al final no es la joven enamorada, sino la sociedad" (The comparison between comedies and serious works reveals that who wins in the end is not the young woman in love, rather society) (224), especially since he presents comedy as a prelude to tragedy. Regarding women, he adds, "En conjunto la comedia española nos presenta a mujeres libres y respetables" (Taken together, Spanish comedies present to us free and respectable women) (224), and "Estas jóvenes vencedoras son indomables en su búsqueda de la libertad" (These young victorious women are indomitable in their search for freedom) (223), but the following statement modulates and restricts that search for liberty: "La meta de la mujer en la comedia coincide con la meta de la propia comedia: 'casarse'. Es decir, levantar [sic] una casa o una familia" (woman's goal in comedy coincides with comedy's goal: marriage. That is to say, to raise a home or family) (232). There is nothing to gain from attacking that last statement from a contemporary ideological or feminist stance; rather, we should consider the conclusion in its context, as a general observation about comedy: women's goals conflate with comedy's conventional ending.

For Frye, literature is a highly nuanced circle around which one moves smoothly, almost seamlessly, from tragedy to irony to comedy to romance and on around again to tragedy passing through different phases along the way. For Wardropper, Spanish *comedia* (drama) is polar, admitting two modes, comedy and tragedy, "en la España del Siglo de Oro la comedia es preludio de una tragedia en potencia" (in Golden Age Spain comedy is a prelude to potential tragedy) (227). What separates comedy from tragedy is, simply, the marital state of the protagonists. In comedy there may be serious topics but a play becomes truly grave when the principals are married. Why is this so? Because Spain's theater is Counter-Reformation Catholic, and in a world view where marriage is sacramental, marriage effectively marks the end of one kind of life and the beginning of another. Focusing on marriage as the goal of Spanish comedy inevitably promotes a preoccupation with marriage and shifts attention away from the action that precedes it.

If we look at the antitheatrical writers from this period, marriage as the end or goal of the comedies scarcely occurs to them. Of the tracts I have read, only one even mentions marriage and then backhandedly, "No saben los poetas escribir comedia sin amores torpes, porque les parece que después se salvan y se honestan con el matrimonio" (Poets do not know how to write a comedy that does not deal with lewd love because it seems to them that in the end they can save and make honest [the lewd acts] by marriage) (D. Gonzalo Navarro Castellanos, *Controversias,* in Cotarelo 1904, 488b). For him, last-minute marriages are a subterfuge, a camoflage for the lasciviousness that is the comedies' real content. Last-minute marriages, he suggests, are not enough to reverse the plays' effects because they simply put the seal of approval on deceit, passion, and illicit ways. What the audience will remember is lust and deception, and perhaps they might even view marriage as a reward for such carryings-on. Moreover, when that final marriage is blessed by a father figure, an authority figure who was the butt of the jokes and deceptions throughout, any credence in the "righting of society" and *comedia*'s moral values slips away.

If we shift our perspective away from marriage as goal, and yet still admit its power as a comedic-structural convention, we can then see that the plays are also, perhaps mainly, about the beginnings of desire, though the antitheatrical moralist writers would surely have preferred the term "lust." The plays promote the search for the self in the various mirror images of the self, and thus the comedies unfold a gradual learning process of who and what the self and the other are. For a modern reader, perhaps the most satisfying of these plays reveal the gradual recognition and acceptance of difference in, and independence of, the other. In those unions, at least, one might question marriage as a prelude to potential tragedy.

Spanish comedy is "of one piece" only when the focus falls on the conventional endings, only when seen from a cosmic perspective. The paths to marriage, the paths to love, like the paths to tragic death, are many. The fundamental differences among these plays can be marked by looking at the paths rather than the preordained destination. All roads may lead to Rome, but some may be freeways, others costly turnpikes, and yet others tortuous, rut-ridden cartpaths, or dark and labyrinthine city streets. In what follows, I want to examine the paths and the discoveries made along them; I want to look at the process, not the product. I will concentrate on who sees, who guides, leads, and teaches, who knows what love is and can distinguish between a sudden infatuation and the clear-eyed devotion that results from the tests and trials to be undergone before marriage, all of which may predict a sensible and mutually respectful relationship afterward as well.

In order to study the plays' differences, I must—perhaps sheepishly after Eagleton's pointed, even curt dismissal—return to Northrop Frye. He was right: comedy is about love and the ur-plot he offered holds for every one of the plays I will study, though it might not for later works. With that said, however, I turn to what may be, at least from the perspective of the plays I study, a fundamental flaw in the wording of his formulation: "some twist in the plot enables the *hero* to have *his* will . . . the *hero,* unable to change society, escapes . . . [the *senex iratus*] gives way to the *young man's* desire." The hero, the young man, Frye wrote, controls the action, or at least functions as the focalizer through whom the audience sees the action. In the twenty plays that form the corpus for this study, the "hero" functions thus in only four. In two of those, his role and relation with the woman are positive: *Por el sótano y el torno* and *Desde Toledo a Madrid;* in two, his role and relation are negative: *El hombre pobre todo es trazas* and *El astrólogo fingido.*

In eight of the comedies, however, the young men rarely control any of their circumstances. Rather they tend to be either confused and ineffectual or blustery and sneaky. More often than not, they are the beneficiaries instead of the initiators of the comic action directed at solving the problems. In these plays: *La villana de Vallecas, La celosa de sí misma, Por la puente Juana, Esto sí que es negociar, La dama duende, La toquera vizcaína, ¡Ay, verdades, que en amor . . . !,* and *La huerta de Juan Fernández,* women take the lead, and in the end, the errant or misguided young man along with the father or father figure learn from, relent to, and agree with her superior knowledge.

In the third group of plays, men lead and teach other men—*El astrólogo fingido, El hombre pobre todo es trazas, El premio del bien hablar* and *El examen de maridos*—and women teach other women, *En Madrid y en una casa.* In my final grouping, both the men and the women see clearly what they want, cooperate in the main, and work together to overcome the obstacles in their path as they reinforce to each other the correctness of their view. Those plays include *Amor, pleito y desafío, Amar sin saber a quien,* and *Desde Toledo a Madrid,* along with parts of *Por el sótano y el torno,* and *Los balcones de Madrid.*[3]

Women Teach Men

I start with this group because it contains the greatest number of plays. In these works, women guide men sometimes forcefully, sometimes gently, into a position where they can finally see what it was they wanted all along but were too blind to recognize. Often, to carry out their plans, women must adopt a disguise and/or a "new personality" by means of which they can correct the men's view. Disguise, thus, through misdirection and then redirection, challenges the men to ask themselves anew how they should see a woman. Must a woman be the sun or a diamond or a lily to be loved? Does her characterization through the man's eyes as the radical other, as demon or whore, as fickle, weak, or unworthy have any basis in reality? The women use the disguises and new personalities, plus the awkward and dangerous situations into which they thrust the men, to propel them toward a more complex view that in turn, serves to stimulate the men's minds. The men eventually modify their traditional thinking when they see that those perspectives are insufficient. As this slowly happens, they speak (and think) less often in clichés after they learn from experience that the women and the world are less conventional than they had believed. The men begin to move away from the "authoritative voice" of traditional thought patterns and start paying attention to what is actually going on around them. In many of these plays, the men's preconceived or received notions of the necessary perfection of their objects of desire, as well as their opposite portrayal of the women as demonic other, uncover an underlying arrogance toward and ignorance of the "real woman" they eventually discover and come to love.

In several of these works, the men's conventional, poetically derived ideal of woman comes in for some hard knocks so that they can

---

3. The other two plays are *La moza de cántaro* (which presents a hybrid stance between the women teach/men teach position and will be discussed under the latter denomination) and *Casa con dos puertas mala es de guardar* (which offers parallels to *La dama duende* and will be referred to appropriately. For a complete list of the plays to be considered here, see the Appendix.

begin to glimpse the person behind the veil of language the men themselves have thrown over women. Angela, for example, in her well-known response to Manuel in *La dama duende,* denies each of his traditional epithets one by one in an attempt to make clear one of the lessons he should learn: that the "object" of his desire is a subject as well, or can adopt a subject position if only, as here, to deny object positioning predetermined by male discourse:

> No soy alba, pues la risa
> me falta en contento tanto;
> ni aurora, pues que mi llanto
> de mi dolor no os avisa;
> no soy sol, pues no divisa
> mi luz la verdad que adoro,
> y así, lo que soy ignoro;
> que sólo sé que no soy
> alba, aurora o sol; pues hoy
> no alumbro, río ni lloro.
> Y así os ruego que digáis
> señor Don Manuel, de mí
> que una mujer soy y fui
> (Calderón, *Obras completas*
>   2:264a)

(I am not dawn for I lack its contented smile, nor aurora as my suffering tears should make clear to you, I am not the sun because my light does not herald the truth I adore, and so, I do not know what I am; I only know that I am not dawn, aurora, or a sun; since today I neither enlighten, laugh or cry. Thus I beg of you Manuel that you say of me that I am and have been a woman.)

In *Casa con dos puertas mala es de guardar,* Félix so hypostasizes Laura that he turns a living woman into a statue. In his descriptive speech to Lisardo, he tells of seeing her reclining near a pool in the Aranjuez gardens. He casts his vision as a debate between Nature and Art wherein the former brags to the latter:

> No blasones, no te alabes,
> de que lo muerto desmientes
> con más fuerza en esta parte,
> que yo desmiento lo vivo;
> pues en lo contrario iguales,

sé hacer una estatua yo,
si hacer tú una mujer sabes,
o mira un alma sin vida,
donde está con vida un jaspe"
(Calderón, *Obras completas*
2:278b)

(Neither brag nor praise yourself for being able to give the lie
to death with such force for I give the lie to life; we are equals
in contradiction since I know how to make a statue and you to
make a woman, only look at a lifeless soul where there is living
jasper)

If men cannot see what they are looking at, or if they can see only
with inherited eyes, then the woman must become someone or something else that they can see in order to get them to look again with
fresh eyes beyond the surface, beyond the preconceptions. Angela
wants Manuel to learn to see past his imagined identities for her;
Leonisa, in *Esto sí que es negociar,* wants Rogerio to look beyond the
peasant dress to qualities more profound, as Diego does in *La moza de
cántaro.* It is not that social status, clothes, beauty, or wealth are
unimportant in practical terms in this society; it is that human qualities, as opposed to the traditional abstractions, are more important if
marriage is to be a real conjoining of individuals and not just stock
types going through their paces toward a stock ending.

If marriage, the traditional ending of comedy as Frye insists, is to
speak the true language of the social, the individual, and the erotic
self, if it is to be "the point at which the spontaneity of individual
feelings and the stability of public institutions harmoniously inter-
lock," as Terry Eagleton (1986, 21) describes it, then it must arise
from knowledge. It must reside in mutual understanding, in a recognition of the other, in a giving and receiving of "the fullest mutuality
of minds" (21). To approach this ideal, the men must learn to see
beyond preprogrammed notions.

In *La celosa de sí misma,* seeing incorrectly is precisely Melchor's
greatest problem; even when he looks directly at Magdalena, he cannot see her. Melchor, accompanied by his servant, Ventura, comes to
Madrid from León for an arranged marriage to Magdalena, daughter
of his father's friend, Alonso. Melchor is poor but noble; his intended
is the wealthy offspring of an *indiano* (a wealthy returnee from the
Indies). Upon arriving, he and his servant first go to the La Vitoria
church to hear Mass, and as Melchor kneels beside a veiled woman,
he catches a glimpse of her hand. He sees not an ordinary hand, he

later exclaims to Ventura, but, "¡Ay qué mano! ¡qué belleza! / ¡Qué blancura! ¡qué donaire! / ¡Qué hoyuelos! ¡qué tez, qué venas! / ¡Ay qué dedos tan hermosos!" (Oh what a hand, what beauty, what whiteness, what grace, what dimples, what complexion, what veins, oh what lovely fingers) (Tirso 1944, 130a). When she raised her hand to her forehead to make the sign of the cross, Melchor saw what he was programmed to see, "jazmines, vi mosquetas, / Vi alabastros, vi diamantes / Vi, en fin, nieve en fuego envuelta" (jasmines, I saw globe flowers, I saw alabaster, I saw diamonds, I saw, in sum, snow wrapped in fire) (130a). After a thief cut the lady's pursestrings, Melchor recovered the purse but instead of returning it to her, he substituted his own. To avoid further attention from onlookers, she takes the purse and agrees to meet him there tomorrow to try to find its true owner. As a sign by which he can identify her, she takes off her glove and shows him the hand he so covets.

Of course the unknown woman is his promised bride, and when Melchor next goes to her house to present his credentials, she recognizes him instantly. But Melchor does not know her, for in the church she was veiled, so when he looks at her, his blunt reaction is "fea mujer" (ugly woman). She offers him her hand to kiss, after which his relative and rival, asks "¿Pues no es la de vuestra esposa, / Para mano, tan airosa, / Y tan bella?" (Well, isn't your wife's hand as graceful and as beautiful?), Melchor responds, "No por cierto" (Not at all) (135a). Melchor blindly but insightfully knows, however, that he cannot see either her or her hand well, as he later explains to Ventura, since "La memoria / De aquella mano, Ventura, / Como quien ve por antojos, / Tiene ocupados mis ojos." (The memory of that hand, Ventura, has me like someone who looks through glasses, it has my eyes occupied) (134c). Ventura, on the other hand (you should pardon the pun), responds with obvious bewilderment, "¿Qué hermosura / Se igualará a la presente?" (What beauty can equal the present woman's?) He looks carefully at the hand and adds, "Pero dejando la cara, / En la candidez repara / De aquella mano esplendente, / Que es la misma, vive Dios, / Que melindrizó el bolsillo" (But leaving the face aside, look upon the innocence of that hand which is the same one, by God, that sweet talked you out of the purse). Melchor accuses him of blasphemy, whereon Ventura correctly judges his master's state, "No estáis vos, / Señor, con juicio cabal" (You have poor judgment, sir) (134c).

The next day when he returns to the church to meet the unknown woman, she first shows him her hand, as promised, to which he reacts, "¡Ay aurora, ay sol, ay día!" (Oh aurora, oh sun, oh day!) (137a) and then she thrills him beyond imagination when she drops her veil sufficiently to show him an eye. Melchor cries no! do not call this an eye, "Decid nueva maravilla / Del cielo, decid que es sol / Con rayos que vivifican / El alma" (Say a new wonder of Heaven, say that it is the sun whose rays enliven my soul) (138b). He even calls Ventura over so that he too can marvel at this heavenly vision. The unknown woman then tells Melchor that she knows about Magdalena and that she thinks that she is quite lovely. The unknown woman, now dressed as a widow, tries to set Melchor on the right path through argument. She patiently explains, "Que no es Doña Magdalena / Ni más bella, ni más rica, / Ni más moza, ni más sabia, / Ni más noble, ni más digna / De serviros y estimaros / Que yo" (that Magdalena is neither prettier, nor richer, nor younger, nor wiser, nor nobler, nor more deserving than I to serve and esteem you). Melchor rejects any comparison; Magdalena he swears is "ni hermosa, / Ni digna de que compita / Con vos" (neither beautiful nor worthy to compete with you) (137b).

To complicate matters, Doña Angela, Magdalena's neighbor, is attracted to Melchor and begins to plot with her brother, Don Sebastián, who loves Magdalena, to disrupt the intended marriage. In one scene, Angela dresses as the "unknown lady," speaks with Melchor and Ventura, and she too shows them an eye. Melchor is charmed once more, but Ventura is taken aback, "Mas o mi vista se engaña, / O no es ese ojo el de ayer; / Que su niña era mulata / Y hoy se ha vestido de azul / . . . / ¡Vive Dios / Que era endrina toledana / La niñeta que ayer vimos, / Y hoy nos mira turquesada!" (Well, either my eyes are deceived or that is not the one from yesterday because its iris was brown and today it is dressed blue. . . . By God the iris we saw yesterday was dark as a Toledan sloe-berry and today a turquoise one looks at us!) Melchor repudiates Ventura's oath swearing to the veiled woman, "En mi memoria os retrata. / Yo sé que es ese el que adoro" (My mind's eye paints you. I know that that [eye] I see is the one I adore) (144b).

So blinded by his imagination is Melchor that he cannot tell one woman from another. How, then can Magdalena bring Melchor into the fold? First, however, must be the question of why. Magdalena was not thrilled about marrying a man she had never met. When Quiñones, her maid, tells her that Melchor has arrived at the house, Magdalena, hurrying to change clothes after returning home from La Vitoria, confesses, "¡Ay, Quiñones, y qué susto / Me causa aquesta venida! / . . . / ¡Y antes de verle me dan / Esposo! ¡Caso terrible! / ¡Qué tenga tanto poder / La obediencia y el honor!" (Oh Quiñones, and what a fright this arrival gives me. . . . Before I see him they give him to me for a husband! A terrible thing! Must obedience and honor have so much power!) (133c). Distressed at the forced marriage, she laments her lack of choice in so important a matter, "¡He de amar a quien aguardo! / Quiñones, ¿no es caso fiero?" (I must love the one I await! Quiñones, isn't this a cruel thing?) (133c).

She was, however, taken with the stranger she met at Mass, so taken, in fact, that she has dreamily dawdled before meeting her forced intended, "Tenía yo divertida / El alma, y no sé si el gusto, / Con la memoria apacible / Del forastero galán" (My soul was diverted, and perhaps my fancy too, by the pleasant memory of the gallant stranger) (133c). What she found attractive was his grace, his gallant behavior, and nearly perfect physical form. How she wishes she could make Melchor "Si no tan perfeto, / Tan amante o tan discreto" (If not as perfect, then as loving and discreet) (133c). When Quiñones hopes aloud that Melchor could be even better than the stranger, Magdalena retorts, "¿Cómo será eso posible? / ¡Tan cortés urbanidad! / ¡Tanta liberalidad! / Y sazón tan apacible" (How can that be possible? Such courteous urbanity! Such generosity and pleasant maturity) (134a). When she sees that Melchor is the stranger, her surprised joy is tempered with mistrust, "Pensamientos / ¿Qué piélago os ha engolfado / De contrarias suspensiones . . . ?" (Thoughts, what wave has engulfed you in astonishing contraries?) (134c); "No sé deso lo que arguya, / Pensamientos solicitan / Guerra, en mi pecho, cruel, / Y si unos vuelven por él, / Otros le desacreditan" (I do not know what this means. Thoughts bring out cruel war in my breast, and if some fawn on him, others discredit him) (133b). Observing her mistress's perplexity, Quiñones suggests that her fears spring naturally from the step she must take into marriage, but Magdalena denies that. She tries to explain that she already loves Melchor so that "sin él, morir espero" (without him I hope to die) (135c), but her doubts arise because "¿con qué seguridad / Rendiré mi voluntad / A quien, con tan fácil fe, / La primer mujer que ve / Triunfa de su voluntad?" (With what surity will I surrender my will to a man of such facile faith that the first woman he sees conquers his will) (135c). She forecasts an uncertain future for "Quien así desvanece, / Y sin penetrar sus ojos / Lo que, por no ver, ignora, / . . . / ¿. . . quién me asegurará / De voluntad tan lijera, / Que, desposado, no hará / Lo mismo con cuantas mire . . .?" (Whoever faints / falters so easily without even looking into her eyes unable thus to see what he ignores, who can assure me that a man of such weak will, when married, will not do the same with all women he meets?) (1325c). She loves him, but she does not trust him, and the conundrum she faces, of course, as the play's title states, is that she is jealous of herself. To assure herself that Melchor will be true, she will test him, "Eso, pues, quiero probar" (That, then, is what I shall test) (135c).

The causes and effects of her doubled identity I shall study in detail
in Chapter 5; for now, suffice it to say that Magdalena promises to
make Melchor's future a schizophrenic experience even if he passes
the tests, even if they do eventually marry: "Yo le querré eternamente, / Y eternamente también / Se vengará mi desdén / De lo que
en el suyo siente" (I will love him eternally and eternally too will my
disdain avenge the disdain in which he holds me) (140b). After Magdalena and her father agree to let Melchor out of his marriage contract, Magdalena gives him a message from her "friend," the Countess.[4] She has decided to marry a cousin so as to avoid a legal battle
over her estates and to leave promptly for home. Having lost both
women in the blink of an eye, Melchor resolves to return empty-
handed to León.

As he and Ventura pack, the Countess sends him a note saying that
her marriage and her departure were faked to test his love (142c), so
back to La Vitoria they go. Even though he just passed through a
moment of disenchantment, Melchor has not learned to see, since he
instantly reverts to his fetishizing language, "¡Ay mi mano! / ¡Que
otra vez tengo de veros!" (Oh, my hand, once more I can see you)
(142c). Complications arise when Angela, with Quiñones help, dresses
as the Countess and outruns Magdalena to church. When Melchor
meets the disguised Angela, he describes her as *alba* (dawn), *sol*
(sun), and *mañana* (morning) (144a). Magdalena arrives and Melchor
now faces two Countesses. Angela shows him the purse, obtained
from Quiñones, and an eye (and, as noted above, Ventura futilely
swears that it is not the same eye he saw yesterday), and Melchor
begins to believe her his true love. Magdalena still retains the cut
pursestrings and produces those as her proof. Melchor then asks, ironically, to see each woman's hand so that he can know who the real
Countess is, but due to the untimely arrival of both Angela's and
Magdalena's brothers, both women quickly exit. Magdalena then
sends for Melchor to come to her house.

There, as the Countess, she tells Melchor that she really does have
to leave for Italy to marry her cousin. Since their marriage cannot be
and since Magdalena, her true friend, loves Melchor, she begs him to
marry her. Melchor, to prove his love for the Countess, states that
though he does not love Magdalena, he will marry her. The Countess
immediately turns on him, "¡Ay traidor! ¡Y quien tuviera / Fe en voluntades de vidrio, / Que al primer golpe se quiebran!" (Traitor! Who

4. Magdalena as the unknown woman has adopted the name and position of La Condesa de Chirinola. Chirinola, Jane Albrecht (1994) explains meant, among other
things, "enredo, embrollo," or entanglement, mischievous lie, imbroglio.

could have faith in a will of glass so easily shattered at the first blow) (147c). She expected him, she declares, to offer excuses, to insult Magdalena, to die before agreeing (148a), but he has proven faithless once more. Melchor, taking the cue, begins to call Magdalena names, but she modulates her voice, becomes Magdalena, and accuses him of ignoble and discourteous behavior: "Quien habla mal en ausencia / De mujeres principales / . . . / . . . bien será que pierda / Como el crédito conmigo, / El amor de la Condesa" (Who speaks ill of absent principal women, it is right that such a man lose credit with me and lose the Countess's love as well) (148a).

Melchor is now thoroughly deflated. Thus when in the final clarification scene before the reunited cast Magdalena explains all the deceptions, Melchor admits his ignorance and embarrassedly adds, when she shows him her hand, "Conózcola, y con vergüenza / En ella sello mis labios" (I know it and with it I shamefully seal my lips) (148c). His final words stand in stark contrast to his earlier inflated, blind, poetic flights as he admits his errors and kneels, chastened, before his knowing bride.

Magdalena's disguise and her new identity hold the key to her didactic project. Melchor falls for a veiled woman, thus for an idealized image, for a person he literally cannot see. He falls, as Magdalena clearly knows, for a fantasy created by his own imagination. He calls the woman he looks at ugly and repulsive, whereas what attracts him to the unseeable woman is precisely the mystery, the exoticism hidden from him behind the veil like a treasure that only he can find. What repels him about Magdalena is, in part, the quality of the forced marriage. She is not of his choosing, but worse, he must approach her humbly since he is poor and she is wealthy, "yo me vengo a casar / Con sesenta mil ducados, / Y soy pobre" (I am come to marry seventy thousand ducats, being poor) (128b). She is, then, the dutiful daughter, the unwanted wife, and the wealthy hag, all in one, "Es fría. / No me la nombres, Ventura" (She leaves me cold, don't say her name to me, Ventura) (136b).

Magdalena cannot allow Melchor to see her thus nor to pigeonhole her. One fear is that if he accepts the marriage, he will seek the exotic elsewhere; another is that if she simply tells him right away that she was the mystery woman, she can never live up to his fantasy. She must teach him that he can neither demean nor idolize her since any one description would be insufficient. She must show him that she can be both wife and lover, dutiful and free, loyal if he is loyal, ready to make his life miserable should he prove unfaithful—capable, that is, of change and growth. She must demonstrate that she is a multifaceted person and that before she will marry him, he must free himself from received notions and categories and grow too.

This is Angela's problem in *La dama duende*. Both Juan and Luis see her as obedient sister on the one hand and as a dangerous young widow on the other. Every time that Manuel thinks that he knows who and what she is, she glides beyond that definition, manifesting yet another facet of her being. So confused is Manuel and so bound by traditional notions, however, that despite Angela's best efforts, he learns very little—except that he is in a real bind—by the end of the play. In Lope's *¡Ay, verdades, que en amor . . . !* Celia must teach Juan that he cannot take her or her love for granted, that she is neither a submissive, begging lover nor a fickle, vindictive harpy, though she can easily play either role. Juan must learn to prize in her the values he only slowly and painfully discovers.

Standing between Melchor and Magdalena are his romanticized and idealized imaginary constructions based, as Primaj Halkhoree (1989) has correctly observed (89–90), on stylized Neoplatonic preconceptions of how a beautiful woman must look. While this observation is true enough, more important is Magdalena's role as guide to the blind lover.

She, along with the play, seems to ask, Do we love what we see or do we love what we imagine we see? How can we distinguish? What shapes our imagination? What influences how, and thus what we see? *La celosa de sí misma* posits woman as she who sees clearly, as she who must/can lead the man past his preconceptions, past traditional, received idealizations to another way of looking at her, and consequently to another way of looking at himself. The problematics of viewpoint, knowledge, illusion and reality, the representation of illusion and the illusion of representation involve not only the characters in the play, but extend beyond the stage to encompass the audience as well. Given the mixed audience in the *corral* (playhouse), totalizing speculation about audience response is dangerous, but if the audience can see what Melchor cannot, it can laugh at his errors and ridicule his mistakes. However, the audience might also recognize that it occupies a godlike position, able for the duration of the play to see from several or all points at once. If the audience members were to sympathize with Melchor, they might see their viewpoint constrict. Such a recognition could provoke a critical stance that highlights the need to examine how one sees since the audience witnesses a work wherein it has viewed others from a place from which they cannot look at themselves.

Magdalena's basic problem could, in fact, be summarized by appeal to Lacan's (1981) "When in love, I solicit a look, what is profoundly unsatisfying and always missing is that—You never look at me from the place from which I see you" (103). Magdalena wants to get Melchor to see her much as she sees herself. By showing Melchor's misrecognition and the causes thereof, the comedy presents an anatomy of some particular societal problems that produce restricting misperception. By following the woman's schemes, as she works through displacement in disguise, the audience may glimpse not only the problems but also a solution, a way to see differently: examine and reevaluate the cultural givens.

In *La celosa de sí misma,* as well as in other plays, the problem lies in man's traditional (poetic) concepts of woman; in *Esto sí que es negociar,* the barrier is social. Rogerio and Leonisa were raised together in the country where Rogerio had a comparatively easy go of life. Brought up as the son of a lower noble landlord, Rogerio, from this privileged position, sought out the loveliest of the women in the region, Leonisa. He exercises not only economic but also social power over her because she is a *villana* (peasant). But he loves her despite their social differences, believing that her beauty and virtue are merits strong enough to overcome class difference. Besides, as he says to her, "No tienes el gusto tú / A serranos toscos hecho; / Que esa alma erró el hospedaje / Cuando entró a vivir en tu cuerpo: / Tu elección toda es hidalga" (Your tastes are not those of rough mountain people; for that soul selected the wrong home when it came to live in your body. Your choices are all noble) (249c)—no doubt praise for Leonisa but also backhanded self-praise as well as self-justification. Yet he refrains from telling his father, Pinardo, of his intentions toward Leonisa. When he went to school in Paris, there too his path was smooth as he graduated to universal applause in "cánones, leyes y filosofía" (canon law, civil law, and philosophy) (249c). All during his absence, he says, he thought of Leonisa constantly. Upon his return, he is suddenly elevated by the Duke of Bretaña to heir to the dukedom; Rogerio turns out to be the Duke's bastard son. However, problems arise as Rogerio's public persona and the possibility of marriage to the noble Clemencia "require" that he reject Leonisa, "¡Ay Leonisa de mis ojos! / Autor soy de tus enojos; / No ha mucho que prenda tuya / Me llamabas: soy ya duque; / Por fuerza te he de olvidar" (Ah! Leonisa . . . I am the author of your anger; Not long ago you called me your love but now I am a duke and I must forceably forget you) (2532a). Once more the woman must take it upon herself to show the man what is of value and what is not.

Leonisa is no village mouse. Before her current problems, occasioned by Rogerio's unexpected social elevation, she successfully fended off several suitors. She has held one, a local nobleman named Filipo, at bay and she rejected her father's advice and her overlord's request that she marry the latter (248c/49a), always believing in her greater worth, in values hidden by her lowly clothes and social position. Thus she is anything but abashed when Rogerio tells her he must now reject her. To lead Rogerio to a new understanding, she counts on Enrique, Clemencia's now discarded noble lover, to help. But in the unfolding plot, he is more passive than active, taking on the roles and speaking the words Leonisa gives him. At first Enrique looks down on all social inferiors, including Rogerio, whom he considers an upstart bumpkin, "Hoy un duque, ayer villano" (Today a duke, yesterday a peasant) (251a). But the more contact he has with the clever and attractive Leonisa, the more his attitudes change. In the final act, he compares Leonisa most favorably to Clemencia, "Perlas enseña su risa, / Cielos logra su presencia; / ¿Qué tiene que ver Clemencia / Con los ojos de Leonisa?" (Her smile offers pearls, her presence is heavenly, how can Clemencia compare with Leonisa's eyes?) (260b).

To lead Rogerio to discovery, then, Leonisa counts on Enrique, but counts more on her intelligence, on her ability to improvise, and on an unwavering faith in her own worth. In the course of the play, she presents several ringing endorsements of true worth; here is one:

> Porque Clemencia nació
> Duquesa, ¿es bien que me impida
> Ser de Rogerio querida?
> Si es el alma la que da
> Valor, aquélla será,
> Que es mejor, mas bien nacida.
> ¿No es más noble el alma, cielo,
> De pensamientos mejores? . . .
> Yo, que de mi esfera salgo
> Con mejores pensamientos,
> Animando atrevimientos,
> Merezco más, pues más valgo . . .
>
> (253c)

(Just because Clemencia was born a duchess, is it right for that to prevent Rogerio's loving me? If the soul is what gives one worth, the well-born soul is best. Thus, is not the nobler soul, the one that has the best thoughts? Since I surpass the state I

was born in by means of better, even daring, thoughts then I
deserve more because I am worth more.)

Her conviction of her own worth plus her constancy carry the day.

When the situation demands it, she can appear abrupt, even
loutish. For example, when Rogerio is about to kiss Clemencia's hand
during their first meeting in the countryside, Leonisa rushes in and
pushes the two apart saying that she is looking for an earring she lost
right where these two are standing. When Clemencia upbraids her for
pushing her aside, Leonisa responds, "¿No estoy en mi casa yo? / Cada
cual manda en la suya" (Am I not in my own home? Everyone is
queen in her own castle." (252a), and then she insults Clemencia.

Later in the play, Leonisa says that she will marry Filipo. Rogerio,
burning with jealousy, counsels Filipo not to marry her because of
their social difference (259a). When Filipo insists, Rogerio turns on
Leonisa accusing her of fickleness, but then recognizes that her "error" was originally his: "*Ap. ¡Ay Leonisa! al fin lijera. / Mas si estoy
culpado yo, / ¿Por qué a mudanza atribuyo / Lo que en ti fue discreción?*) (*Aside*. Ah! Leonisa, in the end fickle. But if I am really to
blame, why do I attribute to fickleness what was really discretion in
you?) (259b). That is to say, he begins to note the double standard; he
damns her for what he too has done. He has taken the first steps
along the path that Leonisa has prepared for him learning, to modify
an old proverb, that what's right for the gander is also right for the
goose.

In a subplot, Leonisa disguises herself as Margarita, a noblewoman
come to Britanny to escape the wrath of the king of Scotland. As Margarita—and Rogerio cannot fail to note the physical symmetry between Leonisa and the noblewoman though he marvels at the linguistic distance that separates the two—she proposes to marry Enrique.
Rogerio had thought that he had a way out of his conflict: marry
Margarita, Leonisa's mirror image, "Es de Leonisa retrato" (She is
the very picture of Leonisa) (209a), in his words. Calling Margarita
aside, Rogerio asks her to forget Enrique as he will forgo Clemencia
and the two will marry. She tells him that while she does not really
love Enrique, and while she feels a certain inclination toward him,
she does not trust him. What, she asks, would you do, for instance, if
my fortunes changed and I were suddenly poor? Rogerio, nearing the
end of Leonisa's prepared path, swears, "No prosigas; que aunque
fueses, / No Duquesa, una serrana" (Stop, for even if you were not a
duchess, but rather a mountain girl) (261c), he would marry her.

Calling Enrique aside, he now orders him not to marry Margarita.

Enrique agrees and says that he did not really want to marry her anyway because he has fallen in love with "Una serrana hay aquí, / Que en esta sierra es hechizo / Del amor . . ." (A peasant girl around here who is the mountain's love enchantress) (262b). Rogerio threatens to kill Enrique if he proceeds. In the prior scene, Rogerio proposed to Margarita and gave her a ring. In the subsequent scene, he proposes to Leonisa and gives her a ring as well. Now, he approaches madness:

> ¡Yo estoy loco! ¿Qué he de hacer?
> La mano y anillo di
> A Margarita, ¡ay de mí!
> Pues si ha de ser mi mujer,
> ¿Cómo me desposo agora
> Con Leonisa? . . .
> ¡Y con las dos me he casado!
> ¿Qué haré? ¡Cielos, triste yo!
> ¿Desposado allá y aquí?
> Con la misma semejanza sí,
> Mas con las personas no.
> Remediadlo vos, fortuna,
> Amor, mostrad que sois Dios;
> O haced que me parta en dos,
> O convertidlas en una.
>
> (263c)

(I've gone mad. What can I do? I gave my hand and a ring to Margarita, woe is me. So if she is to be my wife, how can I now propose to Leonisa? . . . I've promised myself to two women. What will I do? Heavens, how sad I am. Engaged over here and over there? They both look alike but they are separate persons. Fortune, please fix it, Love, show that you are a god; either split me into two or make them one.)

Before the *dea ex machina* ending, Rogerio publicly confesses to the Duke his love for, and proposals to, both women. For proposing to Margarita and abandoning Clemencia, he offers as the principal reason the duration and constancy of Enrique's love for the latter. For proposing to Leonisa, he offers his own long-standing love, stating that he will marry her even if it means giving up his rights of succession, even if it means his own death. Central to his declaration was Leonisa's role as guide, which combined with her many abilities directed at showing Rogerio what was really important: that she was greater than his limited "class perspective" would allow. Nowhere does Rogerio show more clearly the lesson learned than when he deliberately repeats part of the speech Filipo made to him:

> No mancha al mar una gota
> De tinta, ni en sangre noble . . .
> Podrá Leonisa manchar
> Mi calidad. ¿De qué roble
> no sale una imagen bella
> Que el mundo después adora?
> Si es roble por ser pastora,
> Amor piensa sacar della
> Una imagen soberana.
> En mi real tapicería
> La industria igualar porfía
> Al oro y seda la lana;
> Con ella se mezcla y teje,
> Y siendo por sí tan baja,
> Al brocado se aventaja
>
> (259b)

(A drop of ink cannot stain the sea, nor could Leonisa stain my noble blood. . . . Cannot a beautiful statue admired by all the world come forth from a rough oak? If because she is a shepherdess, and thus like the oak, love will make her into a lovely icon. In my royal looms, skill strives to equalize wool with silk and gold, with it they are mixed and woven, and though so lowly by itself, it then becomes better than brocade.)

This speech recalls the parallel situation of Perdita and Florizel in *The Winter's Tale* and the exchange over nature/nurture between the maid and Polixenes. His royal son, Florizel, has fallen in love with a (presumed) shepherd's daughter, Perdita. In an exchange between the shepherdess and the king, she hands him a bouquet of rosemary and rue, rather than the seasonal flowers because:

> the fairest o' th' season
> Are our carnations and streak'd gillyvors,
> Which some call nature's bastards: of that kind
> Our rustic garden's barren; and I care not
> To get slips of them.
>
> (IV, iv, 81–85)

To the king's perplexed why? she answers that those flowers are unnatural, for nurture, or the gardener's art, has crossbred the flowers, changed them, made them bastards. Polixenes counters:

> Yet nature is made better by no mean
> But nature make that mean: so, over that art,
> Which you say adds to nature, is an art,
> That nature makes. You see, sweet maid, we marry
> A gentler scion to the wildest stock
> And conceive a bark of baser kind
> By bud of nobler race. This is an art
> Which does mend nature—change it rather—but
> The art itself is nature.
>
> (89–97)

As in the Rogerio/Filipo speech where from a rough oak a beautiful icon can emerge, or as in a tapestry where the interweaving of silk and wool produces a richer fabric, so too does grafting one plant onto another produce a better bud. While not a profound discovery, it is an important observation in a period when marriages between estates were not the norm.[5] In addition, it may also point to the "created" nature of nobility itself rather than to its "natural" status.

5. Víctor García Ruiz, in his introduction to *Esto sí que es negociar* (Tirso de Molina 1985), speculates that "Los matrimonios desiguales no debían de ser frecuentes pero tampoco inusitados" (misalliances were probably not frequent but they were not unheard of either) (134). I have searched in vain for hard statistical data about marriages across class boundaries. However, there is some anecdotal evidence. Jack W. Sage (1973) says that "by the end of the sixteenth century social advancement linked with misalliance had become very significant factors in more or less ordinary Spanish life. As early as 1487, Diego Rodríguez de Almella, making valuable progress towards factual history with his *Valerio,* had devoted the whole of título 4 to 'aquellos que nacidos de bajo lugar fueron hechos claros y nobles . . . .'" (Those who had a low birth became famous and noble.) The *Valerio* was republished in 1584 and 1587. Sage reminds us that Domínguez Ortiz stresses social mobility and the "ensuing struggle . . . with the subversive notion of nobility-through-works" (250). Sage offers examples of misalliance, for example, "the grandfather of Lope's employer (the fifth Duke of Sessa) had married, in 1538, a girl far below his own rank who was the daughter of our model upstart-secretary, Francisco de Cobos himself. And in this same household of the third Duke of Sessa lived the celebrated black slave, Juan Latino, who married a Veinticuatro's daughter" (252). Appealing to literary evidence, Sage lists a number of plays between 1590 and 1630 wherein misalliances occur (264–65). Jaime Fernández (1989) lists six misalliance plays by Lope including *El perro del hortelano* and *El villano en su rincón.* In *Emigrants and Society,* a study of sixteenth-century Extremadura and America, Ida Altman (1989) notes, again without statistics, that "among the lower-ranking hidalgos intermarriage with non-hidalgos was common, further blurring distinctions between individuals at this level" (54).

Rogerio, blinded by his sudden rise and by the social prejudice he believes such an elevation entails, classifies Leonisa and rejects her, but the rejection conflicts with his feelings, thus like the *perro del hortelano* (the dog in the manger), he threatens any suitor who comes forward. He wants to settle on her simulacrum, Margarita, but still cannot release the "rustic" woman he has loved so long. He prays for a way out of his conflict even as he approaches madness. The way out is to accept his inability to define her once and for all, to accept change as the only constant and trust in her and in himself and in a love that can withstand any challenge. She is "fickle" and constant, but so too is he. Leonisa's is a bastard's condition—rustic and noble— and so is Rogerio's; he is an educated rustic, noble and illegitimate. From that crossbreeding, a better bud may appear, but one whose nature is not fixed but mixed. No single social category, no single linguistic construct is sufficient to contain either Rogerio or the woman he loves.

In the final scenes, Rogerio does accept, and now faces down everyone with his public declaration of love for Leonisa:

> Yo me crié con Leonisa
> En estas sierras; y niño
> Amor, siendo ya gigante,
> ¿Qué mucho engendre prodigios?
> Su esposo tengo de ser,
> Aunque el patrimonio rico
> Pierda que en Bretaña adquiero,
> Y otra vez viva estos riscos.
>
> (264b)

(I was raised with Leonisa in these mountains, and the child Cupid, now become a giant, can he not work wonders? I must be her husband even if I lose Brittany's rich heritage and once more live among these hills.)

It turns out, of course, that Leonisa is noble: she is the long-lost daughter of the real Margarita's uncle. The "surprise" ending would not have been much of a surprise for anyone in the audience since something of that kind had been hinted at throughout, and since Leonisa played Margarita's role so well. For some, the ending might seem a letdown, a return to the norm, a rejection of the play's potential subversiveness: by elevating Leonisa to the nobility, any real possibility of marriage outside of traditional boundaries is averted.

Equally important, however, is that Rogerio confess his love for Leonisa and offer to give up his inheritance *before* she is recognized as Margarita's cousin. Rogerio has learned to perceive and accept what is of value in Leonisa and in himself, to admit the possibility of change, to reject social prejudice, to accept joy and pain, growth and decay, loss and gain, to prize in Leonisa what she has shown him is of true worth to both of them.

In Juan Pérez de Montalván's *La toquera vizcaína* (1629), we see one more variation on the "women-know-and-lead" motif. This play begins at the opposite pole from Melchor's high-flying rhetorical infatuation (*La celosa de sí misma*) when Juan sees his beloved Elena speaking with his rival, Diego. And indeed, Elena has met Diego in a secluded spot but only to beg him to desist from following and loving her because she loves Juan. But Juan can only see "¿Tú hablando con mi enemigo? / ¿Tú en el campo? ¿Tú tapada?" (You speaking to my enemy? You in the countryside? You veiled?) (*Dramáticos contemporáneos de Lope de Vega* 1924, 2:514c). Juan launches a lengthy degradation of Elena decrying her false tears, her deceitfulness, her changeability, her "dos caras" (two-facedness). She tries to get him to listen but he rudely rejoins, "Elena, cierra los labios" (Elena, shut up) (515a); she tries to get him to see but he insists, "Ya lo he visto" (I have already seen enough) (515a). Juan rushes off but later returns to tell her that he has killed Diego and that he now leaves her forever.

In the secondary plot, Lisardo, in Madrid, pursues a *mujer esquiva* (disdainful woman), Flora. Since she rejects any open expression of love, he must hide his feelings, dealing with her as a courteous but suffering man forbidden to speak his love. Flora had earlier rejected the many love notes left at her door by other suitors, since the notes were filled with poetic clichés she then ridicules by taking them literally. One begins, "Estoy tan muerto. . ." (I am so dead) and she immediately stops reading, saying, nonsense, "Porque a estar muerto ese amante, / No sintiera como siente" (Well if this lover were dead, he wouldn't feel as he does) (516b); when another compares her to the sun, she objects, "¿Qué tiene que ver / Con el sol una mujer?" (What does a woman have to do with the sun?) (516c); when one says that he saw her yesterday and burns today, she wonders, well, if he burns today, what will be left for tomorrow? Yet, though funny, the situation is laced with irony since she calls herself, tritely, a *mujer esquiva*.

When we next see Juan, three months have passed and he now lodges in his friend Lisardo's house, afraid to go out except at night because the man he killed has many relations in the capital. Juan now pines for Elena, who he now recognizes as his true love. Luquete, his servant, says that she loves him more because women love more than men: "Sí puede, porque es mujer / Y dellas tengo entendido / . . . que . . . / Quiere cualquier mujer / Muchísimo más que un hombre; / Porque, en fin, el más amante / Ronda, visita, pasea, / Juega, mira, y aun desea / Divertido e inconstante; / Mas una pobre señora, / Que no sale por la villa, / Y asida a una almohadilla, / Con lo mismo que llora, / Claro está que querrá más / Y que guardará más ley" (Yes, she does, because she is a woman, and from them I have learned that any woman loves much more strongly than a man because even the most loving man goes about, visits, walks around, gambles, looks, and even desires, distracted and fickle, but a poor woman can't wander about town rather she [stays in] clutching a pillow into which she weeps, obviously she loves more deeply and she will be more faithful) (519a/b). We soon discover that Juan indeed does go out; further, that Luquete says he's interested in Flora. Juan ridicules the accusation, saying that not only does he not love her, but she refuses all love, and moreover, that his best friend loves her (519b).

In the interim, Elena has gotten her servant Beatriz's sister to stay in a convent in Valladolid pretending to be her while she and Beatriz have come to Madrid searching for Juan. Elena has taken the name Doña Antonia de la Cerda where she lodges, but is also Luisa de Licoalde, *la toquera vizcaína* (The Basque hat/veil-seller) in which disguise she can search the streets and enter many ladies' houses seeking her beloved. Though convinced in her heart of hearts that Juan loves her, she fears that he may be living with another woman since after searching for him for a month she has had no luck. Aiding her is Magdalena, a real *toquera,* and now Elena's friend.

Lisardo invites Juan to Flora's house for an evening chat. Curiously, Flora has fallen for Juan because of his constancy toward Elena. As they speak, Luquete arrives with a packet of letters from Elena, which Juan sits down to read as Flora burns. From offstage, the audience hears Magdalena's cries, "¿Compran tocas? ¿Quieren tocas?" (Who will buy headcoverings? Who wants headcoverings?) (522b) and Flora calls the vendor in. Elena and Beatriz enter while Magdalena waits outside. As they display their wares, Elena spies Juan, gets angry, and leaves. Juan, believing the *toquera* to be Elena, follows her to a house, pounds on the door only to discover neither Elena nor Luisa, but Antonia de la Cerda. She tells him that she cannot be the woman he seeks because she has been married for ten years, but she wonders if he is not the man who has been wandering about under her balcony at night. If he is, she says, he should be more discreet and write her rather than risk her husband's jealous attack. Juan leaves trying to sort out the enigmas, "lo que yo he sacado / De aquesas enigmas es, / Que Elena está en un convento, / Que es suya [the letter] aquesta que ves; / Que la toquera de hoy / Es doña Elena también, / Y lo mismo doña Antonia" (what I have gotten out of these enigmas is, that Elena is in a convent because this letter you see is hers; That the hat/veil-seller of today is Elena too, and so is Antonia) (524b). Since he cannot find the *toquera,* "Pretenderé a doña Antonia, / . . . / Mis penas entretendré / Hasta salir deste encanto" (I shall court Antonia to divert my suffering until escaping from this enchantment) (524c), thereby partially confirming Luquete's observation on men's diversion.

Elena too sorts out her feelings, "Don Juan es cuerdo y galán, / Cortés, gallardo, entendido, / Puntual y bien nacido" (Juan is sensible and gallant, courteous, elegant, smart, punctual, and well-born) she says, but "Y con todo eso, don Juan / A un mismo tiempo enamora / a cuatro" (and with all that, Juan courts four women) (524c); that is, Elena, Luisa, Antonia, and Flora. She wonders aloud, if Juan is the best of men, what can the others be like? She, like Magdalena in *La celosa de sí misma,* decides to test him, "Examino su verdad, / Conozco su voluntad" (I shall examine his truthfulness; I shall learn his intentions) (525b). First, disguised as Doña Leonor de Peralta, she will visit Flora to see if they love each other. Then, as Elena, she sends Juan a letter "from Valladolid" asking him to return immediately; she sends him a letter from Luisa declaring her love; and she sends him a message from Antonia saying that her husband is out of town and that he can meet her at the Prado. As Leonor, she tells Flora that Juan loves many women and Flora repents of falling for such a philanderer. As Luisa, she goes to Lisardo's house to see if Juan might really have a woman hidden there. Juan receives Elena's letter and Antonia's invitation as Luisa declares her love for him. Juan, though confused, holds firm and prepares to leave for Valladolid. In the last scene, Elena explains all of the disguises, Flora enters, declares Lisardo the only faithful man in Madrid, and the play ends in multiple marriages.

This play differs from *La celosa de sí misma* in that Juan remains constant to Elena once convinced of her innocence in the Diego matter. He is distracted by Luisa and Antonia but only insofar as they mirror Elena, a situation parallel to Rogerio's love for "Margarita" in *Esto sí que es negociar.* This play differs from the following group— men know and teach—because Juan is neither active nor the focalizer, Elena is. Elena loves Juan but, since she has not seen him since he left Valladolid, she doubts his fidelity. She has received his letters wherein he swears his loyalty and love, but she says, in letters, "Dicen locuras los hombres / Y mienten a rienda suelta" (Men say crazy things and lie freely) (520c). She has to see for herself that he is true. Thus she plans and puts into operation a series of deceptions, all invitations to Juan to stray from the path. Her tempting disguises then range from the *toquera* to the *casada infiel* (unfaithful wife), but Juan holds the line. Flora, whom she cannot control, represents a threat so she creates a philandering image for her true love, and Flora desists. Yet even with Flora, Juan has shown himself true to his word: he would not love her no matter what since he loves Elena and since his best friend, Lisardo, loves Flora. Juan passes all of Elena's tests well, and though often confused, his fidelity holds. Elena, finally convinced of his real qualities, drops the deceptions and marries him.

In other plays we have variations on the theme; for instance, in Lope's *Por la puente Juana,* a noblewoman disguised as a serving maid is pursued by several noblemen even as she assures her beloved that in the face of such trials a woman can be as hard as a diamond. Yet he still does not trust her. Nonetheless, the strength of her character bring the two together in the end. In *La huerta de Juan Fernández,* Doña Petronila must bring Hernando into her arms by showing him what he should seek in a wife, by illustrating the dangers of not keeping his word, and by disrupting his love for an Italian noblewoman. Finally, in the meanest of these plays, mean because Violante, *La villana de Vallecas,* was seduced and abandoned by her ex-soldier lover Gabriel, she must shove the deceptive man into an increasingly tight corner from which he can only get out by admitting what he has done and gratefully accepting Violante's hand.

In many of these plays, men's misperception of women springs from inherited social, cultural, and linguistic categories. At the beginning of their trials no middle ground exists: woman is either idolized or degraded, but rarely ever "seen." But to say that the men do not see the women is not correct: they do see them, but with other men's eyes, or with the eyes of tradition, of poetic formula, or cultural or social stereotype, with eyes inherited from the past. René Girard (1965) examined a similar triangulation of desire in *Don Quijote,* showing the hell that can come from such a way of seeing (2–25; see also Blue 1986). In the intercalated novel, *El curioso impertinente,* Cardenio wanted to believe his lover true, but believed more in woman's inherent deceitfulness. Thus when he "saw" his beloved Luscinda prove faithless and marry another man, he went mad. Anselmo wanted to believe Camila "tan perfeta como yo pienso" (as perfect as I think she is), but could not: "no puedo enterarme en esta verdad" (I cannot make myself believe this truth) (Cervantes, *Don Quijote* 1:330). Don Quijote, on the other hand, follows his model, Amadís, maintaining his faith in his idealized construct, Dulcinea, no matter what Sancho might say.

In the plays described above, fantasy is debunked, stereotyping decried, degradation reversed. The women lead men through trials and tests to give them the experience from which more adequately to judge. When early on men speak from within received patterns, in clichés, they bring into play their "pre-knowledge" of what woman is. The women's task is to shake the men from their inherited blinders and lead them to a different understanding, tempered by experience, of woman and consequently of themselves.

From another angle, Jacques Lacan got at the root of these problems through his ideas about language. How do we express to ourselves and to others, he asks, through and within a structure imposed upon us, the distinction between what we see and what we feel? In some of these plays, the men seem to sense discontinuity as they doubt whether the woman is as they see her. Preconceived notions exist in the language the men and women inherit, as do the myths they live by. It is through preconceptions, myths, language, and their division of the world into arbitrary categories that they organize their experiences. When desire disturbs the connections among the men's impressions of the women and their thinking and talking about them, the men necessarily make faulty links. For the women who can see well, their task, desire, and goal then, is to rewire the men, connect the circuits, and redirect the current; to see the world through fixed categories and received myths is to limit the enormous surprise that life can hold.[6] The women in these plays through masquerade, disguise, plotting, and the rest show men some of what women can be; they do indeed surprise the men and thereby introduce an enriched

6. Though above I focus on the men, both men and women are subject to desire, both are constructs of the symbolic, with the difference that women's self-definition is based, as Ragland-Sullivan (1991) observes, on the "not-all" rather than the "all." While "woman is essentialized by males as containing secret truths, the answers to enigmas, answers from, or to, the Otherness that the masculine denies and rejects and projects onto others" (60), she "knows no one is whole because she has not identified with difference as an imaginary universal" (62). "Feminine sexuality," Ragland-Sullivan continues, "—not necessarily correlated with gender—is a masquerade not only because s/he can disguise her desire, can fake it, can cover her body with cosmetics and jewels and make of it a phallus, but also because her masquerade hides a fact—that masculine sexuality is a tenuous matter" (71).

freshness into the men's conception of life. "Mutually constitutive relations between the self and other," W. Thomas MacCary (1985) writes, "are possible only through the creative efforts of the individual who simultaneously confirms and denies his derivation from his society and its traditions" (69).

Central to these plays and to the women's plans is theatricality itself—role-playing, plotting, deception, disguise—which spotlights appearance by shining a light on the mask. These plays, in other words, re-present representation so that the male and female characters, and potentially the audience, can perhaps begin to see the createdness of traditional categories of thought, the myths, and the ideological power of language, and thus the power and limitations of these inherited categories. Theater underscores, as Barbara Freedman (1991) insists, the split between looking and seeing: theater "shows that it knows that it is showing" (69). The women's masks and adopted personalities foreground the display of displacement and thus force the men (and invite the audience) into a search for the other and the consequent search for the self since the disguises highlight the insufficiencies of received categories. The women in these plays know more and must teach the men how to see anew. The question of the sufficiency of marriage as the "solution" still nags, but I must postpone addressing that problem until the end of this chapter, as the rest of the plays end in marriage too. For now I turn to plays that cast men in the docent's role.

Men Guide Women

As *La toquera vizcaína* showed, not all men are blinded by social prejudice as was Rogerio (*Esto sí que es negociar*) nor encased by poetic fetichism as Melchor (*La celosa de sí misma*). Although Don Juan (*La toquera vizcaína*) can see, after his moment of jealous outrage, he is more passive than active; it is Elena who initiates the search, dons the disguises, creates the characters, and leads Juan eventually to confirmation. In other words, it is through Elena that the audience focalizes the action. In the plays discussed in this section, the audience sees through the man's eyes and deeds. In Lope's *La moza de cántaro,* for example, another Don Juan sees past María's humble disguise to the qualities he esteems. But the play does not begin with the presentation of a man in the active role. Quite the contrary: the aged Bernardo, María's father, comes home one day bemoaning his fate; because of a disagreement, he was slapped in public by Diego. Unable to defend himself, he laments (to Maria) his son's absence. She then goes to Diego's jail cell to offer herself to him in marriage as a means of putting the dispute and inevitable round of revenge to rest. Diego praises her angelic and wise decision, and as he embraces his lovely peacemaker, she pulls out a dagger and kills him, "¿En canas tan venerables / pusiste la mano, perro? / Pues estas hazañas hacen / las mujeres varoniles" (You put your hand on his venerable head, dog? Well such deeds do manly women make) (104). Before her father's return, however, María had been discussing her various suitors—so great is her beauty that she has attracted men from all around Seville—with her maid. As Luisa hands her their letters, María rejects them all, as did Flora in *La toquera vizcaína*, and as Inés will do in *El examen de maridos* on stylistic grounds. One fails for being *culto* (writing in an affected way); another for being prolix. Her rejection on stylistic grounds while amusing, nonetheless, obeys a greater mandate: she calls all of her suitors "esos Narcisos" (those Narcissuses). That is to say, María is beautiful, noble, and rich and those are the only qualities her petitioners see in her. What they see, in other words, is a beautiful prize wrapped in a golden inheritance; for them, as she well knows, she is nothing more than a mirror for their own vanity. She marks the distance between how they see her, plainly visible in the stylistic banalities of their letters, and how she sees herself when she rejects them and marriage itself, "Nací con esta arrogancia; / no me puedo sujetar / si es sujetar el casar" (I was born with this arrogance; I cannot allow myself to be subjugated if marriage equals bondage) (86). The suitors' writing style is a signifier for the signified, narcissism.

After killing Diego, she adopts a *moza*'s (maid's) disguise and flees to Madrid. On the road, she is hired by a stingy, domineering, and soon to prove randy *indiano* (wealthy returnee from the Indies), thus María decries how far her fortunes have fallen (139). Later, in Madrid, the play introduces the Conde who has fallen in love with the noble widow, Ana who, in turn, loves his cousin, Juan. In an evening get-together, each offers a sonnet to the others. The Conde, as befits his position and duty, speaks of the recent Spanish victory over the English in Cádiz (1625); Ana, reflecting on her situation, speaks of unrequited love; and Juan sings the praises of a beautiful *moza de cántaro* (maid with a waterjug [a water carrier]) who has enchanted him. As in the first scene with María and the letters, a round of critical comments follows wherein both Ana and the Count censure Juan's sonnet, not for stylistic reasons, but because they deem the subject

unworthy of such noble praise. When Ana jealously queries, "¿Un caballero discreto / escribe a tan vil sujeto?" (Would a prudent gentleman write to such a vile subject?) (156), Juan vigorously defends his
choice which, he says, was no choice at all:

> No es elección
> amor; diferentes son
> los efetos de su nombre.
> Es, desde el cabello al pie,
> tan bizarra y aliñosa,
> que no es tan limpia la rosa,
> por más que el alba lo esté.
> Tiene un grave señorío,
> en medio desta humildad,
> que aumenta su honestidad
> y no deshace su brío.
> Finalmente, yo no vi
> dama que merezca amor
> con más fe, con más rigor.
>
> (158)

(There is no choice in love; it affects people differently. From
her head to her feet, she is so lovely and neat that no rose is as
pure, no dawn so perfect. In her humbleness she demonstrates
a dignity which magnifies her modesty without diminishing
her charm. And finally, I never saw a lady who deserved more
tenacious, faithful love.)

Now while the audience probably guesses who the *moza* is (Isabel, as
María now calls herself), Juan does not know but yet he gazes beyond
the humble clothes, beyond the surface to qualities within. Both the
jealous Ana and the class-bound Count heap disdain on the lowly object of Juan's affections yet he persists.

But Juan does not know exactly how to approach the woman so, in a
later encounter, he praises her in *culto* terms. Isabel chides him as she
did her Sevillan suitors, "¿Espejo y despejo? Bueno. / Ya con cuidado me
habláis" (Reflect and deflect? Well, now you speak to me contrivedly)
(166). If you speak to me, she continues, let your words show me who
you are, "Habladme como quien sois" (Speak to me from your heart)
(167). She then accuses him of coming on too strong, as wealthy and
noble men often do to humble women. Juan swears to improve his language and his behavior and insists, in a style that recalls Lope's earlier
Peribáñez, that he loves her for who and what she is:

> . . . más estimo y precio
> un listón de tus chinelas
> que las perlas de su [Ana's] cuello;
> más precio . . .
> . . . ir contigo a tu casa
> en tus brazos o en tu pecho,
> que ver cómo cierta dama
> baja en su coche soberbio,
> . . . Yo me contento que digas,
> dulce Isabel, "yo te quiero,"
> que también quiero yo el alma,
> no todo amor es cuerpo.
>
> (170)

(I esteem and value more a ribbon from your clogs than the pearls from around Ana's neck. . . . I would prize more going to your home in your arms or in your heart than seeing how a certain lady comes down in her haughty coach. . . . I would be happy to hear you say, sweet Isabel, "I love you" because I love your soul, love is not just for the body.)

Juan's reply, now simple and direct, impresses María who begins to think that perhaps there may be something good in this fellow. She gives him the highest compliment she has ever offered a man, "que el primer hombre sois vos / a quien amor agradezco" (you are the first man whose love I am thankful for) (170).

Later when she sees Juan accompany Ana to the spring where Isabel must go for water, she challenges him to desist from courting her; that is to say, to cease courting Isabel. Her challenge is couched in a poem to herself but addressed to her "*cántaro*":

> Sois barro, no hay que fiar;
> . . . lo que es barro humilde,
> en fin, por barro se queda.
> No volváis más a la fuente;
> de que estoy segura y cierta
> que no es bien que vos hagáis
> a los coches competencia.
>
> (192)

(You are clay, do not trust; . . . what is humble mud must always be so. Do not return to the spring again, for I am absolutely sure that it is not wise for you to try to compete with noble carriages.)

Next, after María joins Ana's household, escaping from the unwarranted attentions of the aforementioned *indiano,* Juan corners her and insists: "Vive Dios, que te he querido / y te quiero y te querré / con tanta firmeza y fe" (I swear to God that I have loved you and that I love you and that I will always love you with such firmness and faith) (222). At this point, María learns that she has been granted a pardon by the king for killing Diego; thus, she feels she must return home to be with her father. Without telling him any of the details the audience knows, she asks Juan to help her arrange the journey, all the while assuring him of her love, "Yo os quiero bien, aunque soy / de naturaleza esquiva; / pero hay otro amor que priva / por quien os dejo y me voy" (I do love you even though by nature I am disdainful, but there is another love that calls me and for whom I must leave you) (223). Juan, though jealous and confused, faithfully promises to help always in the knowledge that "amor le volverá de barro en plata" (love will transform her from clay into silver) (228).

In the final scene, María prepares to leave; she is now dressed in fine clothing, thus creating an appearance that impresses even the class-conscious Count, "a no conocerla yo, / y a saber sus bajas prendas, / hiciera un alto conceto / de su gallarda presencia" (if I didn't know her nor know her low birth, I would make up a fine poetic conceit about her elegant presence) (238). Juan can wait no longer and announces to all gathered:

> . . . el más alto poder
> que reconoce la tierra,
> el cetro, la monarquía,
> la corona, la grandeza, . . .
> . . . es amor; pues siendo así,
> y que ninguno lo niega,
> que yo por amor me case,
> que yo por amor me pierda . . .
> Cuando esto en público digo,
> no quiero que nadie pueda
> contradecirme el casarme,
> pues hoy me caso con ella.
> Sed testigos que le doy
> la mano.
>
>   (240)

(The highest power that the earth, the scepter, the monarchy,
the crown, and majesty . . . recognize is love, that is true, let no
one deny it, because I shall marry for love, as for love I shall
give up all. . . . When I declare this publicly let no one try to
impede my marriage, witness all how I give her my hand.)

Ana believes he has gone totally mad; the Conde threatens to kill
him, "que antes os quite la vida / que permitir tal bajeza" (before
permitting such a vile act, I shall kill you). Furthermore, he will have
María killed for being a witch, "¡Echad / esta mujer hechicera / por un
corredor, matadla!" (throw that witch out into the hallway and kill
her) (240). Juan steps forth to defend her with his life, to the Conde's
utter disgust, "¿Un hombre de vuestras prendas / quiere infamar su
linaje?" (A man of your stature wants to defame his lineage?) (240).

María's disguise cannot serve as a means of escape from the problems she created in Seville because (1) it functions as a stumbling
block for the class-bound Conde; (2) it increases Ana's jealousy, and
since her beauty shines forth from under the humble costume, she
attracts the priapic *indiano*'s attention as well as the unwanted gestures of a number of male servants in Madrid; and (3) it serves as an
unplanned test for Juan. Often the woman's problems require that
she adopt a disguise that involves a descent in the social register—*La
villana de Vallecas, La toquera vizcaína, Por la puente Juana*—but
from that position she can better teach the man to search beyond the
superficial boundary, to seek in the woman-as-other for "hidden"
qualities. In the plays where the woman leads, the man must be
taught to admire in her what he admires in himself: bravery, intelligence, wit, constancy, etc.

In Lope's play, Juan needs no coaching; he sees in her from the
outset what she had given up hope that any man would be able to see.
All her Sevillian suitors saw that María was beautiful, and knew she
was connected by blood to the Medina Sidonia family, "una de las
familias más influyentes, ricas y prestigiadas de la nobleza del siglo
xvii" (one of the most influential, wealthy, and prestigious noble families in the seventeenth century), as Díez Borque (1990) explains in a
footnote to his edition of the text (80); for that reason they saw her
only as a means to improve themselves. What she learns to admire in
Juan is his ability to penetrate the accidental externals, to prize in
her what she admires in herself and eventually in him. His act of
publicly declaring his love for this person *before* learning her real
identity, thereby facing down social censure and death threats, parallels in another dimension her assassination of her father's offender

and thereby bonds the pair: as she went against all traditionally held gender expectations, so Juan violates traditional patriarchal social laws. Their marriage, then, harmoniously unites two brave souls who, of course, turn out to be of the same social order so that "official society" can stamp its seal of approval on the fait accompli. But like Rogerio in *Esto sí que es negociar,* Juan declares his love *before* learning her real social status (see J. Fernández 1989). And it is just possible that Lope did that on purpose just as it is possible that he attempted to make his play and its message "applicable" to all in his audience by naming the principals Juan and María.

In Tirso's *Por el sótano y el torno,* another man must show a woman how to trust. At the beginning of the play, Fernando rescues Bernarda from an overturned coach in which she was carrying her younger sister, Jusepa, to Madrid for an economically beneficial but unwanted and distasteful (from the younger woman's perspective) marriage to the geriatric, wealthy Capitán. Here, I want to look briefly at only Fernando/Bernarda. Bernarda takes the role of the "heavy" in the play since she arranged her sister's marriage, tries to keep her prisoner in the conventlike house the Captain has built for them, and constantly prevents Jusepa from exercising any choice in her own life. Yet Bernarda has had a hard time in life. She married young, was widowed young, and her husband apparently left her little but despair and debt. She does not want her sister to go through what she has. While her motives may be understandable, the altruistic picture Bernarda paints fades when she says that as compensation for arranging her sister's marriage, she will receive ten thousand *ducados* (ducats). As a result, Bernarda sees marriage as an utterly cold and calculating decision designed to assure both her and her sister's financial future; desire, feeling, or love have been excised from the formula.

Bernarda wants her sister to marry the rich, old *perulero* (returnee from America) in whom she can invest a minimum of time and emotion to reap, upon his prompt demise, a maximum dividend. When he dies, Bernarda says, Jusepa can then do whatever she wants including spend emotion to the limit but always in the sure possession of a mattress stuffed full of money to cushion any future, unforeseen blow. From this hard position must Fernando move her. Fernando penetrates Bernarda's formidable, self-protective exterior to the beauty, sensitivity, and possibly the hurt, certainly the capacity for love, beneath to teach her to find a more moderate position between lynx-eyed calculation and blind passion. She must understand that she cannot totally plan her or her sister's life because, while terrible accidents can happen, so too can happiness. She must learn to accept the rough with the smooth; to try to sand down life in advance falsifies living.

He begins by becoming what he is not, a *barbero* (bloodletter) called to bleed his lady to cure any injury she may have suffered in the earlier accident. Thrilled to be in her presence yet unwilling to chance causing her any injury, he takes her arm, caresses her veins, ties a tourniquet, holds her hand, and begins to ask her a series of questions. His trick is shortly discovered and he escapes, but only after one of Bernarda's servants notes of his mistress, "¡Qué despacio le miró!" (How slowly she looked him up and down!) (561b).

Bernarda blusters, swearing public vengeance against the imposter as she sends a servant, Santillana, off to investigate him. He returns with confirmation of the trick plus some information about the perpetrator. As she sends him off again to find out where the malefactor lives, she suddenly calls him back:

BERNARDA.   Volved acá.
SANTILLANA.   ¿Qué mandáis?
BERNARDA.   ¿Y que el hombre es
caballero?
SANTILLANA.   Ansí lo afirma
la tienda.
BERNARDA.   Y él lo confirma
de la cabeza a los pies,
que tiene extremado talle.
SANTILLANA.   ¿Eso tenemos ahora?
BERNARDA.   Andad, sabed dónde mora;
que yo, hasta hacer castigalle,
no puedo vivir contenta.
SANTILLANA.   Eso pido y eso quiero.
BERNARDA.   ¿Oís? Y ese caballero,
¿qué tanto tendrá de renta?
SANTILLANA.   No tuve cuenta con eso.
BERNARDA.   Pues, sabedlo todo, andad.
SANTILLANA.   —(*Aparte*)
Sangróla en la voluntad
el barberito sin seso.
                    (567b/68a)

(B: Come back here. S: What do you wish? B: And is the man noble? S: So they say in the shop. B: And he confirms it from his head to his toes, he has extraordinary looks. S: Is that the topic now? B: Go, find out where he lives, for I cannot be happy until I punish him. S: That's what I want too. B: Listen. How much income does that gentleman receive? S: I didn't find that out. B: Well find out, go. S: (*Aside*) The crazy little barber bled her willpower.)

Immediately afterward, Bernarda begins buying new clothes.

When she later discovers that Fernando receives six thousand *ducados de renta* (ducats of income), her instant reaction is mercenarily joyous, "Alto viudez, esto es hecho; / perdone Dios al difunto" (Whoa, widowhood, that's the end; may God pardon the dead man) (573a). If she had begun to find Fernando daring and somewhat attractive, what seals it for her is his money. Now, factoring in what she expects to earn from the old Captain with Fernando's income, she calculates that "Mejor me sale la cuenta / de lo que yo había entendido" (this account is turning out better than I had imagined) (573a). With "love" and money in the balance, the scales tip toward financial gain; she sees Fernando as a better version of the Captain even though she recognizes that "La codicia y la afición / pelean dentro de mi pecho, / y cada cual el derecho / alega de su opinión" (Greed and desire are at war in my breast, each side declaring it is right) (582a). Before deciding finally, however, she wants to know more.

Santillana thus continues his investigations and at one point spies Fernando in conversation with a young woman. He reports to Bernarda who burns jealously while interrogating her servant about the other woman: "¿Tenía buen parecer?; ¿Y era persona de suerte?; ¿Muchas galas?; ¿Sabéis vos cómo se nombre / esa mujer?; ¿Buen talle?" (Was she good looking? Was she noble? A lot of finery? Do you know that woman's name? Did she have a good figure?) (584–85). Once more Santillana notes in an aside, "O la viuda tiene celos, / o la pican sabañones" (Either the widow is jealous or chillblains are making her itchy) (585b). Bernarda throws on a shawl and storms over to the inn where Fernando stays. There she upbraids him for his actions, declares that she may marry the Captain's nephew, and then starts to cry. She cries, she says, because of the distress Fernando's lifestyle causes her, "Quiéroos bien como a cristiano / y prójimo, y os quisiera / ver tan reformado en todo" (I love you as a fellow Christian and want to see you reform your ways) (587b). Fernando promises to mend his ways even to the point of leaving the inn and moving to another place so as not to grieve her further. "No," she says hastily, "no quiera / Dios que yo os desacomode. / Más vale que viváis cerca, / porque yo

pueda estorbar / solicitudes traviesas" (God forbid that I inconve-
nience you. It's better for you to live nearby so that I can block
naughty solicitations) (588a). When she is once again at home, however, the audience discerns how far Fernando has moved her:

> Si deste barrio se muda
> a donde después no sé,
> ¿Cómo, ¡cielos! le veré? . . .
> ¡Qué necia fui en no decille
> claramente mi pasión!
>
> (590a)

(If he moves from this precinct to I don't know where, how,
God, will I be able to see him? I was stupid not to declare my
feelings!)

With the finances now taking a back seat to passion, the play drives
rapidly toward the conclusion wherein Fernando and all gather to beg
Bernarda to let Jusepa marry Duarte, and then the entire cast begs
her to accept Fernando's proffered hand. Bernarda openly declares
her love and the play ends. The man here, like Juan in *La moza de
cántaro,* has taught the woman to trust him and in so doing she
learns to trust her own feelings.

In the two plays just discussed, the men see and must bring the
women over to their perspective. In the following plays, the men focus
not on the inner qualities and worth of the women, but rather on
traditional values, and once more, the male character is the one
through whom the audience focalizes the action. In the first two
plays, the male teaches through negative example whereas in the
next two, *El premo del bien hablar* and *El examen de maridos* he
teaches through more traditional positive modeling. In both *El hombre pobre todo es trazas* and *El astrólogo fingido,* Calderón casts the
male leads in disadvantaged positions and, for a while, has them turn
adversity into advantage when their deceptions bring momentary superiority over rivals. In the end, however, those male leads lose not
only their dominance but public esteem as well. From their negative
examples, other men learn. In *El hombre pobre todo es trazas,* Don
Diego de Osorio, son of a poor but noble Granadan house comes to
Madrid to escape the consequences of a duel he had in his homeland.
In the capital he courts two women: the wealthy Doña Clara and the
witty but poor Doña Beatriz. Both women had suitors, Leonelo and
Félix respectively, before Diego's arrival but have apparently aban-

doned them for the dashing newcomer. Diego met Clara when he sought out her father, a friend of his father; he met Beatriz when a friend took him to an *academia* (gathering) she organizes. To avoid pursuit from friends of the man he wounded in Granada, Diego has adopted the identity name Don Dionís de Vela, a soldier recently returned from the wars. He courts Beatriz under that guise but, because Clara's father knows his father, he pursues her under his real name.

In *El astrólogo fingido,* both Juan and Diego love the reticent María who, though wary of expressing her love publicly, adores the former. Thinking that his love will never be reciprocated, Juan decides to leave Madrid for the wars in Flanders, but María declares her love and he stays in Madrid, hiding in a friend Carlos's house so that people will think that he has left town as he said he would. To complicate the situation, a spurned lover, Violante, loves Juan, while Carlos, his friend, loves her. Diego discovers Juan's ruse along with the fact that he visits María nightly; he finds this out through his servant Morón who in turn gets his information from María's maid, Beatriz. In an angry confrontation with María, Diego throws her indiscretions in her face and María turns violently on Beatriz. Morón intervenes to say that not through the maid did Diego learn of María's activities, but rather through his profound knowledge of astrology. Diego not only goes along with the illusion but has this broadcast throughout Madrid. Through the information he gleans from the Morón/Beatriz connection, he manages to seem a great astrologer, to complicate the lives of his rivals, and to embarrass them often.

Both plays end with the *burlador burlado* (trickster tricked) (see Max Oppenheimer on *El astrólogo fingido*) when both Diegos are shown up for the frauds they really are. Besides the endings and the coincidence of the protagonists' names, other similarities between the plays abound, particularly the way both men, or their servant stand-ins, view women. For both Morón and Diego, María is not only ungrateful but hypocritical to boot. When Morón finds out that Juan visits her at night, he says, "¿Aquéste es el santo honor / que tan caro nos vendía? / ¿Cuántas con honor de día, / y de noche con amor / habrá?" (This is the holy honor she would sell to us so dearly? How many women must there be who live their days with honor and their nights with love?) (138a). When Diego learns, he is positively livid, not, he says, because she loves another, but rather because of "tantos extremos / de honrosas estimaciones, / de arrogantes devaneos, / de soberbias fantasías" (so many extremes of honorable esteem, of arrogant ravings, of proud fantasies) (138b). Since he now sees her as the fallen woman, he can treat her as disrespectfully as he wants, "que a mujer de quien se sabe / alguna flaqueza, es cierto / que llega a hablarla el galán / sin aquel cortés respeto / que antes tuvo" (for when one knows a woman's weakness, a gallant may speak to her without the courteous respect he once had) (138b). Once you have the dirt on her, he says, you can do what you will, and that is what he begins to do: in the next scene he tells his friend, Antonio, that Juan has been visiting María in her house at night, not for a few days, but for two years. In a subsequent exchange with María, as mentioned, he calls her honor into question by revealing, in a moment of pique, her indiscretions, which, had she focused her attentions on him rather than on Juan, her actions would have represented the height of *discretion*.

As his fame as an astrologer grows, his opinion not only of women, but of men too drops. At one point, however, he has an attack of scruples when Leonardo, María's father, comes to ask him for help in finding a "lost" jewel. Diego tells the old man that he really knows nothing about astrology. He confesses, he says, because, "Más quiero / perder del crédito mío, / que engañar a un viejo noble" (I would rather lose my credibility than deceive an elderly nobleman) (157b), but his conscience only twitches; in the continuation of that same scene, he tricks Leonardo and further besmirches Juan's honor. He quickly reaches the point of calling everyone *necios* (fools).

In *El hombre pobre*, Diego, as stated, courts two women, Clara and Beatriz, but in his opening narrative to his servant, Rodrigo, he degrades both by reducing the two to generic categories: Clara becomes "la dama del dinero" (the lady with money), Beatriz, "Es de las que discretean" (is one of the clever ladies) (205b). In a poetic debate in Beatriz's house, several men offer answers to the question she proposes, "¿Cuál es mayor pena amando?" (What is love's greatest pain?) (211a). Diego's answer is that to love without hope is worse than Leonelo's proposed "amar con celos" (to love jealously) or Félix's "amar contra su estrella / siendo un hombre aborrecido" (to love against your stars being hated) (211a/b). Diego adds that for a man to be jealous or for him to be hated is terrible but normal. What makes it normal is not the stars, but woman's nature, "porque es fácil de pasar / la mujer de extremo a extremo" (because a woman easily passes from one extreme to the other). Women are so changeable that "es uso pasar / la condición de mujer / desde amar a aborrecer, / también se suele trocar / desde aborrecer a amar" (it is normal for a woman to go from loving to hating, and vice versa from hate to love) (211b/212a).

When he is caught in Clara's house by Beatriz, there visiting her friend, Diego says that he is not who Beatriz believes him to be and that her mistake must be based on a striking physical similarity between himself and this Dionís she refers to. He gets his friends to support the existence of two men who look remarkably alike, but Rodrigo still has doubts as to whether they can carry the ruse off. Diego says not to worry: in the end it will not matter as he is courting two women; even if he loses one, he will have the other to fall back on. He generalizes, "Por eso debe tener / cualquiera amante discreto / una dama de respeto, / por lo que ha de suceder" (Therefore every discreet lover should have a spare lady for what might eventually happen) (219a).

As Diego in *El astrólogo fingido,* Diego in *El hombre pobre* does not limit his tricks to women. He involves his friend, Juan, in a series of deceptions as in the *joya* (jewelry) trick; he enmeshes him in the look-alike deception; he lies to Juan about his (Diego's) poverty and he dupes him out of money with the ease and lack of conscience of a well-seasoned con man (225–26). But he directs his most cynical thoughts toward women. As his plan procedes apace in the final act, he brags to himself, "no hay quien a una mujer / burlar no pueda" (anyone can deceive a woman) (230a).

In the final scene, however, his plan comes unraveled when he must confront the women's ex-lovers and once and for all declare who he is. He boasts:

> Escuchadme, pues los dos,
> de una vez dejando tantas
> disensiones, hasta que
> diga verdades más claras;
> porque un hombre principal
> puede mentir con las damas
> (que engañarlas con industria
> es más buen gusto que infamia,
> y los mayores señores
> lo suelen tener por gala);
> pero con los hombres no.
>
> (232a)

(Listen to me you two once and for all leaving aside dissension, until I declare the naked truth; because an illustrious man can lie to ladies (since cleverly deceiving them is more good taste

than infamy, and the greatest of men often take pride in this)
but he cannot lie to men.)

This speech embodies the double standard (and is a brief anticipation
of Sor Juana's poem, "Hombres necios"), a double standard that Violante, in *El astrólogo fingido*, knows the other side of, as clearly signaled when she complained of Juan's abrupt departure and his failure
to comply with even the most basic of courtesies, for example, saying
goodbye in person:

> Si esto hiciera una mujer
> con un hombre, ¿qué dijera,
> sino que era fácil, vana,
> mudable, inconstante y necia?
> Pues, ¿qué hemos de ser nosotras,
> si ellos mismos nos enseñan?
> Siempre la ocasión es suya,
> y siempre es la culpa nuestra.
>
> (136a)

(If a woman were to do this to a man, what would he say except
that she was wanton, vain, fickle, inconstant, and stupid? Well,
what can we be but what men teach us to be? Opportunity is
always theirs, blame always ours.)

Both the men and the women who have overheard Diego's words
leap on him with both feet. Beatriz stomps on stage, gives her hand to
Félix and says to Diego, "Y castigo su ignorancia / para que vea cuán
poco / le aprovechan sus trazas, / y cuente de aquesta suerte, / cuando
volviere a Granada, / si el engañar a mujeres / se tiene en Madrid por
gala" (And I punish your ignorance so that you can see how little
your schemes got you, and so that thus can you recount, when you
return to Granada, if in Madrid tricking women is to be gloried in)
(232b). Having lost Beatriz, Diego then moves quickly to his "woman
in reserve," "Por lo menos, si he perdido / su hermosura soberana, /
las esperanzas me quedan / de no haber perdido en Clara / la riqueza"
(At least, if I have lost her lofty beauty, I still have hopes of not losing
Clara's riches) (232b), to which Leonelo quickly rejoins, "Yo, que estimo / más su virtud y su fama, / lo estorbaré" (I, who value more her
virtue and honor, will prevent it) (232b). But as they start to draw
swords, Clara enters, gives her hand to Leonelo, and throws Diego's
lines back in his face, "Ved si el mentir con las damas, / y engañarlas

con ingenio, / es más buen gusto que infamia" (Now see if lying to and deceiving ladies is more good taste than infamy) (233a). At that point, Juan too sees what a fool he has been and embarrassedly repents of his complicity in Diego's schemes (233a). Even Diego's servant, Rodrigo, disgustedly belittles his master's schemes.

Calderón leaves the final words to the humiliated Diego. When Rodrigo asks him what all of his *trazas* have been worth, he responds:

> De mucho, si en ellas halla
> desengaños el que es cuerdo
> mirando en mí castigadas
> estas costumbres . . .
> (233b)

(A lot, if in them the wise find the plain truth seeing these customs punished in me.)

It is not common practice for Calderón to make the "message" in his comedies so overt, but here, and in another form in *El astrólogo fingido,* the playwright goes out of his way to be sure that the audience grasps the lesson. To treat women as Diego has done in *El hombre pobre todo es trazas,* and to deceive male friends or rivals is degrading and shameful conduct worthy of the strongest censure. Diego sees women as things to be manipulated for his own benefit with no thought to their real human qualities; he reduces both Clara and Beatriz to substitutable commodities that he can possess for his own benefit, one financially beneficial, the other, socially so. He feels free to lie to them because they are unworthy except insofar as they can provide him benefits. He feels free to deceive men as well until he is caught, whereupon he blusteringly steps forth to defend his "honor," because he swears he cannot lie to men. The other men in the play, through their nearly unwavering fidelity to their beloveds, are upheld in their traditional masculine values and beliefs through Diego's negative example and his final mortification.

Similarly in *El astrólogo fingido,* the other Diego not only goes along with the deception, but has it broadcast far and wide. Yet when he faces that representative of the honor system, Leonardo, he hesitates, attempts to act according to his sense of right, but in the end, opportunistically dupes the old man as well. Calderón sets that play in the context of astrology and of popular beliefs and superstitions about that marginal science.

Between the time of Copernicus (1473–1543) and Newton (1642–

1727), as scientific knowledge advanced, astrology began to wither and petrify into a separate and finally irrelevant system of belief thereby losing its claim to validity and/or symbolic value. But outright skepticism was not the rule when Calderón wrote this play. In this period, for example, the influence of the heavens on disease or agriculture was not totally rejected, although Lope's peasants in *Fuente Ovejuna* show a healthy disdain for astrological predictions and their validity. Astrology stood on the boundary between science and superstition; while religion and astrology offered contradictory explanations for the same events. Natural disasters, famine, plague, crop failures, for example, were seen by many religious people as disasters visited upon mankind for God's own purposes; the astrologers called them the result of an unfortunate conjunction of planets and that smacked of heresy. But the church's position was remarkably subtle: for example, since the stars were quite useful for navigators, then "there was no reason why God should not achieve His purposes by working through them if He pleased" (Keith Thomas 1971, 360). Understanding how they function could only increase respect and admiration for the Creator; after all, He had placed the star in the East as a guide to the magi. Where astrology got into trouble was in the areas of astral determinism, which stood in direct conflict with free will, and in the area of "hoary questions," questions the astrologer could resolve by studying the state of the heavens, as we see Diego pretend to do with the problem of the lost jewel. Moreover, astrology slid over the line, at least in popular opinion, into witchcraft when astrologers claimed they could produce visions, as Diego seems to do when he makes Juan appear before the frightened and duped Violante. Calderón thus situates the play on the border between knowledge and superstition, as he does with *La dama duende;* throughout, his play not only criticizes popular beliefs in astrology and magic but also traditional, degrading beliefs about women. In the end, Diego is rejected as much for his misuse of astrology as for duping everyone, and for demeaning the women he supposedly loved. The men who learn from his negative example prosper in the final scene.

In the following two plays, the male leads offer positive examples, at least from the perspective of some of the other men who learn from them. In Lope's *El premio del bien hablar,* Don Juan comes to Seville from Madrid, accompanied by his sister, Angela, to embark for the Indies after having earlier killed a man who spoke ill of women. His past now repeats itself when after mass one day, he hears Don Diego, surrounded by friends, insult an *indiana* (a female returnee from the Indies). Juan defends the unknown woman, a fight ensues, Juan wounds Diego and escapes. He takes refuge in a nearby house—which, of course, happens to belong to the *indiana,* Doña Leonarda, who hides the noble stranger. Feliciano, Leonarda's brother, and his friend, Pedro, Leonarda's suitor and Diego's brother, enter so that Feliciano can arm himself to help hunt down Diego's attacker. Pedro seeks solace from Leonarda but she says that his brother got exactly what he deserved. Feliciano and Pedro next break into the inn where Angela, Juan's sister, lodges. Pedro insults her but Feliciano defends her, enraptured as he is by her beauty. Returning home, he tells Leonarda of his attraction and they agree to take her into their house.

Juan overhears Antonio, Leonarda's father, promise her in marriage to Pedro and jealously prepares to leave the house. Feliciano enters, sees Juan, and starts to draw his sword, but Juan explains the reason behind his fight with Diego. Feliciano, in part because he loves Angela, in part because he begins to recognize the correctness of Juan's argument, grants him refuge, ironically asking him to keep his presence in the house a secret from Leonarda, "sin que lo sepa mi hermana" (without my sister learning of it) (1267a). Feliciano and Leonarda confess their love for the siblings and promise to work together. In the end, Diego recovers, Juan marries Leonarda, Feliciano marries Angela while Antonio and Pedro bless the marriages.

Juan is the chivalric exemplum. He came to Seville "porque a un hombre / castigué la lengua infame. / Hablaba mal de mujeres, / y yo, que he dado en preciarme / de defenderlas, no pude / sufrir que tan mal hablase" (because I punished a man whose infamous tongue spoke ill of women, and I, who prize in myself their defense, could not suffer him to speak so ill) (1251b). His defense of the unknown *indiana* is one he would mount for any woman based as it is on woman's innate nobility, "que el ser mujer es bastante / nobleza" (because just being a woman is nobility enough) (1252a). That nobility, in turn, he ties to woman as mother, "que es honrar a las mujeres / deuda a que obligados nacen / todos los hombres de bien, / por el primer hospedaje / que de nueve meses, deben / y es razón que se les pague" (all good men are born owing a debt of honor to woman for our first nine months' lodging; it is right for men to pay what they owe) (1252a).[7]

7. Compare Juan's comment on women to María de Zayas's statement, "Con mujeres no hay competencias, quien no las estima es necio, porque las ha menester; y quien las ultraja ingrato, pues falta al reconocimiento del hospedaje que le hicieron en la primera jornada." (There is no dispute about women, any man who does not esteem them is ignorant because he needs them; and whoever insults them is thankless because he fails to recognize that for the first part of his life they gave him lodging.) This citation

Diego, "Aquel necio maldiciente," (that ignorant slanderer) as Leonarda's maid calls him, is Juan's opposite number. Juan cannot stand by while Diego defames all the women he sees, "No salió mujer de misa / a quien un don Diego, un áspid, / helado para gracioso, / para hablador, ignorante, / no infamase en las costumbres, / no deslaciese en el talle, / no afease en la hermosura, / no descubriese el amante" (No woman came away from mass whom that serpent Diejo, too cold to be clever, an ignorant gossip, did not defame her customs, did not discredit her figure, did not defame her beauty, did not tell all who was her lover) (1251b). If Juan sees woman as mother, Diego misogynistically views woman as whore. The views the men espouse are the standard polar ones we have already observed. Since we never again see Diego, we have no way of knowing if he learned anything from his experience.

If Diego cannot be worse and Juan not better, then Lope must array Feliciano and Pedro between these two poles. Feliciano learns from direct contact with Juan and Angela whereas Pedro must learn more offstage than on. Feliciano, his father worries, has fallen in with a bad crowd and thus he fears that something evil will befall him, "Siempre los malos sucesos / vienen por malos amigos" (Bad outcomes from bad friends flow) (1254a). When Antonio learns that Juan defended women, he praises his actions saying "No hay cosa, Leonarda mía, / más digna de un hombre honrado" (Dear Leonarda, there is nothing more worthy in an honorable man) (1254a), and wishes that he could find a way to help the stranger.

Feliciano takes the first step toward changing his behavior when Pedro insults and threatens Angela. Feliciano, instantly attracted to the lovely and defenseless sister of his "enemy," snaps back at Pedro, "Callad, don Pedro, por Dios; / que es bajeza esta palabra. / De lo que don Juan ha hecho, / ¿qué culpa tiene su hermana?" (Shut up, Pedro, for God's sake, that word is mean. What blame can his sister have for what Juan has done?) (1255a). At that point Pedro challenges him to accompany him and be his friend or to defend the woman and fall in his estimation. Feliciano stays with Angela. The second step is his reconciliation with Juan who, after he recounts the reasons for his fight with Pedro, elicits "De todo estoy satisfecho" (I am completely satisfied) (1266b) from his new friend.

Feliciano learns through his love for and defense of Angela the

is from *Tres novelas amorosas y ejemplos y tres desengaños amorosos*, ed. Alicia Redondo Goicoechea (in Zayas y Sotomayor, 49). I thank Margaret Greer for reminding me of the passage from Zayas.

practical application of what he saw Juan do in the action that opens the play. Through contact with the brother and sister, he learns the value and correctness of speaking well of and defending women. What he learns, of course, is not new since his view of woman ends up solidly in line with traditional values, but on the other hand, he does grow up. Leonarda, in one of the opening lines of the play, lumps together all of the "maldicientes" (slanderers)—including her own brother—as "juventud liviana" (fickle youth) (1250a). Antonio, in similar fashion, though from a father's perspective, groups such young men as "los hijos traviesos" (dissolute sons) (1254a). Stressed here is the men's youth: they are adolescents. To orient themselves in this society, these men seek models. Whom Pedro and Feliciano look to, as the play opens, is Diego who is slightly older, but essentially of their age, class, and sex. He leads a group of snide, nasty youths who gather at the church's doors to snipe at women. His, and their, social and sexual immaturity manifests itself in group-centered security from where they can pepper women with hebetic jibes as they hector the men who defend them. Diego belittles even his own younger brother, "¡Que trate / mi hermano por interés / con esta indiana casarse! / . . . / . . . no es bien que se case / mi hermano desigualmente" (That my brother could think of marrying that emigrant for money! . . . it is not right for my brother to marry below his station) (1252a).

These adolescents, caught between dread and desire, need and negation of women, take refuge in the masculine group to disparage women and those who love them. The "threatening woman" turns the young men toward male bonding which, in this case, results in a kind of pathological narcissism. Their slanderous talk is a form of rebelling against their society and adult authority, as the Feliciano/Antonio conflict shows. As the play develops, Feliciano, and to a lesser degree, Pedro, discover new models. Feliciano turns not to his father, but toward Juan. Feliciano comes to revise his conduct through contact with Juan, observing his protective relation with Leonarda and with Angela, who plays a central role in his development (it is no small matter that Lope casts her as the innocent and defenseless woman); she is Angela, "angel," whom Feliciano can "defend and protect." In the end, Feliciano rejects his adolescent rebelliousness and takes his place alongside Juan and Antonio in the traditional patriarchal order.

Juan Ruiz de Alarcón's *El examen de maridos* does not seem, at first blush, to have much to do with men teaching men; rather, it seems to establish a strong and wealthy woman intent on determining her own destiny, and thus in charge of the men who surround her.

On his deathbed, the Marqués wrote a succinct note for his daughter and sole heir, Inés: "Antes que te cases, mira lo que haces" (Before marrying, think twice) (MacCurdy 1971, 334). Though she has felt inclined toward the Marqués Fadrique, she determines not to let those inclinations (passions) rule her reason, "elegir esposo quiero / con tan atentos sentidos / y con tan curioso examen / de sus partes" (I shall select a husband intelligently by means of a diligent test of his abilities) (334b). She will hold a series of tests open to all worthy applicants for her hand.

Don Fernando, Doña Blanca's father, meantime, tells Conde Carlos that their mutual friend, Fadrique loves Blanca; he begs Carlos to ask the Marqués to desist for fear that his love is not aboveboard. Carlos speaks to Fadrique and he readily agrees to abandon Blanca because he has recently officially inherited his title: as a condition of his keeping his title, he must marry neither out of his family line nor below his station; thus he must reject Blanca, who is socially inferior. Blanca, however, not at all happy about being left in the lurch, confronts Fadrique and threatens vengeance for his mutability. At the same time, Carlos, who has loved Inés for some time, feels threatened by her decision to admit all men to the contest for her hand but agrees to play by her rules.

As Act 2 opens, Inés feels even more inclined toward Fadrique, but Blanca enters in disguise to tell Inés that Fadrique has a number of faults: bad breath, a running sore, boastfulness, and lying. From the pain Blanca's story causes her, Inés recognizes the depth of her new feelings for Fadrique (350b). When he defends himself citing a long list of his accomplishments, Inés begins to believe the charge of boastfulness, but he counters saying that his was a simple recounting of the facts. Inés, confused, wonders, "¿Es posible / que tales faltas esconda / tal talle, y no corresponda / lo secreto a lo visible?" (Is it possible for such an apperance to hide so many faults: does not the interior correspond to the exterior?) (352b).

Carlos challenges all of Inés's pretenders to a series of physical tests, and Fadrique agrees, though reluctantly, to compete against his best friend (353a). Beltrán investigated the *tapada* (veiled woman) who told Inés of Fadrique's faults and knows who she is. Since Beltrán supports Inés's desire to marry Fadrique because "El es tu deudo; y por Dios / que fuera bien que se unieran / vuestras dos casas, y hicieran / un rico estado los dos" (He is your relative and, by God, it's right for the two of you to unite your two houses, for you to make one rich state from two) (927–30), he decides to use part of Blanca's story, wherein she said she loved Carlos, and turn Carlos toward her.

In a later conversation between Blanca and Carlos, she decides to let him think it true so that she can use that love to extract further vengeance on the Marqués. Besides, she cynically reasons, if things do not work out as she hopes, a count is better than no one. Carlos by then really does love her.

Fadrique learns of his alleged defects and discovers that Blanca is behind the lie but he decides to keep this to himself so as not to embarrass Carlos. In the final public debate between Fadrique and Carlos—that is to say, in the male competition in which woman is the pretext and the prize—Carlos defends the position that to love an imperfect person is the best choice. He thereby takes the Marqués's case as his own. Fadrique, supporting his best friend, argues for love of a perfect person. Carlos wins the debate by popular acclaim and Inés must give her hand to the victor. But Carlos says that since he defended Fadrique, Inés should marry him and he will marry Blanca.

The play sets up a strong and powerful woman who can choose whomever she wishes only to hoist her on her own petard: she must marry, by her own rules, the contest winner. It is not that Inés cannot see what she wants nor is it that the Marqués cannot see whom he wants; rather, circumstances and Blanca's plot impede their path. For the first part of the play, the men must learn from Inés. Carlos, for example, complains of her mutability, which he opposes to his constancy, comparing her to the tricky cold north wind, "Apaga el cierzo violento / llama que empieza a nacer; / mas en llegando a crecer / le aumenta fuerzas el viento" (The powerful cold north wind puts out the flame but that same wind can also inflame the growing fire) (344a). Such comparisons to nature, to the sun that can be obscured by a cloud, to the waxing and waning moon, to the passage of the seasons, to withered flowers commonly stress woman's fickleness and by contrast highlight the man's constancy. Inés defends her decision to admit all comers saying, in effect, if you are as noble as you say then you will easily win, "Mas si acaso el propio amor / os engaña, y otro amante, / aunque menos arrogante, / en partes es superior, / ni es ofensa ni es error / si en mi provecho me agrada" (But if perchance egotism deceives you, and another, though less arrogant lover, is superior to you, there is neither offence nor error if to my benefit he pleases me more) (344b). Inés then goes on to stress the value of the trials, set up to bring forth the "inner values" as opposed to good looks and facile attraction, "Corta hazaña es por amor / conquistar una mujer; / ilustre vitoria es ser / por méritos vencedor" (It is a minor deed to conquer a woman by love; it is an illustrious victory to win her by merits) (345a). Carlos begins to accept her logic and agrees to enter the fray. By the middle of the play, he has internalized her teachings, and displays both grace and understanding when he learns that the Marqués will compete for Inés's hand (354b).

Inés tells Fadrique that though she is inclined toward him, she has heard of certain defects he has. Instead of turning to her for clarification (for she will give him no further information), he turns instead to Carlos, his best friend and most serious challenger. "Conde, solo estáis conmigo, / mi amigo sois," he says and then adds these important words, "y el amigo / es un *espejo fiel*: / en vos a mirarme vengo" (Count, we're alone, you are my friend and a friend is a *true mirror*: I have come to see myself in you) (369a; my emphasis). Carlos says that he sees no faults and that the infamous accusation must be the result of some *industria* (trick) (369a). Shortly thereafter, Fadrique discovers Blanca's plot, but for the love of his friend Carlos, and possibly to his own detriment, he refuses to name his enemy, "*Aparte*. (Pues ha de ser / Doña Blanca su mujer, / decoro le he de guardar / en callarle que ella ha sido / quien con celosa pasión / se valió desta invención" (Aside [Since Blanca is to be his wife, I must preserve his honor by keeping silent the fact that for/because of jealous passion she made all this up]) (2599–2604). In the final debate, the men take up each other's position as their own and argue for their counterpart.

In the play, then, after Inés puts both Carlos and the Marqués on the right path, the men turn from her to each other and to traditional values for lessons on how to proceed. When the Marqués must look to someone, he looks to his friend/rival in the belief that male friendship is more powerful, more valuable, and trustworthy than desire for a woman. When the Marqués looks at the "*espejo fiel*" and at the man in the mirror, he sees reflected back those qualities he most seeks in himself, qualities he knows he can find in Carlos. Satisfied, he can now be prepared to sacrifice himself, if need be, to lose the contest by not reporting Blanca's schemes, since his friend loves her, in the name of those nobler values the men embody. Likewise, Lope's *Amar sin saber a quien* centers on the love between Juan and Leonarda but works along the male-to-male lines described in Alarcón's play. In Lope's play, Juan goes to jail for a murder he did not commit and there, because of his sense of honor, refuses to identify Fernando as the real killer. Luis, who loves Leonarda, gives her up to his friend, Juan, saying, "Quien piensa mal del valor / de su amigo es enemigo: / que el amigo de su amigo / siempre piensa lo mejor" (Whoever thinks badly of his friend's worth is his enemy because a true friend always thinks the best of his friend) (317b).

Alarcón's play, then, sets up a seemingly strong woman, Inés, and creates a deceitful and vicious one, Blanca, only to have the men empty them of power and meaning. Blanca's deceptions and Inés's trials could eventually threaten the friendship between Carlos and Fadrique especially since they are rivals for Inés's hand. Inés's power and Blanca's demonic scheme re-present masculine fears of feminine threats to the men's self-concept. Therefore, both men set traditional values and male-to-male friendship, male bonding above their disputes, even above their love for a woman and thereby make the spiteful Blanca and the all-too-easily-duped Inés look small and petty by contrast to the men who must step in in the final scenes to right the wrongs wrought by women.

El examen de maridos, while apparently parting from a "radical" position—a rich and powerful woman who can choose any man she wishes—turns into an utterly conservative reinforcement of male-to-male teaching, of patriarchal authority. What the two men see in each other is what they do not find in the women, namely, a mutually satisfactory reflected image of their own idealized view of masculine values. Inés's ability to choose is effectively nullified, then, because she does not control her choosing at the end any more than she did at the beginning. There, as the play opens, Inés "decides" to follow her father's advice about how to choose—and in so doing fails and must be rescued by Carlos—but that she *must* choose, that she *must* marry is never once questioned: "forzoso es / señora, tomar estado" (You must marry, my lady) (3–4); "a mi padre he de ser / tan obediente en la muerte / como en la vida lo fui" (I shall be as obedient to my father in death as I was to him in life) (11–13). In the end as in the beginning, father knows best.

The men in these plays learn not so much from the women, whom they persist in seeing as either perfect or fickle, headstrong, and/or deceptive—thereby confirming certain stereotyped notions—as from other men who stand as "positive" or "negative" examples of accepted and acceptable masculine behavior. Through modeling themselves on or against other men, the "heroes" of the plays restore order to a disfigured world as they reinscribe themselves and the women in the patriarchal pattern.

Women Teach Women

In Tirso's *En Madrid y en una casa,* by the time that Manuela, the young widow from Seville, meets her future friend and confidant,

Leonor, the latter has already learned the salient points of Manuela's life from Ortiz, Manuela's maid and Leonor's former duenna. Manuela was married at the tender age of fourteen, by her parents, to an old Sicilian count. The marriage lasted two years before the venerable fellow died. Shortly thereafter, her parents died leaving her titled, wealthy, young, widowed, and orphaned. She has been pursuing a young man, Gabriel, who, though the son of a nobleman, has squandered his fortune and misspent his life. She found him one day after he had been in a fight, unconscious, bleeding, and apparently near death. With all due references to Angelica and Medoro, she rested his head in her lap, bound his wounds, fell in love, and gave him over to a trusted servant for care. Since Gabriel was unconscious, he never saw her, but she has followed him to Toledo and from there to Madrid. In Toledo, an old friend of Gabriel's deceased father arranged for him to marry Serafina, cloistered daughter of a wealthy man. Gabriel spent six days there, never saw Serafina, agreed to the marriage, and is now in Madrid living downstairs from Manuela's apartments in a house owned by Leonor and her brother, Luis. Manuela, in disguise, stopped Gabriel as he was entering Madrid to tell him that a wealthy woman loved him and that he should mend his ways should he ever hope to meet her.

All this Leonor learns from Ortiz and then from Manuela herself. Leonor, however, is not a disinterested party; she has recently fallen in love with Gonzalo, Luis's friend. Gonzalo has loved Serafina since they were children, though he has been unable to communicate with her directly for some time. He found out about Gabriel and followed him to Madrid where he has arranged with Luis to stay with him, watch Gabriel, and devise a plan to interrupt the planned marriage. Both Luis and Gonzalo want Leonor to help with their scheme, but she has plans of her own now that she is attracted to Gonzalo.

When a servant enters to say that Gabriel is on his way up to speak with Leonor, Manuela fears that her fickle lover will fall for Leonor, "¡Ay cielos, si te ha visto / no dudes que te adora! / . . . / temerte puedo competidora: / de tu nueva amistad, Leonor, desisto" (Ah Heavens, when he sees you, doubt not that he will love you! . . . I must now fear you as a competitor; from our newfound friendship, Leonor, I desist) (1275a). But worse, so powerfully attractive does Manuela consider Gabriel that she believes the mere sight of him "hechiza visto, y voluntades muda" (bewitches the sight and twists the will) (1275a); thus Leonor must surely fall for him. Leonor tries to reassure her new friend, reminding her that she loves another and, in addition, she has her own jealousy to contend with; thus Gabriel can have no effect on her. She chides her new friend, "¡Qué fácil me has juzgado!" (How easy you have judged me) (1275a).

Later Manuela confides her misgivings to Ortiz, "Es, Ortiz, Leonor muy bella, / y don Gabriel muy hechizo" (Ortiz, Leonor is very beautiful and Gabriel is a charmer) but Ortiz, who knows Leonor well, rejoins, "No hará su amor tornadizo / en su firme valor mella" (He will not make her love fickle nor make a dent in her firm steadfastness) and projects a tough time ahead for Gabriel, "Tú verás el don Gabriel / los purgatorios que pasa / en pena de ser mudable" (You will see the purgatories Gabriel will go through as punishment for his fickleness) (1276b). Manuela, though socially and financially superior to Gabriel, and even though she is a widow, and according to popular opinion, "experienced" in the world, is still quite a young and innocent person. Her attempts to "court" Gabriel have amounted to little more than pining away at home, following him around Spain, accosting him in disguise once, and throwing a purse full of money and a cryptic note through his window. Now, in the company of the wily *madrileña,* she will begin to learn to trust her newfound friend, gain self-confidence, and then to make Gabriel and several other men dance to her tune. Through her visit with Luis, she begins to understand the power of her beauty, presence, status, and wealth when the young man stumbles and stutters upon being presented to her. To her confused, "what's the matter with this guy?" Ortiz responds, "Desbaratada has su aviso / porque el donaire que tienes, / es como pedrada en los sienes" (You have thrown his introduction of himself to you into confusion because your grace/presence is like a stoning) (1277a). So, when Gabriel unexpectedly enters, Manuela controls her emotions and the situation as she sends Gabriel off half-jealous so that she can have a "private talk" with Luis.

Leonor next creates the illusion that Serafina has left the convent school and is now in the house under her protection. While the men rush off to search for her, Manuela once more trembles, but also hopes that this new turn is part of Leonor's plan, "¡Cielos! ¡Si esto no es quimera, / y Serafina ha venido / a deslucirme esperanzas, / muerta soy, en balde vivo!" (Heavens! If this is not a trick and Serafina has come to dull my hopes, I am dead, I live in vain) (1281b). Manuela begs her friend for assurance and Leonor responds that all's well and that this is just the beginning.

When Manuela then fears that Gabriel is preparing to leave the house, Leonor once more devises a plan to confine him to the house. By now Manuela is starting to see how all of this works; thus when Leonor tells her of the house's secret, she understands completely that "La invención, cuanto engañosa, / nos puede ser provechosa" (The invention, since it's deceptively clever, can be of benefit to us) (1285b). And in the subsequent deception scene (1290–93), no difference exists any longer between the "teacher" and the "student." In fact, when Ortiz begins to feel pity for "poor" Gabriel because of what Manuela is putting him through, Manuela advises her servant to stem her pity because "Desta suerte estimará [Gabriel] / más, Ortiz, la pena mía" (Thus, Oritz, will [Gabriel] appreciate more my suffering) (1293b).

From that point on, Manuela is in charge. She takes Luis aside and involves him in her and Leonor's plot, to the point where he tells his friend, Gonzalo, that Leonor is really Serafina. When Gonzalo gives her, Leonor, his hand, Manuela questions him, "¿si la toledana, / sin salir de sus retiros, / sustituyese sus gracias / en la que tenéis presente, / siendo de don Luis hermana, / dirimiréis desposorios?" (if you were to discover that the Toledan woman had never left her retreat and that the woman here with all her grace had been substituted for her, and that she was Luis's sister, would you annul the marriage?) (1297b). When Gonzalo says no, she tells him that the woman whose hand he holds is in fact Leonor, and Gonzalo reconfirms his marriage pledge. Having quickly resolved that situation, "Ya aqueste par de pichones / están pareados: vayan / al palomar" (Now that these two doves are paired, let them go to the dovecote) she turns to the next one, "y otros vengan, / que el encanto se remata" (and let others come so that the spell can be put to an end) (1297b). She takes Gabriel's hand, and as Luis, who thought he was the man who would marry the Countess, begins to swagger and object, sends him packing off to Toledo to seek Serafina's hand.

Seen from one angle, since after all this is a play about women written by a man, a case could be made that what Manuela learns falls easily into stereotypical notions about the "wily woman." She learns to lie, to deceive, to manipulate, and thereby only reinforces notions, like those broadcast by the moralists in their antitheatrical tracts, about woman's inherent "Eve-ishness." But if we look from another angle, what she learns is how to grow up and take a measure of control over her life—a control she was denied by her social-climbing parents, by her forced marriage to the aged Sicilian count, by her youth and inexperience. To some degree, she was Serafina's analogue. Serafina has been locked away in a convent school since she was ten, and there she has lived prohibited from any contact with the outside world. Manuela, guarded by her parents, married to the Count at fourteen, widowed and orphaned at sixteen has had little or no experience on her own. Though for the last two years she has fended off potential suitors by cloistering herself in her home, on one of her walks she finds the handsome and helpless Gabriel, she is lost with no one to turn to for instruction. She learns from Leonor to gain some understanding of who and what she is or could be. She has to get Gabriel to *see* her, to see her as a capable, intelligent, and worthy woman, not just as a pretty face with a large bank account. That, she says, is how he sees Serafina, "y él avariento, más que enamorado, / gusta que el alma al oro se sujete" (and he, greedy more than in love, willingly subjects his soul to gold) (1274a). She must reform him in the process, change what she calls his "costumbres mozas" (youthful customs) (1259a).

But before he can see her differently, she must learn to see herself differently, and that is where Leonor comes in as model/teacher. Luis and Gonzalo try to involve Leonor in their plot to break up the Gabriel/Serafina match, first by trying to fob off Gonzalo as their cousin. Leonor, however, has some strong doubts about this "relative": "¡Primo en Toledo, hasta ahora / no conocido!" (A cousin in Toledo and until now unknown!) (1265a), she exclaims to herself. She will go along with the men's plan, she tells them, and will offer *noble ayuda* (noble aid) to her "cousin." But once alone, she admits that she feels a more than passing attraction to Gonzalo; thus she would be crazy to help break up the marriage if it meant losing Gonzalo, "a costa de propios daños" (at my own cost) (1270a). No, she says, "negociar quiero por mí, / pues estoy primero que él" (I shall negotiate for myself since I come before him) (1270a). Leonor knows her own desires, knows what she wants, and knows how to get it. That is why when Manuela tells her what a smooth operator the handsome Gabriel is, Leonor can tell her not to worry and not to judge her "fácil" (easy); Gabriel will have no effect on her at all. As Manuela learns to trust her friend, to see her in operation, to observe how easily she can control the men around her, she learns from her and grows from an insecure girl into a self-confident woman once and for all in charge of her situation, her desire, and of the man she wants.

Couples Cooperate

In other plays, both male and female romantic leads know precisely what they want and who they are; together they lead others to their point of view by surmounting the barriers that stand between them and their desires. Two examples of this type of play are Lope's *Amor, pleito y desafío* and Tirso's *Desde Toledo a Madrid*. In the first case, Juan de Padilla and Beatriz have been in love for some time, yet her father, Alvaro de Rojas, opposes the marriage because the young man, though noble, is poor. He wants her to marry the king's favorite, Juan de Aragón, who in turn successfully schemes to get the king to back his marriage to Beatriz. She and Juan Padilla opt to work together in bringing a lawsuit against the father and the favorite (involvement in the legal system will be taken up in a later chapter). Throughout the *pleito* (lawsuit) and the many complications that arise, Juan Padilla and Beatriz confide in each other, trust one another, counterscheme together, and finally bring about their desired goals.

Tirso's *Desde Toledo a Madrid* backshifts a parallel situation— lovers collaborating—to the couple's first meeting. But that first meeting and the instant "love" it initiates is so improbable that the dramatist apparently felt the need to supplement the standard love-at-first-sight convention and in so doing, show how the young couple come to trust in one another. In the opening scene, Don Baltasar enters sheathing his sword, breathlessly speaking of his fight with, and the possible death of, an adversary, of his ill-timed arrival in Toledo, and, in an attempt to escape from the law, of having broken into the house where he now finds himself. When he enters the room, the door shuts and locks behind him. Inventorying the room with its "sillas bajas, contadores, / Bufetillos de marfil / Y ébano, ajuar femenil, / Arquillas, aguas de olores" (low chairs, small marble and ebony desks, feminine trousseau, little chests, scented waters) (434b), he knows it to be a wealthy woman's bedroom. He paces about, rehearses speeches he could offer her or her father when they find him there, and finally, exhausted, sits down and soon falls asleep.

Doña Mayor and her maid, Casilda, enter, candle in hand, without seeing the sleeping Baltasar. Casilda leaves and Mayor begins to lament her upcoming forced marriage:

> El alma, que al gusto entrego
> De mi padre, mas que al mío.
> A casarme a Madrid voy,
> Y enamorada no estoy.
> (435b)

(I hand over my soul to my father's desire, not to my own. I am off to Madrid to marry and I am not in love.)

As she moves toward the bed, she suddenly sees Baltasar, faints, and drops the candle. The noise awakens the man. Surprised, and in the dark room, Baltasar stumbles over Mayor's body. He reaches down to touch her hair and clothing, her neck and forehead, and then places his hand over her heart, lifts and tries to revive her.

As she comes to, frightened, her first reaction is that he is Don Luis, her future husband, who is perhaps too impatient to wait for the marriage ceremony, but when Baltasar says that he is not Luis, Mayor's fears increase incrementally. He presents a brief summary of how he wound up in her room and begs for her understanding and compassion. Somewhat moved but still wary, Mayor seeks a light; when Baltasar sees her, he exclaims, "¡Qué divina perfección!" (What divine perfection!) (484b). In the ensuing conversation, Mayor informs him that she must leave on the morrow for Madrid and the unwanted marriage, and that her future husband is in Toledo. When Baltasar reacts calling Luis "mi enemigo" (my enemy) and swearing that he burns with jealousy, Mayor exclaims, "¡Qué adelante pasáis!" (How far ahead you jump!) (484c). Baltasar, surprised at his own passion rejoins, "Más / De lo que pensé jamás" (More than I would have ever imagined) (484c). Mayor, now more than half-believing the man's words, complains, "¿De qué sirve edificar / Torres que se han de quedar / En los cimientos?" (What good does it do to build castles if they must stop at the foundation?) (485a). As the sun begins to rise and as Baltasar slowly exits, lamenting losing her as fast as he found her, Mayor's last words follow him out, "Don Baltasar, / Creed que me he casar, / Por vos, muy de mala gana" (Baltasar, believe that because of you I marry most unwillingly) (485c).

Later, and still reeling from his adventure, Baltasar recounts yet another chapter in the story to his friend and confidant Felipe. That very morning, he says, Mayor's maid came to his lodging to tell him how her mistress was "llorando por vos" (crying for you) (486c) and gave him a letter naming him heir to her lost soul. Baltasar asks Felipe's help in what will follow promising that it will be better than anything he could find in Ovid (487a).

While falling in love instantly is a tried-and-true device in many Golden Age comedies, falling in love with a possible murderer or thief or rapist who has broken into your house and has you trapped in your bedroom, or falling in love with a woman you have never seen on the night before her already announced marriage, and with her father and future groom waiting in the wings, stretches credibility. Even though their situations offer certain parallels—Mayor trapped by her father in an arranged marriage she does not want, Baltasar trapped in a house with the police looking for him; Mayor seeking escape from a man she does not love, Baltasar, we find out later, also seeking escape from a woman, Doña Ana, he does not love—that Mayor and Baltasar could really be in love after their first brief encounter not even the characters would have us believe. The rest of the play, in fact, though chronologically brief (as the trip from Toledo to Madrid would prove), is set up in such a way that, through delaying tactics organized by the pair, they can converse, get to know and trust each other, outfox the opposition, and move toward a more convincing conclusion than their breakneck courtship might otherwise allow.

The next morning, Mayor devises the first delay. "Stop the coach," she cries out, for the rough ride is about to do her in, "Parad el coche, hermano, / Que voy muerta" (Stop the coach, friend, for I'm dying) (487a). She then explains her complaint much more graphically, "Señores, ¿quieren que eche las entrañas?" (Gentlemen, do you want me to puke?) (487b). To Luis's "Poco hay de aquí a Cabañas," (It is only a little way from here to Cabañas) Mayor retorts, "Menos hay de la boca a las entrañas" (It's even shorter from my guts to my mouth) (487c). She has noticed that Baltasar, dressed as a *mozo de mulas* (muleteer), has joined their small caravan. Her plan to slow their progress and have the opportunity to talk with Baltasar depends on escaping the coach and riding at his side on his gentle mule.

Later, as soon as the sun goes down, Baltasar pokes the mule with some thorns and, with Mayor aboard, off they gallop into the night so that they can speak at leisure. Then, he and Mayor pretend that Baltasar, or Lucas Berrío as he calls himself, is a simpleton and that for diversion on their journey she will pretend, with her father's laughing consent and Luis's grumbling acceptance, to prefer Lucas over Luis and even to marry him in a mock ceremony.

Their collusion gives them the time to get to investigate each other for, as Mayor says, despite her strong inclinations toward Baltasar, "Tengo preguntas / Considerables que haceros" (I have substantial questions to ask you) (489c); "El poco conocimiento / Que tengo de vos, rehusa / Lo que el corazón otorga" (My little knowledge of you refuses what my heart grants) (489a). Love, she explains, can be your lawyer in this cross-examination for love consists in understanding who and what you and I really are. In their lengthy interview, Baltasar explains that he is a noble, wealthy, soon-to-be-titled Cordoban (patrimony, lineage, future prospects); moreover, he takes time to clarify his motives or intentions, "Cortés amaros pretendo / Con deseo casto y limpio, / Segura mi voluntad / Y mis gustos comedidos. / Sin manos viene mi amor; / Solo en la lengua y oídos / Jurisdicción limitada /

Que os respete, les permito" (I offer you only courteous love with chaste and pure desire, my will is certain, my pleasures courteous, my love without hands, only to my tongue and ears do I give it the limited jurisdiction to state my case) (492a).

Mayor says that that is all well and good, but she has more questions, so now, down to details, "¿Tenéis en la corte empleo?" (Do you have business at court?) (492b). When he answers yes, she asks him why he left and warns him not to lie to her (492b). Baltasar swears to tell the truth and admits that he had to get away from an insistent woman. Her name? Mayor requests. Her social state? Was your problem jealousy? She continues like a good attorney interrogating a client she may defend in a later court case. Baltasar answers each and every question with neither hesitation nor evasiveness. Given Baltasar's cooperation and honesty, Mayor then promises him she will not marry as planned (492c), but she wants to investigate matters more when they get to Madrid. Charmed by, even infatuated with, this man, Mayor remains cautious, questions, probes, and carefully scrutinizes her possible future husband.

With Luis, she has apparently had no similar opportunity since her father's peremptory action took away any possibility for her to express herself and explore whatever similarities or differences she might have discovered between herself and Luis. She sets out a model plan, as careful and cautious as any her father might have devised, for finding an appropriate marriage partner and thereby shows herself her father's match and, later, her father's better.

The more Baltasar deals with her, the more he appreciates her ingenuity, wit, intelligence, and discretion; thus the more he knows that she is his other half. Parting from the highly contrived and pressurized spontaneous combustion of mutual, perhaps desperate, attraction between two people in impossible circumstances, the play slows to reciprocal investigation, to joint action in the more controlled but warm fire of symmetrical give-and-take.

Near the end, through a momentary misunderstanding, Mayor believes Baltasar *mudable* (fickle), and he believes her a fury, but that brief disturbance serves as a final test of their true feelings for each other. Thus when Baltasar, before the united cast, says that he spoke true during the mock marriage and Mayor swears she did as well, their marriage promises are seconded by her father. Luis, however, leaves in a huff threatening a breach of contract suit in the Madrid courts, but with Alfonso's blessing securely in hand and with the love, respect, and cooperation already witnessed between the future spouses, even if Luis throws a final impediment in their path, surely together they can overcome.

Now this is a comedy, not a treatise on marriage and the brief look at the play does not do justice to the complications that arise through secondary plots and characters, through other blocking forces, through the often ridiculous, sometimes tense situations that are part and parcel of the mode. But despite those complications, the audience knows what will happen in the end; the interest lies in how. In comparison to *La villana de Vallecas, La dama duende* or *Por el sótano y el torno,* both *Desde Toledo a Madrid* and *Amor, pleito y desafío* are less theatrically compelling since they lack the constantly whirling, frenetic action, the nimble costume and scene change that are the hallmarks of those other comedies. In their place, however, these two plays offer a sensitive (for comedy) portrayal of two young people working together, talking together, and striving for a goal they both want. These plays, and to them we could add *Amar sin saber a quien* and as well part of the plots of *El premio del bien hablar, Por el sótano y el torno,* and *Los balcones de Madrid,* demonstrate how two people work to bring desire to a stable form. The lovers respect each other, and after some cautious investigation, trust in each other and in their abilities to overcome any obstacle in their way. They come as close as anyone in the comedies to actualizing what Terry Eagleton (1986) describes as love's ideal goal:

> Marriage is not an arbitrary force which coercively hems in desire, but reveals its very inward structure—what desire, if only it had known, had wanted all the time. When you discover your appropriate marriage partner you can look back, rewrite your autobiography and recognize that all your previous coveted objects were in fact treacherous, displaced parodies of the real thing, shadows of the true substance. This, broadly speaking, is the moment of the end of the comedies. . . . [Marriage] is the true language of the erotic self, the point at which the spontaneity of individual feeling and the stability of public institutions harmoniously interlock. It is at once free personal choice and impersonal bond, "subjective" and "objective" together, an exchange of bodies which becomes the medium of the fullest mutuality of minds. (21)

I would only emphasize, as all of these plays do, the role of knowledge and understanding, the role of personal choice. Marriage is a solution so simple, so implausible, yet so obvious that it makes us laugh. Marriage ends the plays but learning how to love is what the comedies are all about.

This chapter posits that if marriage is the only goal of the love comedies, then indeed they all do look pretty much the same: two people meet and are attracted to each other, problems arise, problems are circumvented, and the two marry. However, if we turn our attention to the path that leads to marriage, to the problems that occupy the vast majority of the plays' action, then we can reconsider the plays and see just how much one play differs from the rest. I have proposed that one way to see the differences is to follow the one who knows, sees, or teaches the other(s) not only who and what she or he is, but who and what the other is or can be. The disguises and deceptions plus the trials and tests they provoke encourage the characters to see differently, to reevaluate their preconceptions, received notions, or traditional modes of thought. Depending on the play, the lessons learned range from a reaffirmation to a serious questioning of traditional ideas. The plays, seen thus, run the gamut of options open within the overarching, generic comedic structure.

While all the comedies end in marriage, if just marriage were the play's only goal, then several of them could have ended before they began. In five of these plays—*La celosa de sí misma, Por el sótano y el torno, Desde Toledo a Madrid, La villana de Vallecas,* and *Los balcones de Madrid*—an arranged marriage predates the plays' opening scene. In five more—*Esto sí que es negociar, La toquera vizcaína, La huerta de Juan Fernández, El premio del bien hablar, Amor, pleito y desafío*—a marriage is arranged shortly after the play begins. But in nearly all cases, the woman or the man or both, instead of happy acceptance of comedy's declared goal, exhibit growling submissiveness, vacillation, or outright obstruction. Even in cases where the arranged marriage does take place (for instance, in *La celosa de sí misma*), there comes a moment where the arrangements break down.

Arranged marriages, normal in the socioeconomic realities of seventeenth-century Spain left little room for initial romantic love; yet mutual love was a powerful cultural fantasy. In most of the plays, arranged marriages are overthrown in favor of personal choice and mutual love. Marriage was the gateway to the adult world; marriage and raising a family were considered woman's true mission in life, unless she became a nun. In these plays, all written by men, no matter how strong, clever, capable, or powerful the female lead might be, she ends up married. That is to say that she is a controlled element in a set of fantasies that extend and protect male profit and power. In the real world of the seventeenth century, marriage represented for most women legal submissiveness.

For men, marriage could represent personal privilege, legal prerogative, social advancement and political empowerment. For instance, when the *junta grande* (Great Council) came into existence on 3 September 1622, it paid great attention to what it saw as the monarchy's greatest danger: population decline. To counteract a depopulation, it encouraged marriage offering "special exemptions and privileges . . . to the newly married and to anyone with six male children or more, while conversely, anyone still unmarried at the age of twenty-five was to be penalized" (Elliott 1986, 117). In the Royal Proclamation of 11 February 1623 (I quote here from the contemporary translation) Philip states:

> We doe ordaine and command, that foure years after the day of any bodies marriage, he shall be free of all charges and publick offices, recouries, hosts, souldiers and others; and the two first years of these foure, of all royall taxations and offices . . . and if any marry before the age of eighteene yeares, hee may administer and enter in the eighteenth on his goods; and those of his wife, although shee bee younger, without asking any leave of Authoritie. And to those which are full five and twenty yeares, and are not married, may bee put to the sayd charges and publicke offices, and are bound to serve them, although they are in the power and house of their fathers.
> Item, That he which shall have six male children aliue, shall be free for all his life time from the said charges, and publike offices. (*A Proclamation* 59–60)

Arranged marriages function to guarantee the smooth transferral of power from one man to another promising to each and to their heirs their place in the traditional socioeconomic, political power structure. The brides in such arrangements are figuratively or literally commodities to be bargained with or for to assure the passing down or gaining of wealth, land, or title. While a socially or economically poor marriage could adversely affect a man's prospects, men did not suffer the loss of identity experienced by many women upon solemnizing their vows. Bernarda "sells" Jusepa to the aged, wealthy Captain in *Por el sótano y el torno* to guarantee both her and her sister's economic well-being. In *Amor, pleito y desafío*, a father organizes his daughter's marriage to the king's favorite to advance his, and his heirs', political position. Marriages are arranged between cousins in *La huerta de Juan Fernández* to end disputes and consolidate family holdings dispersed in the past; in all of these situations, the women's desires are immaterial. With so many arranged marriages, what ought we to make, then, of the overturning of the arrangements in so many plays?

There are a number of ways to formulate an answer to that question. For instance, we could easily see the overthrow of "parental authority" as representing generational conflict, as does Frye when he describes the standard blocking figure as *senex iratus*. He says, "The obstacles are usually parental, hence comedy often turns on a clash between a son's and a father's will. Thus the comic dramatist as a rule writes for the younger men in his audience, and the older members of almost any society are apt to feel that comedy has something subversive about it" (164). Such "subversiveness" was felt keenly, for example, by P. Juan Ferrer in his *Tratado de las comedias . . .* (1613) (Cotarelo 1904) when he complains of the evil effects comedy can have on daughters, "Espántase el padre . . . de que [a su hija] se le casó por los rincones y dio la palabra sin su consentimiento, y siéntelo y llóralo, y el triste padre no ve que la raíz de todo el mal de sus hijas fue la comedia donde las dejó ir" (The father becomes frightened . . . that his daughter married secretly and gave her word without his consent, he regrets it and weeps because of it and the sad father does not recognize that the root of his daughter's wrongdoing was the comedy he let them attend) (*Controversias* in Cotarelo 1904, 253).

In these plays, marriage seems to resolve certain real conflicts, but it can only do so by highlighting those conflicts in powerful ways. Such illustrations of the problems are an admission of the demands the characters explore as well as the subtle projection of a "better world" wherein they may be satisfied. These plays, then, show prevailing order and traditions simultaneously affirmed and questioned, undermined and reinforced. Although there are many ways to look at the overthrow of the norm, I turn to the social and political arena for a final analogy. The 1620s saw a change in government and a change in public attitude upon the death of Philip III, and Philip IV's assumption of power. Many people were fed up with the status quo, fed up with Philip III's ministers, their policies, their cronyism, and their self-aggrandizing greed. "The late king's ministers," Elliott (1986) says, "had made themselves deeply unpopular, and a regime which moved against these bloodsuckers of the commonwealth was automatically assured of a warm welcome" (103). Philip IV and Olivares caught the reformist spirit of the time and during the first months of the new administration set out to rid the government of many of Lerma's cronies. "The initial measures of the new administration," Elliott (1986) recounts, "were *well-calculated* to *create an impression* of purification and renewal" (103; my emphasis). Almanso y Mendoza, "a professional writer of newsletters from the court was sufficiently uplifted to write: '[T]he reign of the king our lord, Philip IV, is a golden age (*siglo de oro*) for Spain, and such happy beginnings promise a prosperous end.'" Elliott summarizes, "The *symbols* of change were from the beginning very much in evidence" (103–4; my emphasis).

Behind the scenes, however, Olivares operated along the same lines as did his predecessor, filling offices with friends and relatives; he was clever enough, however, to create the impression that many offices were being filled on merit. There were some positions that he could not touch; "on the other hand, there were no restraints on the creation and bestowal of knighthoods (*hábitos*) in the Orders. While these yielded no income, their conferment . . . [was] highly coveted . . . [and there was] an immediate and spectacular increase on the number of those bestowed by its predecessor [the Lerma administration]: 515 in the Order of Santiago alone between 1621 and 1625, as against 168 between 1616 and 1620" (Elliott 1986, 137). In addition, Olivares rewarded faithful soldiers and "made sure that some of the *hábitos* went to military men—thirty, for instance, to soldiers of the army of Flanders in 1621—he also distributed them generously as a means of winning adherents and rewarding supporters" (137). His largesse "created a climate of expectation in which he could set about the major enterprise of fashioning an administration that would reflect his hopes and desires" (137). R. A. Stradling (1988), commenting on the same phenomenon adds, "Dozens of obscure men were in this way made socially eligible for office, not only in the household, but also in government, civil service, and the armed forces" (47). The recruitment and advancement of "new men," plus, in the cultural field, the mustering of Quevedo, Antonio Hurtado de Mendoza, and the young Diego de Velázquez, who in 1622 "came to court under the patronage of the count-duke and a year later succeeded to the post of official court painter" (Stradling 1988, 46), along with the rehabilitation of persecuted critics such as Mariana and Alamos may have created the impression that perhaps merit rather than old political and hereditary ties might be more valuable for getting ahead.

With the foregoing in mind, I propose that in these comedies arranged marriages can be seen as metaphors for traditional power structures; in play after play, mutual love overturns the arrangements. Mutual love was the fantasy ideal and the development of that love, the plays show, depends on recognizing the merit of the other. Marriage for love, then, can be seen as a poetic, displaced metaphor for achievement by merit rather than by traditional ties. Therefore, the love comedies of the 1620s can be read as re-presentations in a different register of the hopes and dreams of many people who flocked to Madrid seeking advancement and a better life. Those same people went to the *corrales* and saw the comedies wherein the exercise of personal choice along with the recognition of the merits of the other led to a projected fulfilling future for many of the couples at the end of the plays. In those plays, perhaps, some people in the audience caught a glimpse of their own hopes and dreams.

2

COMEDY AND MADRID

The way a group describes, depicts, and structures its geography whether in maps, narratives, poetry, or drama, entails a set of beliefs about how its locale is and thus how the people who inhabit that space are. If we look at a map of the world that used to be found in grade school textbooks in the United States when I was growing up, we see a flattened, distorted world. We see land masses relative to oceans with those land masses divided by boundary lines, colors delineating nation-states and their possessions plus the names of significant areas, geological formations, and cities. In the center of that map rests North America, more specifically the United States, thereby implying its central role in the "natural order" of a worldwide political geography, mediating, as it were, the distorted and fragmented world. None of my teachers ever questioned the representation—though my childrens' teachers likely would, and they do not use such maps in my childrens' public school—rather, their silence on this matter led one to see the map as accurate and legitimate, a true representation. Geographical depiction re-creates the way that people see their space, and vice versa, and is a vital clue to how they understand their space and themselves.

Bruce Wardropper (1978) states that the cape and sword plays take place in the here and now, often in Madrid, but, he adds, that the young lovers live in the city as though the city did not exist (216), carrying out "la ilógica búsqueda de la Arcadia en el corazón de la capital" (the illogical search for Arcadia in the heart of the capital) (216). The analyses in this chapter will show that not only do the young lovers in the plays from the 1620s know very well that they are in the city and in the court, but that many of the schemes they devise to resolve their problems depend on an intimate knowledge of Madrid, of how the city works, of its geographical, economic, and architectural features, as well as of the atmosphere that reigns there. Far from living in the city as though the city did not exist, the main characters are, or quickly become, "streetwise." The playwrights, in turn, depend upon the audiences' knowledge of the city to fill out the connotations of the things and places the characters speak of and work in and with.

In many of the plays from this period (*La villana de Vallecas, La celosa de sí misma, En Madrid y en una casa, Los balcones de Madrid, La dama duende, Desde Toledo a Madrid, El hombre pobre todo es trazas, La toquera vizcaína, La moza de cántaro, El examen de maridos, Por el sótano y el torno, El astrólogo fingido, La dama duende, La huerta de Juan Fernández,* and *¡Ay, verdades, que en amor . . . !* characters are already in, or on the road to, Madrid, and the capital is where most or all of the action takes place. More specifically, much of the action takes place in and around the Santa Cruz and San Sebastián parishes; that is to say, in the quarters where the two *corrales* stood. During the 1620s, Madrid was definitely the capital and the court and everyone, it seemed, was headed there.

Throughout these plays, characters tell us where they are going in Madrid and where they have been; among those places are:

El Prado: *Hombre pobre todo es trazas; ¡Ay verdades que en amor. . .!; El astrólogo fingido; La villana de Vallecas; Los balcones de Madrid*

Calle Mayor: *La celosa de sí misma; ¡Ay verdades que en amor . . .!; Por el sótano y el torno*

Calle del Príncipe: *Hombre pobre todo es trazas; En Madrid y en una casa*

Calle de Silva: *La celosa de sí misma*

Calle de Alcalá: *¡Ay verdades que en amor . . .!*

Calle de Arenal: *¡Ay verdades que en amor . . .!*

Calle de la Gorguera: *La huerta de Juan Fernández*

Calle del Lobo: *Los balcones de Madrid*

Calle de Carretas: *Por el sótano y el torno*

Foncarral: *El astrólogo fingido*

The corrales: *En Madrid y en una casa; El astrólogo fingido, ¡Ay verdades que en amor . . .!*

Descalzas: *Hombre pobre todo es trazas*

San Jerónimo: *Hombre pobre todo es trazas*

San Sebastián: *Hombre pobre todo es trazas*; *La huerta de Juan Fernández*

La Vitoria: *La celosa de sí misma; ¡Ay verdades que en amor . . .!; Por el sótano y el torno*

Santa Cruz: *¡Ay verdades que en amor . . .!*

El Buen Suceso: *¡Ay verdades que en amor . . .!; Por el sótano y el torno*

San Blas: *En Madrid y en una casa*

San Felipe: *Por el sótano y el torno*

Rastro: *Hombre pobre todo es trazas*

Puerta Cerrada: *La huerta de Juan Fernández*

Puerta del Sol: *El astrólogo fingido; Por el sótano y el torno*

Puerta de Guadalajara: *Por el sótano y el torno*

La Casa del Campo: *La moza de cántaro*

La Plaza de Palacio: *La moza de cántaro; La dama duende*

Lavapiés: *El astrólogo fingido, La villana de Vallecas*

La huerta de Juan Fernández: *La huerta de Juan Fernández*

On Madrid's labyrinthine streets, newcomers easily become lost or confused; indeed, confusion seems to be one of the standard reactions to the capital. Madrid is a *selva encantada* (enchanted forest) (*Hombre pobre todo es trazas*), a *mar* (sea) (*¡Ay verdades que en amor . . .!, La* *villana de Vallecas*), a *golfo* (gulf) (*En Madrid y en una casa*), a *Creta encantada* (enchanted Crete) (*La villana de Vallecas*), a *casa de orates* (madhouse) (*La villana de Vallecas*). In this sprawling urban complex, no one knows even their next-door neighbor (*En Madrid y en una casa, La celosa de sí misma*), and everyone is in a hurry tending to his or her business: "Como tan presto se pasa / El tiempo en Madrid, no da / Lugar aun de conocerse / Los vecinos, ni poderse / Hablar" (Since time passes so quickly in Madrid, neighbors cannot even get to know each other nor even converse) (*La celosa de sí misma* 128c); "No tiene en Madrid el ocio / lugar, ni tiempo dilatar. / No, señora, sólo trata cada cual de su negocio / aquí" (Idleness has no place in Madrid, nor does time slow. No madam, everyone only goes about his business here) (*En Madrid y en una casa* 1263a/b). Here everything is for sale: "Es una tienda / De toda mercadería" (It is a shop filled with every imaginable merchandise) (*La celosa de sí misma* 139b); and deception is a way of life: "Esta corte / Es toda engaños y hechizos" (This court is all deception and magic) (*La celosa de sí misma* 140c); "En la corte viven todos / De industria, y hasta los lodos / Cubren aquí su malicia. / Písalos, si contradices / Esta común opinión, / Y te dirá lo que son / La ofensa de tus narices" (In the court everyone lives by their wits and even the mud covers up its malice. If you doubt this common truth, step in the mud and the offense done to your nose will tell you what you're really stepping in) (*La villana de Vallecas* 52a). But also in Madrid one can find beauty, justice, and true nobility, "¡Tanto señor, tanto grande, / honra del mundo . . .!" (So many gentlemen, so many grandees, the honor of the world!) (*Amar sin saber a quien* 302b); "Es infinita / la nobleza que le habita: / toda Castilla se pasa / a la corte" (The nobility that lives here is infinite, all Castile is coming to the court) (*En Madrid y en una casa* 1263a). There is no one single description of Madrid that suffices: it is, as one character states "todo el mundo en mapa breve" (it's a small map of the whole world) (*Hombre pobre todo es trazas* 204b). Madrid is the center; Madrid is the court.

The choice of Madrid as capital of Spain was purely political. No other European capital was so poorly located, from a commercial or trading standpoint, nor was so utterly dependent on a politically administered economic life. Without a navigable river, the city was subject to the vagaries of overland transportation that, especially in the winter and during times of heavy rains, frequent in the 1620s, was most unreliable. Since the city lacked any major industrial or commercial base, yet attracted the politically and economically powerful, throughout the sixteenth century Madrid undermined the economic position and functions of the other towns in the Spanish interior. In the seventeenth century, Madrid's growth caused, in its environs, the development of a rural society, low-order central places, and market and land usage that left few incentives to local powers (as per Ringrose 1983, 108–39).

When Madrid became the capital under Philip II in 1560, the population was around 20,000. By 1600, it had grown to 65,000 and by 1620 to 130,000 plus a floating, transient population of near 25,000; in total the estimates are between 150,000 and 155,000 at the time Philip IV ascends the throne (see Ringrose 1983, 34–65). Philip himself seemed concerned about the capital's population. In the royal proclamation prepared by the Junta de Reformación and published on 11 February 1623, the king states:

> Likewise, because of the great concourse of people in this our Court, . . . there arise many inconveniences, as well as by the number which liue Idely, and the danger wherein they liue, in such confusion . . . , Wee doe Commaund, that as touching the Gouernment of this our Court, that therein there may not bee more persons then needfull, and so great a concourse be diminished. (*A Proclamation* 74)

An obviously weak order since in the next decade, population growth remains strong so that by 1630 there are around 175,000 people, that is to say that between 1606 and 1630, the population effectively tripled. During the same period, David Ringrose (1983) notes, *peso mayor* revenues, which reflected regional market activity, declined; thus prices rose, wages fell, and the new immigrants found themselves in increasingly poor straits. In addition, the Arganda tolls, which measured long-distance trade, rose, leading Ringrose to conclude that Madrid's market was dividing sharply between the rich who could afford expensive imports and the poor who had trouble making ends meet, with the later group shifting their buying to basic commodities (Ringrose 1983, 24–31).

Between 1600 and 1630 petitions for citizenship in Madrid substantiate the picture of a rapidly expanding city; the predominant number of such requests came from artisans, skilled laborers, food and service industry workers, and traders (Ringrose 1983, 88–90). After 1630, more requests came from the political, governmental, and royal service quarter. Madrid became a center for the elite, for those with access to state-controlled wealth and power. Affluent families moved to the city, bringing with them the income from their estates and thereby creating a consumption-oriented market with all its attendant inequities. Such a market "locked urban crafts into quality production that further separated the city from the hinterland which could afford few luxuries. The city increasingly attracted long distance trade from the seaports; and as income became more concentrated, the preference of the elite became more cosmopolitan and the city purchased an increasingly narrow range of goods from its own hinterlands. Thus the city provided a kind of cash economy for the landed elites, while encouraging a more rudimentary and self-sufficient rural economy" (Ringrose 1983, 314). The agglomeration of wealthy families abetted the immigration to the city of artisans and merchants who created an intense and competitive business atmosphere. As quoted above, one of Tirso's characters notes, "Madrid es tienda / de toda mercadería." But the industry, the manufacture, was of the small, family-owned and -oriented "casa-taller" variety, dedicated to immediately salable utilitarian goods or to luxury items for the wealthy court dwellers. Among these groups were: *cedaceros* (sievemakers), *boneteros* (hatmakers), *calceteros* (stockingmakers), *jubeteros* (doubletmakers), *cofreros* (trunkmakers), *doradores* (gilders), *peineros* (combmakers), *cuchilleros* (knifemakers), *latoneros* (brassworkers), *tintoreros* (dyers), *curtidores* (tanners), *bordadores* (embroiderers), *pellejeros* (leather dressers), *zurradores* (leather curriers), *zapateros* (shoemakers) (Deleito y Piñuela 1942, 183–84). Many had their shops on the lowest floor of their houses on streets named for their profession or product: Cuchilleros, Latoneros, Platerías, Boteros, Cabestreros, Panaderos (see Martínez Kleiser 1926, 28). Commercial areas were located between Calle Mayor and the Plaza de Santa Cruz (Mesonero Romanos 1990, 1:265) wherein Calle de Postas was well known for its cloth and linen goods, as well as for the *valonas* (Vandyke collars) made there. On the Puerta del Sol one could buy bread and there also were small shops, *baratillos,* where goods of inferior quality were sold. In the Plaza Mayor only bread, milk, and fruit could be obtained but on its corners were bootmakers, dry goods dealers, and mattress makers. In the Plaza de Puerta Cerrada, bladed weapons and fish could be found, and in La Plaza de la Cebada, firewood. The Plaza de los Herradores as well as at the Puerta de Santa Cruz were centers for rentals of coaches and sedan chairs. The Calle Mayor was the chic shopping center of the city. From San Felipe to Amarguras were the jewelers; further up were clothing dealers, *pretineros* (girdle or belt makers), furriers, and silk dealers. The central part of the street belonged to the famous silversmiths and to elegant clothing shops. This area, near the Puerta de Guadalajara appears in several Golden Age plays.

But besides the established shops and shopping areas, there were many small shops called *confiterías,* which sold baubles of all sorts. Moreover, itinerant salespersons set up stalls in the Plaza de Santa Cruz to sell secondhand clothing and shoes as well as books, fruits, herbs, knives or whatever (see Calderón's *entremés, La Plaza de Santa Cruz).* In addition there were numerous places where one could eat, from the established taverns and bodegas to the so-called *bodegones de punta pié* where one could eat standing up—a sort of precursor to the fast food stand. Many of these places served *empanadillas* or meat pies (which Pablos in Quevedo's *Buscón* always crossed himself before eating in the belief that the mystery meat inside the pies came from executed criminals whose bodies had been displayed the day before at the city gates).

In the area where the two theaters were located people lived, played, and strolled.[1] The sector was a popular locale for *la gente moza* (lively/young people). But, this area was also known for its public institutions. Nearby were Nuestra Señora de los Desamparados, an orphanage, San Nicolás de Bari for ill and handicapped women, Santa Rosalía for dying clerics, a home for beggars, the Hospital General, and the Cárcel de la Corte on the Plaza de Santa Cruz. In the same sector were the congregations of Caridad y Paz whose task was to assist condemned criminals. They celebrated a mass for the soul of the doomed man on the day he was to be executed and they accompanied him on his final journey. And just down the way from the Corral de la Cruz, for example, was the Hospital de San Juan de Dios, founded in 1552 for those suffering from venereal diseases. Herrero y García locates the hospital on Atocha at the confluence of Magdalena and Amor de Dios and adds that in the plays from this period, "todos los versos que hablan de unción y de pelarse aluden a la terapéutica y efectos de las enfermedades específicas del hospital" (all verses that speak of unction [treatment with mercurial ointments] and of cutting hair allude to the therapy for, and effect of, the illness specific to the hospital) (*Madrid en el teatro* 124).

In Santa Cruz, near the theaters, gaming houses or *casas de juego*

---

1. Thomas Middleton (1976; 1982) argues that the area around the theaters "no era ni rica ni pobre, sino generalmente de clase media . . . era un barrio de sólidos burgueses con casas burguesas" (was neither rich nor poor but generally rather middle class . . . it was a solidly bourgeois quarter with bourgeois houses) (144). He suggests that the reason the *corrales* were located here was that "este barrio era el centro comercial y social de Madrid. El barrio donde una gran mayoría de los habitantes pululaban desde el amanecer hasta el anochecer" (this quarter was the commercial and social center of Madrid. The quarter wherein the inhabitants swarmed from dawn to dusk) (148).

were a popular attraction. In fact, in a house across the street from the Príncipe lived the *alguacil* (bailiff) Pedro Vergel—frequent butt of Villamediana's satirical verse—who, along with some friends, was arrested for gambling in 1627 (see Del Corral, 1990, 26–27). On Calle de Francos was a well-known house of prostitution "frecuentada por la gente de alto copete" (frequented by aristocratic people) (Deleito y Piñuela, 1948, 51). This area was also well known as a favorite precinct for prostitutes of the roaming variety, *busconas* (streetwalkers), as well as for its public houses of prostitution or *mancebías*. It is not for nothing that the heroines in Castillo Solórzano's *Las harpías de Madrid* head immediately for this area and rent a house almost next door to the Teatro del Príncipe in which to set up shop. On such streets as Huertas, San Juan, and Amor the ladies practiced their craft. Needless to say, the confluence of gambling, theatergoing, actresses and actors, whorehouses, *gente moza*, and soldiers on leave who tended to congregate here made this area a center for scandal and for often violent arguments. According to Deleito y Piñuela, "los alguaciles, impotentes y temorosos ante la violencia audaz de las pendencieras tropas, no solo no evitaban sus desmanes, sino que rehuían el tenerlos que ver" (bailiffs, impotent and fearful when faced by the outlandish violence of the quarrelsome troops not only avoided their misbehavior but fled from all contact with them) (1948, 48–49). Going to the theater, then, would have been a truly cultural experience.

What did the city look like? Deleito y Piñuela and Mesonero Romanos, from whom the former takes many of his descriptions, offer what has perhaps become the standard view. Here is a sample of some of their better known descriptions:

> Si el recinto de la Corte española era ahogado y mezquino, su aspecto interior tenía poco de cómodo, grandioso, ni siquiera agradable. . . . Apiñábanse en él innumerables callejuelas feas, empinadas, sucias y tortuosas, cuyo tránsito era difícil o penoso. . . . Solo con excepción se contaban algunas vías transitables y espaciosas, largas y rectas. (Deleito y Piñuela 1942, 21–22)

> (The Court enclosure was suffocating and wretched, in its interior zone there was little comfortable, grand, or even agreeable. . . . Jammed together were innumerable ugly, cramped, dirty, and twisting little streets whose transit was difficult or painful. . . . There were only a few wide long and straight streets.)

La construcción del caserío era en general impropia y mezquina. . . . Generalmente . . . la vida interior del pueblo debía de ser tan modesta y poca ganosa de comodidades, que quedaba satisfecha con cualquier cosa, con un hediondo portal, con una oscura y empinada escalera y con media docena de estrechos y desnudos aposentos, coronados por un mezquino zaquizamí; todo esto formado y multiplicado en el reducido espacio que toleraban los conventos. (Mesonero Romanos 1990, xxxix)

(Housing construction was improper and wretched. . . . In general . . . life in the central city must have been so modest and so bereft of conveniences that one was satisfied with anything, with a filthy doorway, a dark and crooked stairway, and with a half dozen narrow, bare rooms crowned by a wretched attic, and all of this crammed into less space than convents would tolerate.)

. . . dice [Alcide de Bonnecase], refiriéndose a los habitantes de Madrid: "Han aprendido la arquitectura de los topos. La mayor parte de sus casas no son más que de tierra, a manera de toperas de solo un piso. . . ." Las aberturas de las fachadas eran estrechas y, generalmente, sin cristales, por ser estos caros. (Deleito y Piñuela 1942, 21–22)

([Alcide de Bonnecase] says, referring to Madrid's citizens: "They learned architecture from moles. Most of their houses are made of dirt and, like molehills, only one story high. . . ." The openings in the facade were narrow and generally lacked glass because it was so costly.)

El aspecto de las calles era lastimosa. Abríanse al azar, sin los desmontes y terraplenes que sus bruscos desniveles exigían, ni la menor idea de rasante para las fachadas, perspectivas, comodidad ni ornato público. (Deleito y Piñuela 1942, 21–22)

(The streets looked pitiful. They opened haphazardly without the cuts or fills their abrupt differences in levels demanded [houses were built] without the slightest notion of grade lines for the facades, without perspective, convenience, or public adornment [style]")

. . . pocos, muy contados edificios civiles de alguna importancia: multitud de conventos de ambos sexos . . . y un general caserío comparable por su mezquindad de una pobre aldea; escasos y mal dispuestos establecimientos de beneficiencia, de instrucción y de industria; dos míseras corrales para representar los inmortales dramas de Lope y Calderón . . . las calles tortuosas, desiguales costaneras, y en el más completo abandono; sin empedrar, sin alumbrar de noche, y sirviendo de albañal perpetuo, y barranca abierta a todas las inmundicias . . . bajo el aspecto material y civil, muy poco o nada puede interesarnos la descuidada capital del siglo xvii. (Mesonero Romanos 1990, xii–xiii)

(few public buildings of any importance; a multitude of convents and monasteries . . . and housing comparable in its shabbiness to a poor village; scant and poorly arranged charitable institutions for instruction or training; two miserable playhouses in which to stage the immortal plays of Lope and Calderón . . . twisting streets, uneven sidestreets in complete abandon; without paving stones, unlighted at night, and which served as a perpetual toilet and channel for all sorts of filth . . . in its material or civil aspect, the neglected capital of the seventeenth century offers us little of interest.)

Some of the foreign visitors to the city seem to confirm this picture of a dilapidated city, for example, Roos:

. . . la poca armonía que guardan unas casas con otras la hace desigual y desagradable a la vista . . . en la edificación de Madrid, si se comparan unas partes con otras, hacen que parezca más bien un sueño que una cosa real, y como si, en una noche, todos sus vecinos hubieran decidido edificar sus casas sin conocerse unos a otros. (Díez Borque 1990, 250–51)

(the little harmony among the houses makes the city look rough and disagreeable. . . . Madrid's construction, if one compares some areas with others, makes it seem more dreamlike than real, as though one night all the inhabitants had decided to build their homes without looking at their neighbors'.)

But other reports stand in opposition (Díez Borque 1990):

BERTAUT: la mayor parte de las casas razonables tienen cuatro cuerpos de edificación, algunos de los cuales hasta son dobles. . . . Hay pocos que no tienen una fuente. (239)

(the better part of the fair houses have four areas for rooms, some even double that. . . . There are few without a fountain.)

Hay multitud de plazas bastante hermosas, y en todas ellas hay también fuentes con estatuas de marmol (239)

(There is a multitude of rather lovely plazas, in all of which there are fountains with marble statuary)

LADY FANSHAWE: Nuestra casa estaba ricamente montada, tanto los aposentos de mi marido como los míos, pues la peor pieza de mis habitaciones, donde dormía mi criada, tenía colgaduras de damasco; y todas las piezas tenían los suelos cubiertos de alfombras persas. (239)

(Our house was richly set up, both my husband's suites and mine, even the poorest of my rooms wherein my maid slept had damask wallhangings, and all of the floors were covered by Persian rugs.)

D'AULNOY: Ordinariamente hay en todas las casas diez o doce grandes habitaciones en la planta. En algunas llegan hasta veinte o más. (240)

(Normally all the houses have ten to twelve large rooms on each floor. In some there are twenty or more.)

BRUNEL: Por la parte que nos aproximamos a esa ciudad no se ve gran cosa; pero desde aquel donde está el Buen Retiro, la vista es sumamente agradable. . . . Sus calles son anchas, pero las peores olientes del mundo. . . . De ese modo esa ciudad, que es nueva y la mayor parte de la cual ha sido construida muy a la ligera . . . se embellece hoy y se mejora todos los días. (253)

(The way we entered the city we did not see much; but from another road one sees the most agreeable sight of the Buen Retiro. . . . Its streets are broad, but the worst smelling in the world. . . . In this way, that city, which is new and in which most has been built quickly, beautifies and betters itself daily.)

Part of the reason for ascribing a rundown look to the city goes back to the time of Philip II and the *regalía de aposento* (lodging exemption). That decree stated that homeowners had to divide their house into two parts, making one available to court functionaries or else pay a special fee for an exemption. This led, we are told, to the construction of one-story houses that could not be so subdivided—the *casas a la malicia*—or to ones that had one story on the street side but "un tejado que se elevaba oblicuamente desde la fachada al interior, originando en él otro piso espacioso con vistas de un patio grande" (a roof that obliquely rose from the facade toward the interior, making room for another spacious floor that looked out onto a large patio) (Deleito y Piñuela 1942, 25).

This description of these houses has been repeated over and over again, but in 1982, José del Corral published *Las composiciones de aposento y las casas a la malicia,* substantially revising the traditional view. Such houses, "de incómoda repartición" (of incommodious division) could have two or even three stories street side, but were arranged in such a way inside that no convenient or workable division into two living spaces could be accomplished:

> Por ejemplo, en los pisos bajos se disponían pesebres como de cuadras, aunque en la vida ordinaria fueron aquellas habitaciones destinadas a salas, con lo que pasaban como no utilizables para la vida hogareña y en los pisos altos se disponían como desvanes—los que se llamaban desvanes altos o vivideros—y, aunque ordinariamente eran utilizados como habitaciones ordinarias [when officials would come to inspect the house] pasaban como simples trasteros. (78)

> (For example, on the lower floor rooms were built to serve as mangers. Though in reality they were to be used for living rooms, though they passed as unsuitable for family life, and the upper floor were arranged as attics—they were usually called upper lofts or habitable garrets—and though normally used as bedrooms [when officials would come to inspect the house] they passed for simple storage spaces.)

The size of houses varied greatly. Del Corral's (1982) study of 850 houses inspected and reported on in the 1622–24 period shows that the facade extension could be as minute as 7 *pies* (one *pie* = .28 m) or as large as 90. The enclosed space ranges from 117 square *pies* (about 90 square meters) to more than 100,000 square *pies* including gardens. Of the 850 houses, 48%, or 411 houses, were one-story buildings; 43% were of two stories or more (up to five). The remaining 9%

were "solares, jardines, huertos, casas en construcción" (plots, gardens, orchards, houses under construction) (20). Two-story homes, like those portrayed in *Los balcones de Madrid* and *En Madrid y en una casa,* plays to be discussed shortly, constitute 33% of the total.

Moreover, Del Corral adds, there were numerous open spaces in and around the houses:

> Todas las casas estudiadas ofrecen patios o corrales y aún éstos es lo usual que tengan una considerable extensión. Considerable en cuanto a la proporción de la superficie disponible.
>
> Estos espacios libres, no construidos, tienen muy diversos usos y destinos. Los de patio y corral se repiten habitualmente. Algunas veces aparecen como jardincillos, pero muy frecuentemente tienen destinos laborales. Talleres, obradores, aún de materias delicadas como tejidos y sedas, como elaboración de tocas por ejemplo. (21)

(All of the houses studied had patios or corrals, and these usually were of considerable extension. Considerable, that is, in relation to the disposable land. These open, free spaces had many uses and purposes. The patio or corral being standard. Sometimes they appear as small gardens, but frequently they were for work. Workshops, shops, even of delicate materials like textiles and silks or for the making of headdresses for example.)

He reaches the following conclusion about the standard view of the *casas a la malicia* and about the standard view of the city:

> Mucho se ha hablado por los comentarios madrileños de las casas a la malicia y mucho también de la Regalía de Aposento y del daño que hizo a la visión urbana de la Villa, llenando sus calles de casuchas desmedradas que ni tenían vuelo ni gracia y más semejaban poblado primitivo o aduar africano que ciudad europea capital de dos mundos. Creemos, a la vista de la documentación que presentamos, que se exageró demasiado al hablar así. Las casas a la malicia, como puede verse, no eran tantas ni tan pequeñas y pobretuelas como se ha pretendido. Seguramente la Regalía de Aposento hizo daño a la urbanización madrileña, ciertamente, pero como tantas veces, se ha exagerado ese daño y se aumentaron las consecuencias lleván-

dolas a extremos que, a la vista de la documentación, están lejos de la realidad. (30)

(Much has been said by commentators of Madrid about the houses *a la malicia* and much too about the Housing Exemption and the harm it did to the city's urban aspect, filling its streets with deteriorated ugly houses with neither flair nor grace and which approximated a primitive village or an African camp more than a European city capital of two worlds. We believe, given the documentation we have presented, that such talk has been greatly exaggerated. The houses *a la malicia,* as can be seen, were neither so numerous nor so small and poor as has been imagined. Surely the Housing Exemption harmed Madrid's city planning, certainly, but as often happens, the harm has been exaggerated and the consequences extremely enlarged, and according to the documentation, such a view is far from reality.)

In her massive study of Madrid's architecture, Virginia Martín Tovar (1983) argues as well for a revised view of the city. She says that during the reigns of Philip III and Philip IV, streets were straightened and broadened thereby offering new vistas, new perspectives; monuments were built as were parks, promenades, fountains, hospitals, "colegios, asilos, plazas, mesones, pósitos, academias, edificios para la amplia burocracia del Estado" (schools, asylums, plazas, taverns, public granaries, academies, buildings for the large state bureaucracy) (10). Along with them came new religious buildings, new houses, inns, and palaces. She argues for a new architectural view of the city as chiefly the product of two court architects and their *escuela madrileña* (Madrid school) or the *escuela cortesana* (court school). She sees the interplay of buildings, streets, and parks creating "efectos de perspectiva en interior y en exterior, resultado de escenificación compleja en ambientes públicos en los propios monumentos" (effects of interior and exterior perspective, the result of a complex staging in public settings and monuments) (10), a staging that could be interestingly correlated not only with painters' use of space, light, color, and perspective, but also with the development of stagecraft, perspective scenery, and *tramoyas* (stage machines).

If Madrid was to be the place of the court, the king's residence, the capital visited by princes, cardinals, ambassadors, businessmen, natives and foreigners alike, then Madrid was therefore, the king's stage, "un gran 'escenario' donde reside el Rey y el conjunto de personas que componen su séquito" (a great stage whereon reside the king and his retainers) (8). Surely one of the things the count-duke had in mind when he supervised the construction and decoration of the Buen Retiro was not just the king's new residence, but his new stage. As Martín Tovar (1983) says, "El Retiro . . . fue un escenario para las artes en que el rey representaba su papel bajo los efectos más brillantes" (The Retiro was a stage for the arts on which the king played his part with brilliant effects) (349). The Retiro, surrounded by gardens, lakes, trees, and parks, "se convierte en el escenario de los ritos, funciones y servicios del pueblo en su vinculación casi cotidiana con el Soberano reinante" (became a stage for rites, functions, and services stressing the links between the people and the reigning sovereign) (10). (The notion of Olivares as Philip's director and stage-manager is explored by Elliott 1986, 171–78.)

When in 1606 Philip III once and for all fixes Madrid as the capital, "Se emiten órdenes reales para la reedificación eficaz de la capital, se piensa en una ciudad nueva con la creación de una gran Plaza Mayor, un nuevo Ayuntamiento, cárceles y otros edificios de uso comunitario, un nuevo trazado de calles rectas, incorporación de nuevas zonas al trazado viario, todo un gran proyecto de urbanización que persigue el ornato y la dignificación de la ciudad" (Royal decrees are issued for the efficient rebuilding of the capital, a new city is imagined with the creation of the Plaza Mayor, a new city hall, jails, and other public use buildings, a new plan for straight streets, with the incorporation of new zones into street planning, a huge urbanization project that seeks the beautification and dignification of the city) (Martín Tovar 1983, 17). Among those plans were orders concerning the shape, the form of individual houses. The city's houses so much preoccupied the primary architect, Francisco de Mora, that he complains that there are "casas por labrar en muchas calles principales, lo cual parece muy mal para el ornato de un lugar tan grandioso como éste" (unfinished houses on many of the main streets, which detracts from the beautification of such a grandiose place as this) (quoted on 20). He stresses his personal interest in his *Informe de Francisco de Mora:*

> estaba proebido que ninguna persona labrase ni hiciese ningún edificio sin licencia y que yo lo viese y diese la traza para que se labrase con la firmeza, Hornato y Pulicia que es nezesario por el peligro que tiene labrar cada uno por su gusto y parecer y es ansi que por haber cesado la dh Junta esto no se hace y habiendo en la Corte muchas obras cada uno labra como se le antoja y de aquí viene que unas casas queden bajas y otras

altas, unas afuera y otras adentro, que causa gran deformidad
y es contra la policía y buen gobierno a que no se debe dar lugar. (quoted by Martín Tovar 1983, 453)

(it was forbidden for anyone to build or make any building
without a license and without my seeing it and okaying the
blueprint so that it may be soundly built, with the beauty and
polish necessary to avoid the danger of everyone building according to his pleasure and opinion that is how things have
been since the aforementioned Junta ceased to exist and thus
there is in the Court today much construction with everyone
building as he pleases, and from this comes some low houses,
other tall ones, here and there, which causes great deformity
and works against harmony and control, and should not be allowed.)

In 1608, a new law was passed modifying the Regalía de Aposento
(housing exemption). The *casas a la malicia* had been a constant preoccupation to all the kings, thus:

por hacer bien y merced a los dueños de las casas de malicia e
incómoda partición y para que con más alivio puedan pagar la
dicha tercera parte y porque el aposento se vaya ensanchando y
la villa enobleciendo y adornando . . . concedemos a los dueños,
exención de huéspedes de aposento de Corte para todo lo que de
nuevo se labrase y edificase en ellas por quince años. (Martín
Tovar 1983, 22–23)

(to favor the owners of houses *a la malicia* and difficult division
and so that they may more easily pay the aforementioned tax
and so that their houses may be enlarged and the city enobled
and adorned we concede to the owners an exemption from housing members of the Court in all new works built [for the next
fifteen years].)

Francisco de Mora dies in 1610 and planning control passes to his
nephew, Juan Gómez de Mora. In 1611, the central government emphasizes that now "Las trazas de las casas que se labran que no tienen exención de la Cámara, da las trazas el mismo Juan Gómez de
Mora, y en su ausencia Gaspar Ordoñez, su teniente" (The plans for
houses to be constructed which do not have an exemption from the
Cámara, Juan Gómez de Mora himself will draw up or in his absence,

his lieutenant Gaspar Ordoñez) (49). It was Juan Gómez de Mora who took over city planning and his name appears on "numerosos dibujos para casas de la ciudad de diversas categorías" (many plans [sketches] for houses of all kinds in the city) as well as on plans for many public works such as "puertas, cercas . . . caminos, calles y plazas" (entrances, walls, . . . roads, streets, and plazas) (49–50). In *Hombre pobre todo es trazas*, Rodrigo complains of the difficulty he has had finding his master, Diego, even though Diego had sent him the name of the street where he now resides. Such is the construction going on that:

> En Madrid, ¿no es cosa llana,
> Señor, que de hoy a mañana
> suele perderse una calle?
> Porque, según cada dia
> se hacen nuevas, imagino
> que desconoce un vecino
> hoy adonde ayer vivía.
> (203B)

(In Madrid, isn't it true, Sir, that from one day to the next a street can be lost? Since every day they make new ones. I imagine that today a citizen does not recognize where he lived yesterday.)

So completely does this architect think out the city's revitalization that, according to Martín Tovar,

> No mira a un solo estamento, los contempla todos, y traza para cada medio de vida, para cada necesidad común, para atender costumbres populares, necesidades de la Monarquía, caprichos de la aristocracia, o deseos y necesidades de la máquina buro- crática, todo un sistema arquitectónico puntual en su función y en su situación artística. (50)

(He looks not just to one estate, but he contemplates them all, and he designs for people of all means, for every civic need, to take care of popular customs, the needs of the monarchy, aristocratic caprices, or desires, and the needs of the bureaucratic machine, an entire architectural system perfectly suited to function and art.)

In 1626, new plans are published for street cleaning, garbage collection, and for "paving" (*empedrado*) of the streets, plazas, and entrances to the city, paying special attention to Atocha, Alcalá, Toledo, Convalecientes, and Mayor. For garbage disposal, Mora plans "unos Corrales grandes 'para que la basura se eche dentro'" (some large corrals, into which to throw garbage) outside the city gates because "parece muy mal que a las entradas desta villa lo primero con que topen los forasteros que vienen, sea con tan grandes muladares" (it is not right that the first things visitors see at the entrances to the city are huge trash heaps) (51).

Perhaps in the facade of the Alcázar, one can find an exemplum of the Mora style. He created a new, more unified face directed toward the city itself, toward the meeting-ground between the monarch and the citizens. Extending out from the facade were rhythmical archways, like two extended arms embracing the citizens and moving the eye toward the facade, which served as a curtain, a backdrop "para los grandes acontecimientos y para el género de vida festiva que en aquel entorno iba día a día desarrollándose" (for the great events and for the festivities that go on there from day to day) (227). Again we can note contemporary visitors' comments on the place. Brunel remarks that the Alcázar "Tiene por delante una plaza hermosísima" (It has a beautiful plaza in front of it) (Díez Borque 1990, 241); Cosme states, 'Todo este edificio tiene muy buen aspecto, situado como está en el frente de una plaza oblonga" (This whole building is pleasing to the eye, situated as it is before an oblong plaza) (Díez Borque 1990, 242).

The facade's centerpiece was a huge balcony onto which the king, his family, or his distinguished visitors could appear facing the gathered public in the open but embraced space. Such an organization of space permitted the close "encuentro del rey con el pueblo en repetidas solemnidades . . . los bautizos de los príncipes y los funerales, los estrenos teatrales, las mojigangas o juegos de cañas, la nueva estructura del Alcázar es el cierre teatral de fondo del espectáculo, un magno teatro para los momentos de paz, y para los momentos más amargos" (encounter between the king and the people on repeated formal occasions . . . baptisms of princes, funerals, theatrical debuts, farces or cane jousts, the Alcázar's new structure is the theatrical backdrop for all spectacles, a grand theater for peaceful times and for more bitter moments) (Martín Tovar 1983, 232; see also 341–47).

In a similar way did the Moras design houses. They were to be built over slightly projecting socles, constructed of brick and stone, thereby providing a bi-chrome, red and white, constancy that offered "agrado a la vivienda común" (a pleasurable appearance to the normal house)

(Martín Tovar 1983, 380). The houses boasted a rectangular patio with living spaces harmoniously arranged. The exterior was divided along vertical axes into two, three, or more floors with each floor sometimes separated from the others by a slightly jutting band. Each house had numerous, expansive windows. The entrance was incorporated into one of the vertical axes, generally displaced to one side, almost never centered, and the doorways were surrounded by white stone lintels with little decoration. Normally balconies extended from each window.

While the houses may present a certain monotony in their outward appearance, I believe their design may be correlated with the facade of the Alcázar in the sense that the houses' facades were also a *telón de fondo* (back curtain) for celebrations, processions, festivals, and the theatricalized life of the streets. But whether that is true or not, they do not conform to the overall shabby picture Mesonero Romanos and Deleito y Piñuela (along with some visitors to the city) paint. Undoubtedly there were poor areas in the city where construction was minimal, but the plays take place in, on, and around the main thoroughfares. Those houses, buildings, streets, plazas, parks, and gardens appear in *La villana de Vallecas* and *La huerta de Juan Fernández;* houses the interior and exterior of *Los balcones de Madrid* and *En Madrid y en una casa.* In many of the plays from this period, the materiality of Madrid is central to the plot.

In 1620, Tirso de Molina writes *La villana de Vallecas.* The play features four main characters: Vicente and Violante, siblings and natives of Valencia; Gabriel de Herrera, ex-soldier who, using a false name—Don Pedro de Mendoza—seduces Violante and abandons her in her hometown; and the real Pedro de Mendoza, recently arrived in Seville from Mexico and headed to Madrid to marry Serafina, daughter of Don Gómez and sister to Don Juan. Vicente is an inveterate gambler who, according to his servant Luzón, has wasted his inheritance and neglected his sister. Returning home at first light from a long night of gaming, Vicente finds a note from Violante revealing her dishonor, blaming both herself and him, stating the name of her erstwhile lover, Pedro de Mendoza, and declaring that she has taken refuge in a convent until Vicente can arrange something. Violante, in reality, has headed to Madrid in pursuit of her fickle flame. Vicente likewise sets out toward the capital. Gabriel, also headed for Madrid, has stopped for the night in an inn near the capital where he meets, to his surprise, a man with the name he picked at random, none other than Pedro de Mendoza. After dining together and after a very few hours of sleep, Pedro and Agudo set off to Madrid before dawn only to discover later that they have taken Gabriel's bags by mistake. They open the bags to find a letter to the authorities about Gabriel's killing a Tudesco captain in Flanders, a letter that declares him not guilty of murder by reason of a fair duel, some passionate letters from Violante to Gabriel, and little more. They bemoan the loss of money, jewels, and identity papers, and their complaints are witnessed by Violante and her servant, Aguado, recently arrived in Vallecas where the scene takes place.

There, Violante adopts the disguise of *panadera* (breadseller); there she will live in the house of the peasant baker, Blas, and, as itinerant breadseller, will have easy entry to all of the streets and houses in Madrid. Gabriel and his servant, Cornejo, meanwhile, are thrilled to find gold bars, money, jewelry, letters of credit, and identity papers in Pedro's suitcases and, adopting the ready-made new identity, Gabriel heads for Madrid to meet Serafina, into whose house and bosom he is warmly welcomed upon his timely arrival. Shortly after, Pedro shows up, presents himself Serafina's fiance, and is promptly declared mad, or at least mean-minded, for his impersonation. In the midst of these troubles, Vicente arrives, discovers both the impersonation and "Gabriel," brings on an *alguacil* (bailiff) and has "Gabriel" arrested for dishonoring his sister. In short order, the utterly confused and depressed Pedro is hustled off to jail. Violante, disguised as a *villana* (village girl), watches all of this in the company of Juan, Serafina's brother, who has fallen in love with the feisty country girl.

Violante meets Don Luis, Gabriel's cousin, come to Madrid with important news for his relative, and sends him off to the jail to spring his cousin on the condition Gabriel will marry her. Violante, as *villana*, then tells Juan that she will be forced to marry a peasant in Vallecas unless he comes to her rescue. She next asks Serafina to be a witness at her marriage and asks Luis to bring "Gabriel." At the wedding, Violante then steps forth as herself and untangles all of the threads she has twisted together, marries the real Gabriel, and restores the real Pedro to Serafina.

Deceit and underhanded behavior are obviously central to the play's action. Gabriel tricks Violante, takes Pedro's identity and attempts to steal his fiancée, never tries to return the suitcases, uses part of Pedro's money, and colludes in Pedro's arrest. Violante as well resorts to deceit when her options are reduced to death or the convent. Vicente is a gambler, a wastrel, and an inattentive guardian of his sister's and his own honor. Moreover, Tirso counts on shared cultural codes subtly to suggest certain negative aspects about the characters. First, both Violante and Vicente are residents of Valencia. In the seventeenth century, Valencia, Herrero García tells us, was synonymous with "emporios de placeres sensuales y pecaminosa molicie" (emporia of sensual pleasure and sinful softness) (Herrero García 1966, 305). Citing Botero, he describes the men from that area: "Sus vecinos son poco estimados de los demás pueblos; porque estando tan entrañados y envueltos en deleites y regalos . . . valen poco para las armas" (Its male citizens are held in low esteem by the people because being so involved with and wrapped up in pleasures and enjoyment . . . they are of little use as soldiers) (307). In addition, since Vicente is a gambler, we note that Deleito y Piñuela (1948) declares that in this period men schooled in the art of cheating at cards received the honorary degree of "doctor en la valenciana" (doctorate in Valencian trickery) (232).

There is an obvious, strong criticism of gamblers, lying and churlish soldiers, inattentive brothers, susceptible sisters, which suggests a breakdown in social and family values that in turn can lead to such situations as are portrayed in the play. However, there is an equally strong implied criticism of the noble Gómez family's gullibility; they make no inquiries about "Pedro's" identity even after another Pedro appears. Moreover, Juan is easily swayed by the *villana's* beauty, willing to marry below his station, and not only refusing to say anything to his father about his feelings, but also systematically attempting to deceive him at every turn. In general, there is a gross lack of communication among friends, acquaintances, and family members.

Pedro is an *indiano* (a wealthy returnee from the Indies) headed for Madrid and an arranged marriage with the daughter of a noble, established family. *Indianos* had mixed reputations at best since many suspected that their fortunes may have been ill-gotten (Herrero García 1966, 317). In the play, Pedro bemoans the loss of the treasure he carried in his suitcases but, perhaps surprisingly, he does not hurry to the authorities to make a full report; rather, he proceeds only cautiously in writing to friends in Seville who could come to Madrid to help restore his identity. At one point in the play, he states that he was in such a hurry to come to Madrid that, to avoid delay, he did not register all his wealth with the Sevillan authorities. It was against the law in seventeenth-century Spain not to declare gold and silver when returning from the Americas. Pedro carries with him 30,000 *pesos* of gold bars and 5,000 *ducados* worth of coins and jewels. If as part of the money he carried there were coins minted in the colonies from unquinted bullion (bullion on which the 20% severance tax had not been paid), Pedro would be subject to the death penalty for smuggling (see E. Hamilton 1934, 16–17, 24–26). Now the play nowhere overtly states that this is the case, but the suggestion that might be gleaned from Pedro's constant wailing on the one hand and demurring on the other, might lead an informed audience, especially an audience whose prejudices toward *indianos* could be counted on, to doubt this man's utter honesty and perhaps to see a certain ironic humor in his losses. Looked at in this way, the play depends on the audience's beliefs and knowledge to fill in around the characters and perhaps to question their stated values. The play seems bent on marginalizing nearly all of the main characters, not holding anyone up as a model of discretion and goodness. All of the principal characters plays fast and loose with the system that they say they support and which supports them, and to which they supposedly owe allegiance.

Central to Violante's ability to pursue and entangle her faithless and slippery Gabriel is the role she takes as *panadera* (breadseller) to Madrid. The role Tirso creates for Violante is not the bumbling, comic rustic, typified in this play by Blas Serrano's unseen son, Antón, who cannot figure out how to put on the breeches he rented in Madrid for his wedding to the *villana* de Vallecas, "De Madrid / Trujo unos diabros de calzas / De alquiler, y hase perdido / Entre tantas cuchilladas" (From Madrid he brought some devilish breeches he rented, and he has become lost in all their openings) (68c); nor is she the wealthy and wise *labradora* (country girl) like Casilda in *Peribáñez* or Lisarda in *El villano en su rincón;* nor is she the worldly-wise, clever, city-bred servant. Rather, as *panadera,* the "suburban laborer," neither totally countrified nor completely citified, Violante when she wishes can speak rustically though discerningly on the lifestyles and habits of those around her. She can highlight the peasants' hard life in such a mixed society, conflating their woes with her own, as when she appears in the last act selling brooms. When Serafina marvels at her change in office from breadseller, Violante responds, "Todos son de labradora, / Y aun con todo, el pan no alcanza. / Ya vendo trigo, ya escobas, / Y enojos también vendiera, / Si hallara quien los quisiera" (Peasant women do all these, and even then do not make enough for bread. Now I sell wheat, now brooms, and I would sell anger too if I could find someone to buy it) (65a).

In addition, from this "distanced" position, she can also wrap the moon-eyed Juan around her whimsical finger. In an early dialogue with the already smitten swain, who moments before her arrival had praised her blue-green eyes, lovely face, and brown hair (about the importance of which, see Margaret Wilson 1977, 51), Violante shines as the sharply punning "country/city girl." When Juan declares, "Desde que ayer os vio [my soul] os busca," (Since it saw you yesterday [my soul] searches for you) *la villana* retorts, "¿Luego el alma tien buscona?" (Then you have a streetwalker (seeker) soul?) (53c). When he praises her with "Donaire tenéis," she shoots back, "Sin don; / Que en Vallecas mas se usa / El aire al limpiar las parvas, / Que el don que mos las ensucia." This is impossible to translate well to English because of the word play. *Donaire,* cleverness, Violante breaks into two words, *don,* a term of respect, and *aire,* air, and she puns on both. A flat rendition would be "you are clever. Without the *don,* for in Vallecas we use the air to winnow whereas the *don* only dirties the wheat on us" (54a; for more on this exchange, see Ruth L. Kennedy 1974, 303–10). Her humor at times borders the vulgar. Don Juan wants a kiss from the lovely lass so he begs her to cure his malady (love, or perhaps better, desire), by *soplos* (puffs) from her flowerlike, fragrant mouth, "Llegad, sopladme en la boca" (Come here, puff in my mouth). Violante replies, pointing to her mule's anus, "Póngala, si soplos busca, / Aquí, que está el sopladero" (Put it here, if puffs you seek, for here is the blowhole) (54b).

Since Violante fears losing the fickle Gabriel to Serafina, a wealthy *madrileña* (Madrid lady), the court's women come in for particularly gleeful, sarcastic, and sometimes pungent commentary, as in the following passage where she compares them to birds:

> Pardiez, que en eso acertáis;
> Que las aves o avechuchas
> De Madrid son papagayos:
> Pluma hermosa y carne dura.
> ¡Quién se las ve pavonadas,
> Arrastrando catalufas,
> Con más joyas que más andas,
> Y una igreja colgaduras! (. . .)
> Si a pie, nieve sobre corchos,
> Afrenta de la pintura,
> Dando a la plata de coces,
> Que por los lodos ensucian;
> Si a caballo, en cuatro ruedas,
> Y la fortuna sobre una:
> Porque en fin son más mudables
> Tres veces que la fortuna.
> Pues desplumadlas, veréis
> Cuán poco aprovechó el cura
> Cuando les puso en la igreja
> La sal, porque no se pudran.

Puesto que los que las comen,
Nos suelen dar por excusa
Que perdices y mujeres,
Aunque oliscan, no disgustan.

(54b/c)

(By Gosh, you're right about that, the birds or big ugly birds of
Madrid are parrots: beautiful plumage and tough meat. Whoever sees them strutting like peacocks dragging double taffeta,
with more jewels than there are hawked about town and more
things hanging from them than in a church! . . . If [they go
about] on foot, snow on cork sandals, an affront to painting,
kicking against silver which they dirty in the mud; if [they go
about] by horse, on four wheels whereas fortune rides only one:
because, finally, they are three times more fickle than fate. But
pluck them and you will see how little good it did for the priest
to put salt on them in church so that they would not rot. Since
those that enjoy them offer us as an excuse that partridges and
these women, though they smell bad, are not disgusting.)

From her distanced position and in her "rustic" language, *pardiez,
igreja,* Violante criticizes the city women's sweet appearance, which
hides their deceit and hardness: their makeup (*pintura*), their high-
fashion dresses, their love of jewelry (they are like the portable platforms overflowing with junk jewelry hawked around Madrid by itinerant salespersons), they have more things hanging from them than
churches have tapestries and pendants, their high-heeled, silver-deco-
rated shoes, their love of coaches, their fickleness, their rottenness.
Yet when Juan proposes, she adopts (ironically?) all the courtly airs.
She quizzes Juan about what he would do for her if they were to
marry, and to all her questions, Juan dutifully and joyfully answers
yes: "¿Andaré en coche? ¿Traeré puntas? ¿Saldré . . . a toros? Si hay
comedias . . . [¿iré?] ¿Iré al Prado?" (Will I go about in a coach? Will I
wear lace? Will I go to bullfights? If there are plays, [will I go?] Will I
go to the Prado?) (55c–56a).

To further her scheme, whenever she wants, Violante can become a
"noblewoman." First, wearing appropriate clothing, she tells Gabriel's cousin, Luis, of her ill treatment at Gabriel's hands. This is literally true, but the "Gabriel" she refers to and to whom she sends
Luis is in fact the encarcerated Pedro. Next she has Aguado rent a
fully furnished house in Madrid, buy out several stores, and have
enough sewing done to keep three tailors busy so as to become "una

dama mejicana" (a Mexican lady) (61c). With her new residence and regalia, she becomes Doña Inés de Fuen-mayor (62b). She invites Juan to her home and there tells him that Pedro (really Gabriel) seduced her then abandoned her to come to Madrid to marry Serafina. She has followed him to "esta corte . . . confuso Babel" (this court . . . a confusing Babel) (62c) to prevent Serafina from suffering a similar fate as she believes that "luego que se casare / De Madrid se ausentara, / Y sin que en deudas repare, / Tantas mujeres tendrá / Cuantas provincias mudare" (as soon as he marries, he will leave Madrid without recognizing his debts; he will have as many women as there are provinces for him to visit) (62c). Later, disguised as the *villana,* she tells Serafina that Pedro (Gabriel) is living with a "mujer de Indias" (woman from the Indies) (66a) whom he has brought with him from Mexico and who approves of his illicit activities as well as of his plan to marry Serafina (66a).

Violante's strong desire to get what she wants rather than what society might mandate, as well as her native intelligence and wit, along with her various disguises, chief among them breadseller from Vallecas, stress her mobility, fluidity, and her skills necessary to achieve her ends. But why a breadseller? First, in this disguise she can wander the streets of Madrid with access to nearly all houses in search of her lost Gabriel. But what good would it do to have such access if Madrid's population surpasses 150,000 inhabitants? Tirso's knowledge of the city's codes, a knowledge he shares with his audience (in fact, he depends on his audience's knowledge so that his play will not seem utterly unbelievable) provides a means for limiting and focusing Violante's search and offers her entry into just those kinds of houses where she knows Gabriel might be going. The code he employs involves provisioning, foodstuffs.

Feeding a city of 150,000 inhabitants, far from the sea, without a navigable river, with difficult communications, was no small task.[2] In addition, the seventeenth century was a mini–ice age in Europe: agricultural production was tenuous and providing food for a relatively large city a constant struggle. The great droughts of the sixteenth century were followed by drenching rains and floods; Tirso's *La huerta de Juan Fernández* makes direct reference to the Seville floods of 1626. Inundations were recorded in 1610, 1615, 1616, 1617, 1620, 1626, 1627, and 1628 by one man's diary (cited by Espadas Burgos 1977, 8–9). Thus Gabriel's (purportedly Tirso's) claim that "ni rigores

---

2. See Manual Espadas Burgos (1977), to which the following discussion owes much. Also see Viñas y Mey (1955), esp. 476–80.

/ Del cielo hayan afligido / Este reino" (no natural disasters have afflicted this kingdom) during Philip III's time is either a flattering exaggeration or belies his, Gabriel's, ignorance of fact.

As the seventeenth century opened, grain prices were essentially stable except during two crisis years, 1605 and 1615. A *fanega* (about 1 1/2 bushels) of wheat stood at 35 *reales* between 1605 and 1608. Between 1614 and 1616, prices rose, but then from 1618 to 1628 stabilized once more with lower prices especially after the abundant harvests of 1617. By 1623, a *fanega* of wheat sold for four *reales* (Espadas Burgos 1977, 10–11). Thus Gabriel's astoundingly low price of one *real*, "Pues, que en su [Philip III's] tiempo ha alcanzado / Castilla el haber comprado / La hanega de trigo a real" (Since in Philip III's time Castile has been able to buy a *fanega* of wheat for one *real*) (17a) is pure fiction.

Madrid needed between 2,000 and 2,500 *fanegas* a day to provide its bread supply. The breadmaking industry in Madrid, however, was insufficient for its population and thus the "pan de obligación" system was instituted (see Ringrose 1983, 14), requiring surrounding villages to supply the capital with the needed commodity. Among those towns was Vallecas. Bread was sold by *ventureros,* itinerant salespersons, *dispenseros,* those who sold to institutions or priviledged groups, and *registreros,* those who brought bread to the local authorities (Espadas Burgos 1977, 12). Into the first category merges Violante so as to permit her easy movement throughout the city in search for Gabriel. But Madrid was a sprawling city, so just because she could enter the town freely and sell bread on the streets as an itinerant vendor would not necessarily make Violante's search any more directed and fruitful. Thus the play centers on a more specific aspect of the code.

How much and what kind of bread one ate depended upon one's financial condition, social class, and work habits. A normal loaf of bread weighed about two pounds, and a hardy working person of reduced means ate about three pounds of bread, *pan común* (standard bread), per day. Wealthier people with more disposable income to spend on other foodstuffs ate less bread, about a pound per day. The bread sold to wealthier clients was *pan regalado* (delicate bread), or the even more prized *panecillos de leche* (little milk-white loaves), an extremely white, light, and tasty bread, the result of a long and tedious wheat-culling process (Espadas Burgos 1977, 15–16). This is precisely the sort of bread Violante sells. Polonia, Juan's servant, comments that he noticed "la blancura del pan / *Que de leche* nos da" (the whiteness of the milk-white loaves she sells us) (53a; my emphasis). The bread she sells, "de leche," would take Violante to only the most prosperous areas of the city, to the homes of the wealthy where her chances of spotting Gabriel or locating Serafina's house would be best. Tirso thereby ties Violante's new identity in the advancing discovery plot to the economic and social realities of Madrid in the 1620s in order partially to ground the fortuitous detection in a knowledge of everyday reality.

Tirso's understanding and use of the socioeconomic realities of Madrid in the 1620s form more than a flat backdrop against which the discovery plot plays out. A knowledge of everyday "reality" (perhaps not the most efficient of terms) is essential to the development of the play and the creation of character, particularly of the clever, protean woman so often associated with Tirso's comedies. Violante must fully understand the system in order to achieve her ends, and Tirso must be able to count on his prospective audience's knowledge of that same system; to count on its grasp of the everyday reality of the Madrid wherein he sets his play; to count on the audience's ability to fill in the gaps quickly. That is to say, Tirso relies on shared cultural codes (including, of course, the *comedia*'s codes) to which he can refer in dramatic shorthand—shorthand because it is unnecessary to explain fully what everyone already knows simply by living in that society. Such references, however, are fleeting and frequently lost on today's readers since we do not share those same codes.

To manipulate the system, improvisation is a must. Violante must transform other characters' "reality" into a theatrical fiction. She must take "theatrical reality," already a second-level speech-act, to an even higher fictional plane whereon Violante functions as partial dramatist and lead actress to manipulate others, as earlier Gabriel manipulated her. The codes, truths, social responsibilities, and words must be seen as illusions so that she can direct them toward her own goals. From such an "outside" position—"fallen woman," breadseller, *indiana*—she can play with the codes, pun, lie, deceive, and make promises with no intention of ever fulfilling them. She can criticize what she sees around her, make fun freely, and escape censure at the end of the play. In the last scene, she sorts out situations and assigns new roles like the most accomplished of directors as she offers brief excuses to poor Juan, who wanted desperately to marry her, and to poor Pedro, who went to jail when she could have easily prevented his imprisonment.

In order for her to act so freely, she must have plausible roles too. In those fluid roles she can conceal her true desires even as she acts to bring them to fruition. Her improvisation may produce momentary chaos but in the end it serves to reestablish a chastened order: she

marries Gabriel; Serafina marries Pedro. Though the play ends more
or less in orthodoxy, it does so only in the final breathless seconds. All
of the attention, however, has been focused throughout not on order
but on the instability provoked by supposedly noble men acting in the
most ignoble ways; it is only through the clever actions of the potential scapegoat, who turns others toward her and her society's ends,
that a reasonable resolution occurs. In her role as *villana,* as itinerant
breadseller to the wealthy inhabitants of Madrid, may lie an even
greater irony. Those wealthy nobles, even with all their money,
jewels, fine clothes, position and power, might starve to death were it
not for peasants, such as the one Violante plays. The power relations—noble/peasant, man/woman, insider/outsider, rich/poor—come
in for some embarrassing though comic tweaks before being recon-
stituted in chagrined form. Violante as dishonored woman and then
as peasant works from the periphery to the center taking full advantage of her and her audience's knowledge of the cultural codes and
socioeconomic realities of Madrid in the 1620s.

If *La villana de Vallecas* depends on the characters' and the audience's knowledge of provisioning the court, both *En Madrid y en una
casa* and *Los balcones de Madrid* bring the economic atmosphere, the
capital's houses, their furnishings, their architectural features, and
theatricality center stage. Since I have already written on *En Madrid
y en una casa* (see Chapter 1), I shall refer the reader to those pages
for a plot summary and overview of the love problems the comedy
presents. Here is the plot line of the second play.

Don Alonso wants his daughter, Elisa, to marry Don Pedro, but she
loves and is loved by Don Juan. Alonso, however, will not countenance Elisa's wishes because he believes Pedro a better match. After
Juan tells his friend, Conde Carlos, of his love and of Elisa's beauty
the noble ignites with desire and works against his friend toward his
own ends. Elisa's cousin and next-door neighbor, Ana, connives with
Elisa's maid, Leonor, to break up Juan and Elisa because Ana loves
Juan. Juan hears of Alonso's proposed match, Elisa thinks that Juan
loves Ana, and the two accuse each other of perfidy. When Alonso
enters, the two quickly make up and Juan hides in Elisa's room.

The Count bribes Leonor to work on his behalf, then hides in the
maid's room when Alonso, Ana, and Pedro arrive to force Elisa to sign
the marriage contract. Leonor says that her mistress cannot marry
Pedro because she has promised herself to the Count. Ana seconds the
notion and when Elisa is told that this is only a trick to get her out of
having to marry Pedro, she goes along. The Count steps forth to declare his love and intentions; Juan storms out and insults everyone.

The Count leaves, Juan follows and wounds him. Left alone with her father, Elisa begs to marry Juan but Alonso, now spurred by thoughts of the social and economic benefits accruing from her marriage to the Count, tells her she must choose between accepting that marriage or leaving instantly for a convent in Lerma. She chooses the latter. Alfonso calls on a friend, Alvaro, tells him to move out all of Elisa's furnishings, rent new things and redecorate the rooms. He then bundles his daughter into a carriage, seals its windows, and sends her on a circuitous trip to Torrejón. Then, late at night, he returns her to her own "unrecognizable" room, telling her she is in Illescas in her "Uncle Alvaro's" house, that the trip to Lerma was a ruse to throw Juan off the track, and that she will remain here until she either becomes the Countess or dies.

Meantime, Juan has taken refuge in Ana's house where Coral, his servant, enters. Because he had been hiding in Elisa's house, Coral knows all that has transpired, including the fact that she is but a wall away. To permit the lovers to converse, Coral constructs an extendable bridge between the two proximate balconies. Juan visits Elisa, then she goes to his rooms. While she is there, Alonso enters to find a *dama tapada* (veiled lady) who he is sure is his daughter. He rushes back home only to find Elisa sitting disconsolately. He searches the room for a hidden passageway and finding none, goes back to Ana's house where Juan and the *dama tapada* sit in conversation. Unconvinced, he enlists Alvaro's aid to check on Elisa while he visits Juan. The Count, Pedro, and Ana join in, and in the final scene, Ana and Pedro appear on one balcony, the Count, Alvaro, and Alonso on the other; trapped between on the *tramoya* (stage-machine) are Juan, Elisa, Coral, and Leonor. Reconciliations follow as Juan marries Elisa, Ana marries Pedro, and the play ends, as Coral observes, "en el aire" (in the air) (3425).

In both plays, love, trickery, frustrated desire, and the power of money are the sources for much of the action. In *En Madrid*, Manuela inherited a fortune, and now loves Gabriel who, though a descendant of a noble family, had squandered his inheritance and looks to marry Serafina for her money. In *Balcones*, the Count's money and position make both Leonor and Alonso work against Elisa's desires, driven as they both are by greed and thoughts of social improvement. A strong economic subtext is visible in the vocabulary in both plays: *dote, doblón, interés, cobrar, ganar, negociar, alquiler, renta, tesoro, oro, el planeta ginovés* (dowry, doubloon, interest, charge, earn, negotiate, rent, income, treasure, gold, the Genovese planet).

If dreams of economic gain can suborn a supposedly loyal maid,

Leonor (*Balcones*) and cause a father to run roughshod over his daughter, so too can it "buy" Pacheco, enlist a servant in the *escalera levadiza* (staircase that can be raised and lowered) embedded story, and bribe yet another servant to smuggle love letters to the cloistered Serafina (*En Madrid*). In the latter play, Manuela accuses Gabriel of faithlessness, comparing him to a fraudulent merchant, "A ser mercader venís, / confiado en vuestro talle, / de hermosuras, porque os halle / amor, que os vende quimeras, / yendo enamorando a aceras, / gran turco de nuestra calle" (Trusting in your looks, you have come to be a merchant dealing in beautiful women; love, which flatters you, finds you going along the sidewalks courting, the grand Turk of our street) (1209b).

In both plays, deceit and money are closely related, and deceit is joined with theatricality. In *En Madrid,* Manuela plays a *dama tapada* (veiled lady), then the Countess, then Serafina; Leonor plays herself, Serafina, and a *dama tapada* as well. Majuelo compares his master's situation with three lovers to a "comedia de ahora / que la escriben tres poetas" (a current play written by three poets) (1286a), and later wonders aloud if the Countess could be "autora de tanto enredo" (authoress of so much mischief) (1289b). Ortiz, speaking of the drop-down staircase, likens it to devices she has seen in plays, "Donde hay sótanos amantes, / galán fantasma, amor duende, / tornos, casas con dos puertas, / tabiques disimulados, / hurtarán de los tablados / tramoyas que saquen ciertas / esperanzas ya perdidas" (Where there are basement lovers, ghostly gallants, phantom love, revolving dumbwaiters, houses with two doors, false partitions, people will steal tricks from the stage to realize their nearly lost hopes) (1285b). As noted earlier, this was precisely what some moralists feared. To drive the connections home, Tirso locates the house where all the action takes place on *la Calle del Príncipe,* near, so Pacheco tells Gabriel, "La casa de comedia, / . . . en esta misma acera" (The playhouse . . . on this same block) (1266a).

In *Balcones,* besides the obvious references to Coral's portable bridge as a *tramoya* (stage-machine), when Elisa wants to hide the *manto de humo* (gauzy cloak) she used to cover her face when her father burst into Juan's room, she thinks of putting it up Leonor's sleeve. Leonor cautions against that idea, given Alonso's penchant for attending the theater, "Mal consejo, / que en una comedia vi / que le escondieron así, / y todas las oye el viejo" (Bad advice, for once in a comedy I saw them hide it thus, and the old man attends them all) (3156–59). And in fact, when Alonso enters Elisa's rooms, he demands "Despejad las dos las mangas" (Show me your sleeves) (3184).

Deception, money, and theatricality then broaden out to link with the atmosphere of the court itself. In *En Madrid,* the city is a gulf where one can successfully navigate only in a "bajel de metal" (a metal boat) (1259a); Madrid is a labyrinth where "halla ocasiones / toda juventud traviesa" (mischievous youth finds opportunities) (1261b/62a); where the whole world congregates (1262a) and where no one knows his next-door neighbor (1262a); the capital is a huge shopping mart where anything can be bought or sold, "Basta, que Madrid es tienda / de toda mercadería" (Enough, Madrid is a store with every kind of merchandise) (*En Madrid,* 1263b). In *Balcones,* Alonso knows exactly where to go and with whom to speak to when he wants to rent furniture to transform his daughter's room, "pediréis al corredor / Pedro de Avila, el que vive / junto a la Puerta del Sol, / que os alquile por un mes / otra tanta ostentación" (you will ask the broker, Pedro de Avila, who lives next to the Puerta del Sol, to rent you for a month other lovely furnishings) (2201–5). Pedro de Avila was a real person who, among other transactions, lent five hundred *ducados* to "Cristobal de Avendaño y María de Candau, autores de comedias" (directors of acting companies) in March 1623 (Tirso 1982, note to 2202).

Yet even more important and more specific, both plays depend on a knowledge of the architecture of Madrid's houses for the success of the central characters' schemes. The plays offer an inventory of rooms and furnishings. In *En Madrid,* the men rush about searching for the supposedly hidden Serafina, and Gabriel lists for the audience the places they searched, "no habemos los tres dejado / sala, retrete, oficina, / cancel, ángulo / sin registrar" (the three of us have not left unsearched large rooms, small rooms, offices, partitions, or corners) (1286a). In *Balcones,* where the word *casa* (house) appears more than thirty-five times (not counting wordplays on forms of the verb *casar* (to marry) and the phonetically associated *cosa* (thing) and *caso* (circumstance, case), references to architectural features appear more than forty times. Juan describes Elisa, for example, "architecturally" speaking of her *exterior,* the "habitación hermosa / del alma" (beautiful bedroom of her soul) (193–94), of her head as "oficina de tales pensamientos" (office of such thoughts), her eyebrows as the "dos arcos [that] la rematan" (two arches that crown it) (196–97) and later as her "arcos triunfales" (triumphal arches) (203); her eyes are *viriles* (windowpanes) through which one can see "al huésped que en tal casa" (the owner of such a house) (247). Coral compares the *culto* (baroque) poets' accumulations of "aljófar, diamantes, perlas, / nácares, púrpuras, lamas, / soles, auroras, estrellas" (seed pearl, diamond, pearls, nacre, purple, lamé, suns, dawns, stars) (560–67) to the disorder one finds on carts when people move, once more signaling things in a house so that the audience can imaginatively, concretely fill in the sparsely appointed stage:

> ¿Viste mudar una casa,
> cuando sobre una carreta,
> la cargan de baratijas,
> unas con otras revueltas,
> el escritorio y las ollas,
> las sartenes y rodelas,
> el arcabuz y las naguas,
> los platos y la maleta,
> la alfombra y el orinal . . .
> (575–83)

(Have you ever seen moving day at a house when on a cart they load their stuff, all jumbled together are the writing desk and pots, frying pans and bucklers, the harquebus and petticoats, dishes and suitcases, the rug and the chamberpot.)

When Alonso removes Elisa's furnishings, he offers another list:

> despejando aquesta sala
> de cuanto adorno la dio
> la calidad de mi estado
> y de mi hacienda el valor,
> cuadros, colgaduras, sillas,
> escritorio, contador,
> cama, estrado . . .
> (2192–98)[3]

(clearing out everything from this room that bespeaks the quality and worth of my station, paintings, wall hangings, chairs, writing desk, table, bed, drawing room furniture.)

---

3. There are other similar inventories in other plays. In *Desde Toledo a Madrid*, Baltasar lists the items he sees in Mayor's boudoir (434b/c), and in *La dama duende*, Isabel and Angela carefully go through Manuel's and Cosme's bags systematically naming all items found (247a/b). Such inventories, besides filling in the scene, help classify the characters who own the materials by gender, class, and economic condition.

While in *Balcones* both Alonso and Ana are apparently longtime residents of Madrid, well-off owners of two-story private homes, in *En Madrid,* housing is a concern for Gabriel and Manuela. He finds lodging in his uncle's apartments on the ground floor of what is apparently a *casa de vecinos,* or a subdivided house. She searches for private dwellings but can find little, as is readily shown by the following exchange with her aide,

D. JUAN: Vueseñoría
                       perdonara la estrechez
                       deste cuarto que he alquilado . . .
D. MANUELA: Dicen que hay dificultad
                       en Madrid de hallarse casa
                       sola y grande.
D. JUAN: Es infinita
                       la nobleza que le habita:
                       toda Castilla se pasa
                       a la corte.

                                        (1263a)

(J: Your Ladyship must pardon the smallness of this room I have rented. M: They say there is difficulty finding a single, large house in Madrid. J: There is an infinite number of nobles living here: all Castile is coming to the court.)

This house is also two stories but divided into three separate but connected living areas. Occupying the upper floors above Gabriel's rooms are Leonor and her brother. The living area next to theirs is occupied by Manuela.

Whereas *Balcones* takes advantage of the proximity of Madrid's houses, their shared walls, and the standard balconies for comic effect and for the eventual resolution "en el aire" (in the air), *En Madrid* looks to the house's subdivisions and interior design to bring about its most amusing theatrical moment. The house in this play, like the characters who inhabit it and the city where it is located, is not just what it seems. The house too holds its secret, an architectural secret that involves desire, deception, and the power of money. The secret depends on a standard interior design feature in Madrid's houses, a feature mentioned as well in *Balcones.* After her long coach ride when Elisa thinks she is far from the capital, Coral enters her room and tells her to look around carefully at the room she is in, "mira esa alcoba o estufa" (look at that bedroom or stove) (1553), he tells her, and pay particular attention to a feature common to Madrid's houses, "las bovedillas del techo, / que en Illescas poco se usan" (the small vaults in the ceiling, that are little used in Illescas) (2554–55). When she does, she exclaims gleefully, "¡Ay cielo, en la corte estoy!" (Oh heavens, I am in the court!) (2560; see also *La dama duende*, 2626, where Manuel, searching for the suddenly missing "duende" swears to search the "bovedillas del techo" to see if they cover a secret hiding place).

Bovedillas are central to the trick in *En Madrid*. Sometime before Leonor and her brother bought and moved into their house, a guest lived in what are now Leonor's rooms. Directly below, in the rooms where Gabriel now lives, were a young woman, object of the guest's frustrated desire, and her protective aunt. So closely did the aunt keep the young woman that the man could catch only fleeting glimpses of her, but those were enough to inspire his, and apparently her, love. To permit meetings and conversations, when the aunt was off visiting a relative, the man had a carpenter open a section of the floor in his room and in the ceiling of hers and build a drop-down ladder. He then disguised the opening carefully especially in the young lady's room, "Puso otras dos bovedillas, / que con tablas imitó, / y el yeso y arte cubrió, / bastando el arte a fingillas / de suerte que con la pintura, / que ellas con los dos maderos / pasaron por ver-daderos" (He installed two other small vaults made of wood and dis-guised by art and plaster, the art was enough to make them, with a little paint, pass for real ones) (1285a). In his room he covered the trapdoor with a carpet; thus, by means of the ladder, the two could meet, circumvent the aunt, and finally arrange their marriage. Leonor learned of the secret but did not tell her brother "Porque a tener dél noticia / mi hermano, llevara mal / que en casa tan principal / se intentase tal malicia" (Because if my brother heard tell of this, he would not be happy that in such a noble house such malice was at-tempted) (1285a/b).

Now the house, from all appearances, is upright, a noble, clean, and safe residence for Leonor and her brother, Gabriel and his uncle, even for a Countess, yet it holds its deceitful secret. That secret was made possible by the powerful combination of "oro, industrias y deseos" (gold, ingenuity, and desire) (1284b), as Leonor states. The guest bought a maid's compliance "a costa del rey metal" (at the cost of the king of metals) (1284b) to get around a stingy aunt under whose tight-fisted control even the "ventanas pagaban censo / a la avara pesadumbre / de un enfadoso encerado" (windows paid the tax on the miserly grief by means of an annoying waxed paper window covering)

(1284a). He used his money to get the carpenter to do the work, "comprándole el secreto, / para poner en efecto / la industria" (buying his secrecy to carry out the ingenious plan) (1284b). The Madrid house is then a theatrical, deceptive, and labyrinthine construct created by desire and money, externally honorable yet internally adulterated. In the house lived a man driven by desire, a prized and willing woman, and a jealously imprisoning guardian seeking to maintain an outward appearance of honorable demeanor. Leonor makes the connection between the house, money, "art," and Madrid when she invites Manuela to look at the trapdoor and hidden ladder, "Ven a vella, / que la corte siempre vende / sutilezas semejantes" (come and see it, the court always sells such slick tricks) (1285b).

This play works to disfigure power; the house and where it stands are the material analogues for such work. That house, Leonor wants her brother to think, is a "casa tan principal" (so noble a house) that no shenanigans could or can take place there. That house is located on *la calle de Príncipe* (1263b), a noble street "tanto como su apellido," (as [noble] as its name) Don Juan tells Manuela, since "Títulos y caballeros / la ilustran" (titled persons and gentlemen make it illustrious) (1263b). But also passing along that same street are "mirones" (Peeping Toms) who try to peep into ground-floor windows and whom one must constantly guard against. For Pacheco, the house and street gain fame not just from the nobles and grandees who pass along it, but also from "La casa de comedia, / . . . en esta misma acera" (The playhouse on this same block) (1266a) that characterizes it. Nobles, Peeping Toms, visitors, lovers, and actors all converge, each adding their part, to the makeup of the atmosphere where this noble yet secretive and ultimately theatrical house stands. The house that shelters the play's characters, enclosing them, surrounding them, is as open and penetrable as was the Puerta Cerrada, "como está Madrid sin cerca, / a todo gusto da entrada: / nombre hay de Puerta Cerrada, / mas pásala quien se acerca" (since Madrid has no walls, it offers entry to all pleasures; one entrance is called "Closed Gate," but anyone who approaches passes through it) (*La huerta de Juan Fernández* 603). Men enter women's rooms nearly at will and Leonor and Manuela even pass easily through the ceiling. Rules are laid down in the house only to be breached. The house is as labyrinthine as the streets and just as theatrical as the nearby *corral*.

As each of the characters tries to get what he or she wants or desires, each must employ methods seemingly alien to his or her role. The Countess uses disguise and spies on Gabriel to force him to take her part; Luis shamelessly lies to and uses his sister to aid a friend, passing him off as a long absent cousin, in an attempt to help that friend with his love match; Gonzalo initiates the plan and then lies to Gabriel to encourage him to abandon Serafina; Leonor agrees to help her brother and Gonzalo but then undermines their efforts so as to achieve her own ends; Gabriel chases three women at the same time, and the tricks and deceptions do not end there. All the male figures believe that they know what they want, but in the end, their knowledge is proved false. If part of the codes of this period posits a relation between correct seeing and knowledge, then the play works both with and against that equation. It turns women, the presumed objects of desire, into desiring subjects who control and manipulate the men's vision. Their ends are that the men see "correctly": Gabriel must see that he really wants Manuela; Gonzalo must learn that he really wants Leonor; and in the last scene, Luis must be told that he wants Serafina and all she stands for.

But that "corrected vision" partakes of ideological distortion because the women see only one option: marriage. Even the never-seen Serafina will be taken from the convent to marry according to her father's wishes. The play emphasizes throughout a double vision in the portrayal of upright people using questionable means to obtain a "correct" end. But that double vision informs all aspects of the play and its setting: Madrid is the king's court as well as a den of imposters and confidence men, the house is honorable and fraudulent, the streets are populated by the principled and the unprincipled, and everything is theatricalized. While the final arrangements legitimize societal goals, those ends are achieved through unethical means, thereby perhaps calling attention to the distortion inherent in ideological figuration.

From the streets and houses in *La villana de Vallecas, En Madrid y en una casa,* and *Los balcones de Madrid,* the last play I shall discuss in this chapter takes us to one of the city's best-known public and private gardens. Of the plays included in this study, the one that comes closest to incorporating Wardropper's Arcadia and Frye's "green world" is Tirso's *La huerta de Juan Fernández.* The green world, Frye (1957) says, belongs to those comedies of the fourth phase. In those works, "we begin to move out of the world of experience into the ideal world of innocence and romance" (181–82). Among the plays Frye chooses as examples are Shakespeare's *The Two Gentlemen of Verona, A Midsummer Night's Dream, As You Like It,* and *The Winter's Tale.* About those plays, Frye states that "the action of the comedy begins in a world represented as a normal world, moves into the green world, goes into a metamorphosis there in which the comic resolution is achieved, and returns to the normal world. In the English plays, the forest, the fairy world, the Forest of Arden, Windsor Forest, and the pastoral sea coast of Bohemia, respectively, are 'green worlds' wherein the changes occur. Those spaces charge the comedies with the symbolism of the victory of summer over winter [and therefore] the green world has analogues, not only to the world of ritual, but to the dream world that we create out of our own desires" (183). There, in the green world, we see a "genuine form of the world that human life tries to imitate" (183). Frye seems here to posit a bar, a separation between the world of experience, the city, and the green world, the "genuine form," or innocent world of the woods. In a word, he separates culture from nature, implying thereby the superiority of the latter, a superiority springing from natural or uncontaminated forms. Such a separation will not bear close scrutiny in either Shakespeare's plays or these Spanish comedies.

Tirso's play begins in an inn on the road to Madrid, moves from there to the capital, where most of the action of the play takes place in the garden named in the title, and returns from there, in the end, to the world. The garden shelters Laura whose father, the Conde de Valencia del Po, because he had no sons, gave primogeniture to her. Her uncle, however, contested her rights, then took her lands by force. She seeks legal redress in Madrid. Following her there comes Hernando Cortés, a nobleman from Málaga, who two years ago killed a man in a fight over a woman, fled first to Seville, then to Italy to serve with the Duke of Feria until the peace of Piamonte. He came to Madrid, with strong recommendations from the Duke, seeking a position. In Italy, he met Pompeyo, Laura's uncle, and through him, her. Since their meeting, Laura and Hernando have enjoyed a reciprocal love. For the last three months, disguised as a gardener, Hernando works in the garden to be near Laura.

Pursuing him comes Petronila, disguised as a man. On the road to Madrid she meets Tomasa, also disguised as a man, who is pursuing Mansilla, Hernando's servant. When Hernando went to Seville, he stayed with his aunt, Petronila's mother. She hid her daughter so as to avoid possible scandal but Petronila spied on the young man and fell in love. Even though Hernando has never seen the young lady, when he leaves for Italy, he promises to repay his aunt's generosity, "pagarla yerno / mercedes que le hizo prima" (to pay her as her son-in-law the favors she did him as cousin) (885–86). After he left, Seville suffered a horrible flood (24 January 1626), Petronila's mother was killed, and all her worldly possessions were swept away. Petronila's father, meantime, has made a fortune in Peru, and is just making plans to return to Spain, but for the time being, Petronila has nothing. She goes to Madrid knowing Hernando is there to get him to marry her.

In the inn, the women meet Conde Galeazo Malatesta, son of Laura's opponent in the lawsuit, also on the road to Madrid to effect the marriage proposal made by Pompeyo to calm the disputes among the family members. Galeazo develops a deep friendship with "Don Gómez," as Petronila calls herself, and together they go to Madrid. From there on, a series of deceptions, plays within plays, role creations, and lies guide the action until the last scene wherein Petronila marries Hernando; Laura, the Conde Galeazo; and Petronila, Mansilla.

Most of the action takes place, as indicated, in the *huerta de Juan Fernández*. This garden was located where the Palacio Buena Vista, now Cuartel General del Ejército, stands today, and shows up clearly on the Texeira map. That lovely spot was one of the first sights that greeted a tired traveler upon passing through the Puerta de Alcalá, and in the play characters attest to its beauty, its flowers, fruits, and fountains. Laura compares it to the Italian gardens she fondly remembers, "este apacible sitio, / digna elección de un buen gusto, / donde recreaba olvido / los que en Italia curiosos / retratan el paraíso" (this pleasing site, noble choice of good taste, where it called to mind the fascinating ones in Italy which re-created Paradise) (445–49). Hernando calls it "estos jardines elísios" (these Elysian gardens) (517) and Petronila reports her initial reaction upon entering there, "su vista / mis sentidos recreó, / porque en ella se cifró / Chipre, en que Venus asista" (its sight revived my senses because in it Cyprus is recreated, where Venus lived) (1110–14).

Deleito y Piñuela (1942) describes Juan Fernández's gardens:

> Era aquel sitio el predilecto por las damas de alto copete, tales como las duquesas de Lerma y Córdoba, Arión, Béjar y Medina de Rioseco; las marquesas de la Laguna, Ensenada, del Carpio, Mondéjar, Tábara y del Valle; las condesas de Linares, de Campo Alange, Lemus, Alba de Liste; doña Ana Mendoza de la Cerda, esposa de Villamediana, y tantas otras. Allí se solemnizaban con banquetes o jiras las bodas de rumbo, como las del marqués de Villena y el conde de Palma, celebradas el mismo día, de las cuales fué madrina la esposa del Conde-Duque, y que dejaron fama en aquel lugar por su esplendidez. . . . Era el paraíso de la juventud alegre y retozona, especialmente en las tardes de primavera y en las noches estivales. Sin la solemni-

dad palatina del Buen Retiro, pero con el *marchamo* del buen tono, con la intimidad de lugar cerrado y el encanto del césped, el arbolado y las flores, lo mismo ofrecía sitio para las fiestas de concursos numerosos como ocasión propicia a las parejas, a quienes convenía comer en la intimidad del cenador o extraviarse entre la ironda del sendero apartado. (245–46)

(That was the favorite spot for chic ladies, such as the Duchesses of Lerma, Córdoba, Arión, Béjar, Medina de Rioseco; the Marquises of Laguna, Ensenada, del Carpio, Mondéjar, Tábara, and del Valle; the countesses of Linares, de Campo Alange, Lemus, Alba de Liste; Lady Ana Mendoza de la Cerda, Villamediana's wife, and many others. There with banquets they solemnized noble weddings, like that of the Marquis of Villena and the Count of Palma, celebrated the same day, in which the wife of the Count-Duke was godmother, and [the celebrations] made that place famous for their splendor. . . . It was the paradise of gay and frolicsome young people, especially on spring afternoons or summer nights. Lacking the solemnity of the Buen Retiro palace, but with the stamp of elegance, with the intimateness of the closed space and the enchantment of the lawns, the trees and flowers, the site offered the same attraction for numerous get-togethers, such as for couples who needed the privacy to dine in the intimacy of the arbor or walk about together along the leaf-covered isolated paths.)

In his *Antiguallas: crónicas, descripciones y costumbres españolas en los siglos pasados,* Ricardo Sepúlveda (1898) presents an evocative and romantic description of the garden from which Deleito derives part of his "con sus bosquecillos misteriosos, sus macizos exuberantes de flores, sus paseos clandestinos por cerca del laberinto, su explanada de la noria cubierta de verde césped, y el cenador campestre, donde las memorias galantes del siglo xvii suponen que tuvieron lugar escenas de amor y celos" (with its small mysterious forests, its exuberant masses of flowers, its secretive walks near its maze, its irrigated green grass esplanade, and bucolic arbor, where the gallant memories of the seventeenth century imagine that scenes of love and jealousy took place) (Sepúlveda 1898, 59–60; also cited by Berta Pallares in Tirso de Molina 1982b, 247).

Juan Fernández (d. 1632), was a *regidor* (councilman), and in July 1612, was named "comisario de fuentes" (commissioner of waterworks); the garden is also known as the *huerta del Regidor.* Furthermore, he was a "receptor de millones del reino" (collection of the millions tax of the kingdom), or a finance minister after 1607. He was a friend of the Toledan Diego Vargas's (b. around 1604) family. In 1618 at the age of twelve or thirteen, Vargas was named "regidor de Toledo y procurador en Cortes" (councilman from Toledo and member of parliament in Cortes) (Jaime Asensio 1981, 122). In the play, Tomasa in her male disguise calls herself "Bargas" or Vargas. In 1620, the Municipio de Madrid took over part of Juan Fernández's garden "para ensanchar el Prado de Recoletos" (to broaden the Prado de Recoletos) indemnifying the owner (Deleito y Piñuela 1942, 245). Thereafter, the garden was split into two parts, one private "una interior, adonde sólo entraban los dueños y personas por ellos autorizados" (an interior part, wherein entered only the owners and those with their authorization) (245) and where in the play Laura lives, "Hospedáronme ha seis meses / cortesanos deudos míos, / con licencia de su dueño, / en este apacible sitio" (relations of mine in the court have housed me here for six months, with the owner of this lovely site's license) (442–45). The other part was public, "otra exterior, que servía de paseo público, anexo al de Recoletos, y a la que se denominaba también Huerta de Juan Fernández" (another exterior part which served as a public promenade, next to Recoletos and which also was known as Juan Fernández's Garden) (Deleito y Piñuela 1942, 245). Just outside the gardens proper were "fuentes públicas y un lavadero muy frecuentado, que hacía competencia á los ya entonces célebres del Manzanares, de la Pradera del Corregidor y de la Fuente de la Teja" (public fountains and a very frequented washing place which competed with the then well-known ones on the Manzanares river, at the Corregidor's Meadow, and at the Teja fountain) (Sepúlveda 1898, 67–68, also cited by Pallares in Tirso de Molina 1982b, 252). Tirso includes this site in his play when Mansilla discovers Tomasa washing clothes there, "Bien haya quien el jabón / hizo, y inventó las pilas / Bendito sea el regidor [Juan Fernández], / que entre floridos matices / condujo jabonatrices / para que se lave amor! / Ni sus [the garden's] salas ni planteles, / cuadros, estatuas, pinturas, / grutescos, arquitecturas, / rejas, balcones, canceles / se igualan a la invención / que en tanta pila dilata / brazos fregones de plata / entre ninfas de vellón" (Blessed be whoever made soap and invented washbasins. Blessed be the councilman [Juan Fernández], who brought washerwomen in among flowery hues so that love might be washed. Neither its [the gardens] rooms nor nurseries, beds, statues, paintings, grottos, architecture, grills, balconies, or partitions can equal the beauty that spreads out from so many basins, from scrubbing silver arms among copper-coin nymphs)

(2557–70). Such descriptions fix the place within the geographical, cultural horizon of Madrid residents.

Juan Fernández's garden, despite the descriptions of flowers, fountains, and the rest, is not a true green world that stands in opposition to the real world of experience. Rather, it is a garden owned by a powerful man in Madrid; that is to say, a cultural, ideological creation. The garden, as Julián Gallego (1972) writes, "se opone a la selva, como la geometría se opone a la confusión; y representa la naturaleza dominada, humanizada, con un orden terrenal" (is opposed to the forest as geometry opposes confusion; and it represents nature dominated, humanized, with worldly, order) (58). The garden "supplements" nature in the way Derrida (1976) describes:

> The supplement adds itself, it is a surplus, a plenitude enriching another plenitude, the *fullest measure* of presence. It cumulates and accumulates presence. It is thus that art, technē, image, representation, convention, etc., come as supplements to nature and are rich with this entire cumulating function. . . . It is indeed culture or cultivation that must supplement a deficient nature. (145–46)

Here, for example, flowers are not wildflowers, but flowers selected and planted by design and thus they can be "read," as Hernando tells Laura, "que flores tal vez son libros" (that flowers perhaps are books) (531); he then teaches her how to read them:

> Letras estas flores son . . .
> Este jardín es mi escuela . . .
>   Sus hojas
> dan materia a mis cuidados,
> encendidos con las rojas,
> si moradas aliviados,
> si leonadas son congojas.
> Ya con las verdes espero;
> con las azules me abraso,
> con las amarillas muero,
> casto con las blancas paso,
> y con las pardas me altero.
> En las clicies me mejoro,
> con las venus me enamoro,
> presumo con los narcisos,

> y hallando en todas avisos,
> sufro, espero, temo y lloro.
> (1767, 1772, 1777–91)

(These flowers are letters. . . . This garden is my school. . . .
Their petals give substance to my cares, flamed by red ones,
relieved by violet ones, if tawny they are anguish, now with
green ones I have hope; I burn with blue ones, I die with yellow
ones, I become chaste with white ones, I become disturbed with
brown ones. I get better with sunflowers, with Venus flowers
(navelworts?) I fall in love, I become vain with narcissus and
finding admonitions in all of them, I suffer, I hope, I fear, and I
weep.)

Fruits, flowers, and colors were part of a preexisting set of cultural
codes not limited to the literary field, but also belonging to religious
iconography, to the colors worn by priests during different times in
the liturgical year, and of course known and used by painters (see
Julián Gallego 1972, 228–59).

Berta Pallares, in her edition of *La huerta de Juan Fernández*
(Tirso de Molina 1982b), cites Quevedo's "Comparación con el signifi-
cado de los colores" (Simile on the meaning of colors) as an example of
well-understood symbolism:

> Es lo blanco castísima pureza,
> amores significa lo morado,
> crudeza o sujeción es lo encarnado,
> naranjado se entiende que es firmeza.
> Negro oscuro es dolor, claro tristeza,
> rojo claro vergüenza, y colorado
> furor; bayo desprecio, y leonado
> congoja; claro muestra ser alteza.
> Es lo pardo trabajo, azul es celo,
> turquesado es soberbia, y lo amarillo
> es desesperación; verde esperanza
> (note to 1765, 157–58)

(White is the chastest purity, violet signifies love, red is harsh-
ness or subjection, orange is read as resolve. Dark black is
pain, gray sadness, light red shame and dark red anger; red-
dish brown disdain, tawny anguish; clear shows sublimity.

Brown is work, blue is zeal, turquoise is pride, and yellow is desperation; green hope.)

Thus when Petronila enters the garden and sees Hernando hand Laura a bouquet, "un ramillete que aliña, / porque un hilo juntos ciña / celos, amor y desdén" (a bouquet that is organized, because a thread holds together jealousy, love, and disdain) (1151–53), she and the audience understand the "messages" sent by a bouquet of blue, purple, and reddish-brown flowers.

The garden becomes a site for varying interpretations. If for Hernando and Laura, the garden is a book of delights, for Petronila, it is quite the opposite:

> después que hallé entre sus flores
> un áspid que disfrazado
> ponzoña a mi pecho ha dado,
> y aumentos a mis temores,
> volcanes son sus planteles,
> incendios sus fuentes son,
> tormentos su recreación,
> penas su rosa y clavels
>
> (1114–21)

(after I discovered a disguised asp among its flowers, it has poisoned my breast and increased my fears, it nurseries are volcanoes, its fountains are fires its diversion are torments, its roses and carnations, suffering)

In this garden, nothing is just what it seems. Hernando, for example, is a nobleman dressed as a gardener, "Tres meses los sayales / en esta huerta, de Madrid recreo / me ofrecen bienes y me ferian males" (For three months the coarse garments [I wear] in this garden, Madrid's recreation spot, have offered me riches and have given me misfortune) (247–49): no plain gardener is he but "jardinero de amor" (love's gardener) (250), "mis esperanzas cultivo; / mientras que méritos siembro" (I cultivate my hopes; while I sow my merits) (525–26). Here, Tomasa will become el Conde Galeazo and Doña Inés; Petronila, already Don Gómez, will add to her "identities" el Conde Galeazo and "Doña Petronila"; there, the real Conde Galeazo will become a servant in his own retinue.

Into the garden flow other codes. Laura has come to Madrid, to the *huerta de Juan Fernández,* seeking legal redress from her uncle's

physical and legal attacks on her rights, "En Madrid me tienen pleitos / de parientes, que enemigos / usurpándome mi estado, / dieron
causa a mi camino" (Lawsuits against relatives have me in Madrid,
for enemies usurping my state gave rise to my trip) (406–9). The proposed marriage between her and Galeazo, as observed, is an effort at
arriving at an amicable settlement between family members. Petronila seeks out Hernando not only because she loves him but also because he has made a written promise to her dead mother and she
intends for him to keep his word, "vengo a probar lo que valen / pal-
abras que ya son ditas" (I have come to find out how much words
given as bonds are worth) (1026–27). *Dita* means "persona o efecto
que se señala para pagar lo que se debe, o para asegurar la satisfacción de lo que se compra o toma prestado" (a person or effect that one
designates to pay what one owes or to assure the repayment of the
loan for what one buys or borrows) (*Diccionario de autoridades*, 855a).
Nature, nurture, love and marriage are interwoven with the economic and legal concerns.

Thus when Hernando speaks to Laura of his love, it should not surprise to find in this garden legal overtones, "Permitid, Laura mía, /
que mis sabrosos males, / destas flores haciendo tribunales, / sitial y trono
desta fuente fría, / formen de vos querellas, / y os digan mis agravios, /
vos la acusada, los testigos ellas" (Permit, my Laura, my enjoyable mis-
fortunes, making tribunals of these flowers, seat of authority and throne
of this cool fountain, to bring suit against you, and tell you of the of-
fenses done to me, you the accused, they the witnesses) (237–43). Even
though the legal system is supposed to render justice neutrally, Conde
Galeazo prepares to quit his lawsuit before a final verdict is forthcom-
ing. He feels disadvantaged because justice is not impartial:

> Mal su justicia asegura
> quien en pleitos ignora
> que la mujer competidora
> se ampara de su hermosura . . .
> Llora, encarece y intima,
> halla en tribunales gracia . . .
> los jueces templan cuidados:
> que no hay tales abogados
> como son lágrimas bellas
>   (1270–73, 1278–79, 1283–85)

(Whoever involved in a lawsuit is assured of an unjust outcome
if he ignores the fact that a female opponent will use her

beauty. . . . She weeps, urges, intimates and finds grace with the tribunals . . . judges become temperate: for there are no lawyers as good as lovely tears.)

In the garden where Laura is the judge, Hernando makes his appeal. While she is at first favorably disposed toward his case, later he stands no chance when she hears from just the kind of witness Galeazo feared: two beautiful, tearful women who tell the truth, part of the truth, and nothing like the truth. In the final act, Petronila seconds to Laura a story told her by "Don Gómez" about Hernando's perfidy, and Tomasa, dressed as Doña Inés, repeats yet another story, previewed by Don Gómez, about the inconstant Hernando. While Petronila's tale is close to the truth, Tomasa's is pure fiction. As judge, Laura orders Hernando's compliance with her verdict and banishes him from the garden:

> Estos papeles mirad,
> y obligaciones cumplid;
> que aunque es confusión Madrid,
> tiene mucha claridad
> su cielo, con que da luz
> a engaños y deslealtades.
> Empeños y voluntades,
> caballero y andaluz,
> no son pleitos de acreedores
> que se dejen a herederos . . .
> Mirad que se cumple el plazo
> que a estas deudas corresponde . . .
> Escoged entre las dos [Petronila/Inés]
> la más hermosa, y salid
> desta huerta y de Madrid
> o haréos yo salir . . .
> (2367–75, 2391–92, 2399–2401)

(Look at these papers, fulfill your obligations; for though Madrid is confusing, its sky is very clear and shines a light on deceit and disloyalty. Pledges and love, my Andalusian gentlemen, are not creditors' lawsuits to be left to heirs . . . see that you pay these debts on time. . . . Choose the most beautiful of the two, and leave this garden and Madrid or I will make you leave.)

As the legal language is in the garden, so too is the economic. When Laura speaks to Hernando early in the play, she accuses him of weakening in his resolve to love and marry her:

> ¿Dilaciones encareces?
> Caro vendes, o amas tibio, . . .
> Sobre palabra se juega:
> el crédito tengo rico;
> ganancioso te levantas,
> cuando cédulas te libro;
> que no son ditas quebradas,
> pues paga a plazo cumplido
> el que es noble, cuando pierde,
> por palabra o por escrito
> (374–75, 386–91)

(Are you urging delays? You sell yourself dear or you love tepidly. . . . One may gamble based on his word: I hold a lot of your debts; you rise up a winner when I release you from your IOUs; whoever is noble does not break his bonds, rather when he loses, based on his spoken or written word, he pays on time.)

Once more such language does not surprise since the marriages all involve financial concerns. Laura will inherit substantial lands if her lawsuit proves true and Hernando would share in those benefits should she marry him. Petronila, though momentarily without funds, will inherit a vast amount of money from her father or will be given a vast amount as dowry should she marry Hernando. "Tío," she tells Hernando, "mi padre me escribe / que con más de cien mil pesos / viene a cubrir de diamantes / la cruz que os adorna el pecho / si pagáis obligaciones" (Uncle, my father writes me that he comes with more than one hundred thousand *pesos* to cover with diamonds the cross that adorns your breast if you pay what you owe) (2947–51).

The language in the garden is not separate from the language outside of the garden. If Madrid is *confusión* so too confusion reigns in the disguises, plots, and counterplots staged in the garden. If in Madrid, love, money, and desire drive all, "Mas como en Madrid amor, / universal mercader, / todo es comprar y vender, / siendo el gusto corredor" (But in Madrid love, the universal merchant, is all buying and selling, with pleasure acting as his broker) (2199–2202), so too do they hold sway in the garden. If in Madrid roguishness is the rule, so too in the nobleman's garden, "Amor y bellaquerías / que en Madrid y en huertas pasan / tan célebres como ésta" (Love and wickedness occur in Madrid and in gardens as famous as this one) (3455–57). The garden is in Madrid and Madrid is in the garden. There is no antithesis here between the world of experience and the green world of dream or innocence in this play because here "nature" is part of culture. The cultural "supplement" is built into the very design of nature itself.

Juan Fernández's garden is natural and cultural at the same time. But then so too are the woodlands in Shakespeare's plays. In the woods near Athens where *A Midsummer Night's Dream* takes place, hierarchical power struggles over the changeling precipitate the conflict between Titania, queen of the fairies, and Oberon, king of the fairies. They are served by a highly organized retinue; animals have their place in a codified superstructure running from "contagious frogs" to asses, to lions; flowers can be cures or poisons, and Oberon knows the value and use of each as when he sends Puck in search of the once milk-white, now "purple with love's wound" (II, i, 170) Western flower, "love-in-idleness," and whose juice "will make man or woman madly dote / upon the next creature that it sees" (174–75). Windsor woods, a park wherein part of the action of *Merry Wives of Windsor* takes place, by its very name—*Windsor* woods—already is inscribed into a cultural context of noble domain. The melancholy Jacques in *As You Like It* sees nature in the forest of Arden as always already contaminated by man's presence: men "are mere usurpers, tyrants, and what's worse, / to fright the animals and to kill them up / in their assigned and native dwelling place" (64–67). In the *Winter's Tale,* the debate between Perdita and Polixenes (IV, iv, 70–110) underscores the nature/culture crossbreeding. The bar between culture and nature cannot be sustained in those plays nor in Tirso's *La huerta de Juan Fernández,* nor in *Peribáñez,* nor in Calderón's last play, *Hado y divisa de Leonido y Marfisa:* by human presence, nature is acculturated.

Juan Fernández's *huerta* is both part of the city (cultural) and a "natural" setting. It produces plants, flowers, and fruits from nature, but the choice of plants, the order of the garden, the use of fountains and irrigation systems is cultural. The garden is both public and private, owned but partly open to public access, subject to municipal control, open to indemnification procedures. Ownership, economics, and the legal system are built into this place for recreation and love. Love too entangles with these codes and with family ties in this play. Petronila marries Hernando and brings a vast amount of money to their union. Hernando brings social and political recognition as can be seen when he appears sporting his just received *hábito de Santiago* (garb of the knighthood of Saint James). Laura marries Galeazo and their union repairs ruptured family ties, resolves legal disputes, and assures family rights of ownership and control over landholdings. Tomasa marries Mansilla, thereby legally condoning what desire had already brought about; also, their links to Petronila and Hernando reinforce the sense of unity the first marriage delivered. All three marriages underline social, religious, political, and economic order— hierarchies the play treats as "natural." If nature is part of culture, then a culture can be portrayed as natural. All comes together in the garden, which emblematizes the conjunction of the natural and the cultural, rights and responsibilities, the public and the private. Tirso depends on his local audience's understanding of the general symbolic codes of colors and flowers, on the legal and economic codes, on the social and cultural codes, as well as on the local knowledge of the *huerta de Juan Fernández* for the play's meaning and success.

During this period, characters in these plays refer to streets, churches, buildings, plazas, shopping areas, promenades, houses, and gardens where they walk or visit or stay as they make their way through the capital's labyrinthine, expanding environment. Depending on the audience, such references could have different effects. If one of these comedies were performed, for example, in Seville, some of the place names might ring with near mythic resonances—the Prado, Calle Mayor, Atocha. Other references might well be unknown to that audience, yet they would add to the "referential effect" creating thereby a sense of "realism," as when today adventure novelists have their characters walk through the streets of Mexico City or Moscow, mentioning the street or building names. While readers might not recognize but a name or two, references to real or real-sounding places create the impression that characters are "there." When the audience is made up of locals, when the plays are performed before a Madrid audience, the place names and descriptions gain further dimension. When a character goes to La Vitoria, for example, most audience members would know that that church was one of the more tony temples frequented by highborn ladies. Or, when Martín in *¡Ay, verdades, que en amor . . . !* tells Inés how brave he was helping his master in a fight, "Pues si no fuera por mí, / ¿mi amo ya no estuviera / en Santa Cruz, en las andas, / adonde quien fuere sea, / en tanto que se averigua, / le ponen a la vergüenza?" (well, if it weren't for me, wouldn't my master be laid out on the platforms in front of the Santa Cruz church, where until they verify his identity they expose him shamelessly?) (507a). A Sevillan audience might not know what a

Madrid audience would instantly grasp, namely that Santa Cruz, as earlier noted, "servía de depósito de cadáveres adonde venían las familias a reconocer a aquéllos de los suyos que habían sido víctimas de la violencia" (served as an outdoor morgue where families came to identify those who had been victims of violence) (Deleito y Piñuela 1942, 92), and thus the Sevillan audience would miss Martín's macabre joke. These plays then often depend on the denotations and connotations of places and features in Madrid. In the 1620s, Madrid is a theater, literally and figuratively, and the theater, in turn, theatricalizes the city.

3

COMEDY AND ECONOMY

Throughout this decade, characters in the comedies seem more than passingly worried about their past, present, or future financial condition. Many find themselves relatively impoverished, and several of the plays' plots revolve around or begin with the characters' concerns about their economic straits. Angela, in *La dama duende*, has recently returned to Madrid to try to get her financial house in order; Bernarda, in *Por el sótano y el torno*, has struck a deal with an ancient *perulero* (person who has returned wealthy from Peru) in which her younger sister's marriage to the older man will represent financial security for both the seller and the commodity; Don Alvaro, in *Amor, pleito y desafío*, opposes his daughter's marriage to a man whose financial position is anything but secure; and in *La villana de Vallecas*, Vicente has gambled away his inheritance, as has the prodigal young man that the Countess Manuela loves in *En Madrid y en una casa*. In many of these works an economic vocabulary undergirds the action, as for example in *En Madrid y en una casa*, we find the following words among others:

crédito, cobrar, dueño, prenda, interés, dote, reales, doblones, ginoveses, empeñar, adeudar, fiadora, hacienda, mayorazgo, pródigo, avaricia, pobre, negocio, negociar, tienda, mercaduría, usura, deber, tesoro, oro, medula amarilla, regalo, regalar, recibir, heredera, juros, rentas, rico, ganar, ganancia, contrato, contratar, caudalosa, avariento, codicia, costa, costar, comprar, rey metal, dineros, mercader, enriquecer

(credit, to cash, owner, pawn, interest, dowry, real, doubloons, Genovese [bankers], to pawn, to become indebted, bondsman, property, heir to entailed estates, prodigal, avarice, poor, negotiation, to negotiate, store, merchandise, usury, to owe, treasure, gold, yellow marrow, gift, to give, to receive, heir, state bonds, income, rich, to earn, earnings, contract, to contract, wealthy, stingy, greed, cost, to cost, to buy, king of the metals, money, merchant, to enrich)

In this decade, everyone was concerned about finances.[1]

During their reigns the two strongest Habsburg kings, Charles I and Philip II, resisted pressures brought upon them by the enormous

---

1. In this period, the predominant economic system was mercantalism, though vestiges of the feudal system still remained in rural areas just as capitalism or protocapitalism existed in the cities. While this chapter does not pretend to detail what was happening economically in Spain in the 1620s, some observations on the three coexisting economic systems seem appropriate even though these observations are necessarily brief and make no pretense at completeness.

Feudalism, ideally, is a natural economy. Neither workers, tools, land, nor the means of production are commodities for purchase or sale in the marketplace. Producer and product are united with the means of production, the land. The worker is enmeshed in a web of economic and class relations and tied to a geographically specific locale. The worker may keep the products of a particular strip of land he works but he also works land belonging to the nobility in exchange for protection. The feudal lord, in turn, holds his land in fief to higher authorities and his control over his land depends upon his obligation to provide military service for the next higher-up. "At the top of the pyramid is the sovereign who has direct military call on the nobles but only indirect authority over the population as a whole. Thus both property and the state which we understand today as the parameters of control over land are meaningless concepts in feudalism" (Cosgrove 1984, 42). Production's value lies in use and not so much in exchange, though neither markets nor money are missing.

Mercantalism predominated in sixteenth- and seventeenth-century Europe. The mercantalist state was normally one with overseas colonies that served as suppliers of raw materials and consumers of finished goods. The ruler held the state's pieces together by strengthening central governmental control and authority over all aspects of life. Coinage, for example, was concentrated in royal mints and the central government would formulate policies for foreign and national trade. Precious metals were necessary to the state's wealth. War was an instrument of state policy. Population increase was desired so as to provide an increasing labor supply, a growing market, and soldiers. Imported luxury goods were combated as a drain on foreign exchange, thus sumptuary laws were passed. Many of Olivares's policies—minting policies, *erarios, montes de piedad* (state deposit banks, state-owned pawnshops), encouraging thrift, encouraging shop ownership and tradesmen, treading companies, tax breaks for married couples and for large families, the union of arms, wars to curtail the Dutch, the French, and the English— then, can be seen to respond to the mercantalist ideal.

Long-distance trade, which lay near the heart of mercantalism, was of primary importance, according to Ferdinand Braudel (1982), in the development of European capitalism. Enormous profits could be realized from spices, woolens, gold, silver, tobacco, and human labor. Cities grew from trade and the production of luxuries, to be paid for with money, and so attracted rural workers seeking freedom and higher incomes. Trade had an impact on consumption as well in both the middle and upper classes and drove changes in style, diet, furnishings, and housing. The urban mercantile system "operated over and with little reference to the static economy of subsistence agriculture in which population and food supply were in constant unstable equilibrium, and over the economy of local urban markets where primary surplusses were exchanged more for use than for profit" (Cosgrove 1984, 50).

In a capitalist system, supply and demand theoretically regulate prices and the market is central to everything. All production is destined for the market. Buying a commodity gives the purchaser legal rights to it and thus both property rights and property value are subject to exchange and operate independent of use value. Goods, tools, labor, and land are commodities, all available for purchase or sale in the market. The population divides into two groups: the owners of the means of production and workers who own nothing but their labor power. The latter sells their labor to the former to provide for their own survival and thus they become "laboring tools" whose value is regulated too by the market. The market exists in the city and thus land and agriculture become extensions of the city-market. Competition forces owners to derive maximum profit from labor and commodity production because investment in better means of production is necessary to economic survival. The labor force is mobile and can sell its labor to any owner, yet at the same moment, market stresses can put workers out of jobs and inflation, for instance, can eat up salaries.

In the 1620s, we find elements of all three systems in the plays: ties to land (Bras in *La villana de Vallecas*); long-distance trade and profit (the captain in *Por el sótano y el torno*); the *indiano* (person returned wealthy from the Americas in *La moza de cántaro*); labor as commodity (*criadas* [maids] like Ortiz who change mistresses in *En Madrid y en una casa;* Santillana, the *escudero* [squire for hire] in *La celosa de sí misma*); itinerant, small-time merchants (*La villana de Vallecas;* the *toqueras* [headdress sellers] in *La toquera vizcaína*); accomplished merchants or entrepreneurs (Luis de Toledo in *Los balcones de Madrid*); wealthy bureaucrats (Juan Fernández); rich and poor nobles; and even government intervention in production, distribution, and price control over basic necessities (the *pan de obligación* [bread of obligation system] in *La villana de Vallecas*). None of these systems exists in isolation nor in pure form in any of the plays—nor anywhere else for that matter.

What the plays show, then, is the transitional nature of Spain's economy in this period. What they emphasize is the importance of the city; what we see is the characters' concerns with economic matters as those matters have an impact on their own situations and circumstances.

debts created, in part, by imperial wars, periods of crop failures, and overcommitments on a number of fronts to fix the national economic picture by debasing currency, preferring instead to countenance the suspension of debt payment—a sort of bankruptcy. Yet, as Earl Hamilton (1934) observes, "forces were at work . . . that rendered debasement inevitable as soon as a weak ruler ascended the throne" (74). Philip III discovered that crown revenues had been mortgaged for the first two years of his rule and that the expenses accruing from war in Flanders plus the high living style of the court made the measures his forebears had fought irresistible. He issued copper *vellón* in 1599, though in 1602 he reduced its value by half, which did indeed bring some relief to the crown's finances. However, *vellón* currency, which had been near parity with silver, began slowly but inevitably to circulate at a discount. Near the end of his reign, the premium on silver stood at between 4–6% (Hamilton 1934, 74–79, 96). By the time Philip III died, public revenue had decreased, the financial administration had gone from bad to worse, and the result was "an enormous public debt" (Hamilton 1934, 79)

As Philip IV's reign opens, criticism of Philip III's economic policies, his thieving ministers, and the poor financial straits of the nation runs high as does the hope that the new men of the incoming administration could improve the situation. Villamediana, to cite only one example of what was being written, states:

> No ha sido sin gran concierto,
> viendo hurtar tan excesivo,
> remedie Felipe el vivo
> lo que no remedió el muerto.
> Todos tengan por muy cierto
> que no ha de quedar ladrón
> que no salga en el padrón
> que hoy hace Felipe Cuarto,
> viéndose, así, sin un cuarto
> y otros con casa y torreón . . .
>   (Egido López 1973, 94)

(It has not been without general agreement, upon seeing such excessive theivery, that the living Philip remedy what the dead one could not. Let all be assured that no thief will escape the list of infamy that today Philip IV draws up seeing that he has no money and that others have houses and castles.)

In a gloss of the "Padrenuestro," he adds:

> Es muy justo castigar
> a los que, siempre sedientos
> de tus tesoros, intentos
> han tenido de usurpar
> *el tu reino*. . . .
> Nueva ley amaneció,
> con el gobierno nuevo
> más claro se muestra Febo,
> y nuestra España quedó
> *como en el cielo.*
> Los pobres, Señor, estaban
> consumidos y abrasados,
> y tan sólo ellos sobrados,
> porque a todos nos quitaban
> *el pan nuestro*. . . .
> Si vuelves a restaurar,
> como pienso, tus Estados,
> todos andarán sobrados,
> y así podemos pagar
> *nuestras deudas.*
> (Egido López 1973, 98–99)

(It is right to punish those who, always thirsting after your treasure, have tried to usurp thy kingdom. . . . A new law dawned and with the new government more brightly shines our Phoebus, and our Spain is now as it is in Heaven. Sir, the poor were consumed and destroyed and only those others were wealthy because they took from us our daily bread. . . . If you once again restore, as I believe you will, your country we will all be wealthy and thus we can pay our debts.)

Finally, in another poem, Philip III is cast as dying of pure shame, "Su confesor, su duque y su patriarca / reinaron y otros gatos de doblones, / y él de corrido se entregó a la Parca. / Murió, cual Jesucristo, entre ladrones" (His confessor, his duke, and his patriarch reined along with other doubloon thieves, and he from pure shame gave himself over to the Fates. He died like Jesus Christ, among thieves) (101).

Yet, despite public confidence in the "new men," during the first years of Philip IV's government, the situation worsened with the resumption of the war in Flanders after the twelve-year truce, the failure of the *erarios* (deposit savings banks) project, with the "increase in religious foundations under royal patronage, and the emergence of more vigorous international competition by northern Europe" (Hamilton 1934, 79), and with the consequent decline of Castilian commerce. During the first years of his rule, *vellón* was coined to the tune of more than a quarter-billion *maravedís* (Hamilton 1934, 80 n 3, figures from 22 April 1621–6 April 1623). By 1628, the premium on silver hovered between 50 and 60%. By that same year, the commodity index had risen to just over 117 points (215) and prices were outstripping wages (273).

Philip was not unaware of the desperate straits of both his government and his subjects, and, in a letter to his advisors, he demands "Hágase algo aunque se haga mal" (Do something even if it's done badly) (cited by Domínguez Ortiz 1960, 36). To the Consejo de Hacienda (finance council), the king writes, "Donde me va a salvar mis reinos de tan mísera opresión como la del vellón" (Where shall I find salvation for my kingdoms from such miserable oppression as that of copper coinage) (36). Early on in the reign, Olivares had proposed a system of state banks (*erarios*) and pawnshops (*montes de piedad*) only to be blocked by the Cortes. So in 1627, the Crown issued a *pragmática* (pragmatic sanction or royal decree) establishing a network of banks, *diputaciones,* managed by the despised Italian bankers. These banks were to reduce the amount of *vellón* in circulation, receive deposits, make loans, run a lottery, and hold a monopoly on mortgage loans (*censos*) (Elliott 1986, 305–6; Hamilton 1934, 81–82). Elliott points out that the city councils of Castile were incensed by the pragmatic since the Crown seemed to be trying to do by fiat what it could not through legal political process (306). The Cortes presented a summary of their complaints in May 1627 and while they were deliberating what steps they could take to come up with a more palatable solution, voted "to have five hundred masses celebrated for the 'enlightenment of their intelligence' in studying the reform of vellón" (Hamilton 1934, 83, nn 2 and 3).

By 1628, it was obvious that with the cities' open hostility, with general popular antagonism toward the banks, and with the Cortes still working to find other solutions, something had to be done especially since the premium on silver had risen so high. As Lope de Vega among others notes, the economy had come to a virtual standstill. He complains in a letter to the duke of Sessa dated July 1628:

> Lo que aquí se dice de las que quitan no creo, que este lugar todo es mentiras, malos deseos, envidias, pretensiones, quejas y

necedades. Nadie vende, nadie compra, todos parecemos judíos, esperando lo que no ha de venir. (Vega n.d.)

(What is being bantered around here I don't believe, that this place is all lies, evil desires, envidiousness, pretensions, complaints, and folly. No one sells, no one buys, and we all seem like Jews, hoping for what will never come.)

Stagnation was augmented by a price- and wage-fixing decree in September 1627 and by rumors of an impending revaluation. On 7 August 1628, a brutal deflationary measure was proclaimed reducing the tale on copper *vellón* by 50%. Losses to private holders were not idemnified (Hamilton 1934, 83). Lope (n.d.) writes in mid-August 1628, "El golpe de la baja de la moneda bajó ya, aunque no como el cuchillo de Abrahán, pues no hubo ángel que le detuviese: quiero decir, arbitrio que lo estorbase. Tomóse bien generalmente, aunque con lástima de particulares" (The deflationary blow fell, though it was not like Abraham's knife because there was no angel to stop it: that is to say no plan to hinder it. Generally, it was well accepted, though with individual complaints). The premium on silver fell to between 10 and 17%.

The precarious state of national finances had a profound effect on personal finances, producing anxiety, cynicism, and sometimes despair. Such a situation did not pass unnoticed by the dramatists of the period. Comments about money, gold, *vellón*, and money's power abound:

> ¿En el siglo de vellón
> doblones vos? Entraréis
> mejor, si ansí granizáis,
> que el planeta ginovés
> (Tirso 1982a, 132a)

(In the century of copper coins you offer gold doubloons? With those kinds of hailstones, you will become more impressive than the Genovese planet)

> pues después que hay en Castilla
> barbirrubios ginoveses,
> dicen que es cosa rara,
> que no se ha de hallar en ella
> ni doblón ni una doncella
> (*En Madrid y en una casa* 1256/57a)

(Since there have been blond-bearded Genovese in Castile, they say that it's rare to find here either doubloons or virgins)

mas ya no hay desos metales,
porque doncellas y reales
se nos vuelven en vellón
(*En Madrid y en una casa* 1256b)

(but now those kinds of precious metals do not exist, because
virgins and reals turn into copper on us)

En tanta pila dilata
brazos fregones de plata
entre ninfas de vellón
(*La huerta de Juan Fernández,* 630b/31a)

(from so many basins scrubbing silver arms spread out among
copper-coin nymphs)

¿Qué he de hacer?
Andar al uso es razón:
De críticos y vellón
No nos podemos valer
(*Desde Toledo a Madrid* 435b)

(What shall I do? Do what everyone does: we cannot trust flowery poets or copper coins)

pocas veces descansa
el ánimo de los hombres,
aunque sobre el oro y la plata
(*La moza de cántaro* 1009b)

(man's soul finds little rest except on gold and silver)

el oro todo lo vence
(*La toquera vizcaína* 520b)

(gold conquers all)

Mas presumo yo que mira
del oro la cantidad:
dineros son calidad
(*El premio del bien hablar* 1250a)

(I presume that she looks at the amount of gold: money is nobility)

> —Pues escoge desde aquí,
> Clara, vestido o cadena.
> —Cadena es mejor, García,
> que el oro crece el valor.
> (¡Ay verdades que en amor . . . ! 505b)

(Well, choose now, Clara, the dress or the chain. —The chain is better, García, because gold increases in value)

> Todo lo que no es dinero
> en la corte, no es amor
> (La huerta de Juan Fernández 613a)

(In the court anything that is not money is not love)

> Que reales tiran sus oficios reales
> (La villana de Vallecas 52b)

(money brings its royal offices along)

> Alto, viudez, esto es hecho;
> perdone Dios al difunto,
> ¡Seis mil ducados [tiene el nuevo amante de renta]!
> (Por el sótano y el torno 573a)

(Whoa, widowhood, this is over: God forgive the dead man, Six thousand ducats (my new lover has for income)!)

The larger financial issues in this period, then, were inflation, deflation, debt, cost of living, and *vellón* currency. In many of the comedies from the 1620s, characters' concerns and problems arising from the state of their love affairs interweave with the state of their economic affairs. Against and within this background of anxiety over and concern with the public and private economic picture Calderón writes *Hombre pobre todo es trazas*.

Briefly, Don Diego Osorio, son of a poor but noble father, rushes to Madrid to escape the consequences of a love-inspired duel in Granada, his hometown. In the capital, he courts two women: the beautiful, witty, but poor Beatriz and the wealthy Clara. Both ladies have long-standing suitors, Félix and Leonelo respectively, whom they instantly abandon. To avoid problems, Diego courts Clara using his own name while he courts Beatriz as Don Dionís de Vela. Clara and Beatriz turn out to be friends and, at a certain point, Diego is caught by both in Clara's house. Beatriz demands that Diego and Dionís come to her home at the same time but the clever Diego even invents a way out of that. In the end, however, he is shown up for the philanderer he is. Beatriz marries Félix; Clara, Leonelo; D. Juan, Diego's friend, abandons him, and even his servant, Rodrigo, upbraids him. The play might, in some ways, be seen as Calderón's version of Alarcón's *La verdad sospechosa*.

Figuring prominently in this play are references to Madrid's labyrinthine streets (203b), to the war in Flanders (205a), and to theater and theatricality (204a, 217b, 218b, 220b, 231b), but in this chapter I focus primarily on the economic context and its implications for the central character and his schemes. Shortly after the play begins, Diego's servant, Rodrigo, seeks and finds his master to give him a letter from his father:

> Hijo, yo no tengo hacienda para sustentar vuestras travesuras y bellaquerías. Allí va una letra de cuatrocientos reales; mirad cómo gastáis, que quizá no podré enviaros otra. En la corte estáis; dad alguna traza de vivir honradamente, y ved que el pobre todo es trazas. (206a)

> (Son, I do not have enough money to sustain your pranks and wickedness. Here is a letter of credit for four hundred reals; watch how you spend them, for perhaps I will not be able to send you more. You are in the court: make plans to live honorably and remember the poor man is all plans.)

The letter adds a bit more to the background that Diego has begun to sketch. Though noble by birth, Diego hails from a relatively poor family. Evidently, in Granada, Diego has hardly been a model citizen. He has already spoken of having to flee the city because of a duel and now his father insists on a plurality of "travesuras y bellaquerías." The letter succinctly recounts, then, a history of roguish behavior, a father's impatience with an errant son, the family's modest financial state, and the father's hope that with the money he sends, the son will spend wisely and mend his ways especially since he is in Madrid. But the father's hope is futile and his advice arrives all too late. Not only is Diego courting two women at the same time, but he has already been gambling and losing, "gané y perdí; / perdí el dinero y gané / amigos, caudal, en fin, / el mejor" (I won and I lost; I lost money but gained friends a greater wealth by far) (205a). When he values friends over money, the audience might momentarily think that Diego is on the right track, but such thoughts will shortly prove false.

Rodrigo believes that the sum of money they now have is quite sufficient "para quien somos los dos" (for who we two are) (206a), but Diego is crestfallen on the one hand, angry on the other, "¡Que esto mi padre me envía, / cuando yo a la corte vengo! / Sin los que debo, no tengo / para gastar un día" (That my father should send me this when I come to the court! If I take out what I owe, I don't have enough left for one day) (206a). Rodrigo's "para quien somos los dos" has inadvertently hit on the problem. Diego is not who he is and shortly neither will Rodrigo be.

When Don Juan, one of Diego's new friends enters and sees the new arrival so saddened, Diego complains of the paltry sum he has just received. The servant, he says, has just arrived "Con una letra . . . / de solo cuatro *mil* reales" (With a letter of credit for only four *thousand* reals) (206a; my emphasis), inflating the sum by a factor of ten. He then tells Juan that tonight he wants to give Beatriz a piece of jewelry worth one hundred *escudos,* but fears she will be embarrassed by a direct gift. So he proposes that Rodrigo dress as a nobleman and come to Beatriz's nightly gathering as Juan's friend. Then, in a card game, Rodrigo will "lose" the chain to Diego who, in turn, will offer it to their hostess with no opprobium. Juan agrees to participate in "tan linda industria" (such a lovely trick) (206b) so cleverly and generously thought out.

When Juan leaves, Diego tells Rodrigo that the chain is in reality, nearly worthless, "Esta cadena que ves, / solo un doblón me costó" (This chain you see only cost me one doubloon) (207a) and that what he really feared was that if Beatriz found out its true worth, and had he given it to her directly, she would have been annoyed at so cheap a token and thus *he* would have been embarrassed. In one swift and deceptive move, not only does he continue to play Beatriz false—remember, she thinks that he is Don Dionís de Vela, "un soldado, / que en el flamenco país / sirvió al rey" (a soldier who served the king in Flanders) (205a)—but he twice deceives his friend, thereby deflating the audience's momentary hope that he was on the right track.

Rodrigo contextualizes Diego's deceptions by reference to the double-dealing atmosphere of the court, "si engañar es tu norte, / tú no has entrado en la corte, / mas la corte ha entrado en ti" (if deception is your guiding star, you have not so much entered the court as the court has entered you) (205b); "Yo no pienso que he venido / a la corte celebrada, / sino a una selva encantada, / donde todo sueño ha sido" (I do not think that I have come to the famous court but rather to an enchanted forest where everything is a dream) (206a). But, Diego relates his actions directly to his father's advice, "Como mi padre me escribe, / desta manera se vive, / porque el pobre todo es trazas" (As my father writes, this is how one lives, because the poor man is all plans/schemes) (206a).

Traza means "planta o diseño que idea o ejecuta el artífice, para la fábrica de un edificio u otra obra" (floor plan or design the craftsman uses to plan or execute the construction of a building or other work) (*Diccionario de Autoridades* 53a). That is to say, a proto-blueprint, "en lo antiguo, era toda raya o señal que se hacía en la tierra" (in older days, it was a line or mark made in the dirt) (*Diccionario etimológico* 203b), a material mark, something concrete and trustworthy used to guide a builder for setting a foundation. But words, signs, are slippery devils: *traza* is also an "invención, arbitrio, recurso, . . . apariencias o figura de una cosa" (fiction, plan or means, . . . fantasm or figure of a thing) and thus not necessarily so solid, so trustworthy. The Latin root, *tractus, trahere* means to carry along (Spanish, *traer*), influence, attract, win over, as well as to carry off, plunder, rob, drag down in ruins. Diego takes his father's advice "literally" but not in the "literal" way his father meant it. In Lope's *El sembrar en buena tierra,* a similar situation arose when another father advised his son "gastar con prudencia" (to spend with prudence), which he then in fact did, spending large sums on his beloved Prudencia (see Wardropper 1978, 217).

One of Diego's schemes, emblematic, though in nonlinguistic register, of his verbal shiftiness, of his deceitfulness, is his twinning or doubling of himself. I shall address this topic in Chapter 5, but for now I shall note that in many plays from this period, a character will split himself or herself into two apparently dissimilar personages. Here Diego's two selves (really, there is a third self since the "real" Diego is known to Rodrigo) contains elements both similar and dissimilar to the "real Diego." As "Diego" to Clara, he is the noble, polite offspring of a Granadan family whose head is her father's friend. To Beatriz, he is Don Dionís de Vela, a noble warrior, true servant of his king, wealthy and generous. While the true Diego is noble by birth and would perhaps be generous had he the wherewithal, both characters, "Diego" and Dionís, are false inflations of the original. He glosses over his Granadan roguishness, which the audience along with

Rodrigo sees continued in Madrid, keeps his ties to paternal nobility, and creates a dashing, valiant, and wealthy facade that he offers to men and women alike. Those facades circulate freely in Madrid, acquiring a worth that bears little relation to cruder reality. Diego turns himself and his selves into commodities to be bartered for gain. His charm, his verbal skills, and the figures he cuts succeed because of the trust that others have in the implicit but unspoken connection they believe in between face value and intrinsic value, between Diego's word-appearance and reality. But neither the word, nor Diego's identities, nor the chain in which they are links, are what they seem. Through multiple references to theatricality, to role-playing, to *comedia,* the play anticipates a linkage between identity and theatricality to the word or sign. Terry Eagleton (1986) says that "there is no social reality without its admixture of feigning, mask, performance, delusion, just as there is no sign which cannot be used to deceive" (13). The issue Eagleton's observation and Calderón's play present is paradoxical. Eagleton (1986) declares that

> it is "natural" for the human animal to transcend its own limits, yet this creative tendency to exceed oneself is also the source of destructiveness. Being "untrue" to their own nature is natural to human beings; what we call culture or history is an open-ended transformation of fixed boundaries. . . . But when this process transgresses the body's confines too far, it violates the bonds of sensuous comparison and begins its prey on physical life itself. A hubristic, overweening consciousness must be called sharply to order. . . . The problem is how to do this without extinguishing that authentic self-exceeding which distinguishes an animal with history from other natural species. (81; on "excess" see also Paul Julian Smith 1988)

In economics, a similar paradox might be posited. If the money supply were never to change, prices and wages would be stable, but economic stagnation would result. Few if any new products would be manufactured or imported because the amount available for spendable income would not allow for new purchases. Since Spain had mortgaged its income for years ahead and since "hard" currency was required for international exchange, silver and gold became scarce; thus *vellón* seemed an answer to keeping internal exchange afloat. But when the government began to stamp more and more *vellón,* and then restamp it at double its value, it began "to exceed" itself and "prey" on economic development. The paradox was then how to expand the money supply and the economy without falling into runaway inflation and how to control inflation without tumbling into depression.

Despite an acute awareness of the country's, and particularly Castile's, fiscal problems Philip's government failed to bring order. Olivares issued *pragmáticas* (proclamations) attempting to control internal spending. He wanted to establish the *erarios* (state deposit bank) system and he wanted to promote a proto-capitalism by encouraging shop ownership. The government was, however, working at cross-purposes as can be seen by even a casual glance at its growing involvement in expensive European conflicts: Flanders, Mantua, the French problem, and the English problems. Thus the administration lurched from inflationary to deflationary policies and continued to borrow against shrinking future income.

Money and metaphor can be seen to operate in parallel fashion: both offer to exchange two things or two signs with dissimilar values by forcing them into a relation of equality and convertibility (see Eagleton 1986, 22–26). Both depend on a commodification process that exceeds use value and both can lead to inflation, which, in turn, further skews the exchange. In the play, Diego metaphorically transforms Clara from a human being into precious metal and jewels beginning with her hair, "su cabello [es] oro de Orfir, / . . . / su boca joya de perlas / guarnecida de rubís" (her hair is gold from Araby, her mouth pearls lined with rubies) (204b). At the end of his poetically trite transformation, he makes the crude link, "demás de ser hermosa, / lo que me parece a mí / mejor, es tener de renta / largamente doce mil / ducados" (besides being beautiful, what seems better to me, is that she has more than twelve thousand ducats of income) (204b). What attracts him to the poor but beautiful Beatriz is that she "es de las que discretean, / dama crítica y sutil, / hace versos, canta, juega" (she is one of those who try to be clever, a poetical, subtle lady, she writes verses, sings, gambles) (205b). Yet between the two he cannot decide. He views the women as commodities, as desired interchangeable goods, but like a child in a candy store he cannot decide between a chocolate and a jelly. He covets both, yet in his penurious condition he can afford neither.

In the third act, Rodrigo once more worries about his and Diego's financial straits since surely "expiraron / los pasados cuatro cientos" (the past four hundred have expired) (224a). Rodrigo's concerns focus on his own well-being when he punningly complains, as will Clarín some years later in *La vida es sueño,* "si / soy mortal, y como y bebo; / porque ya todos los días / en el filósofo leo / Ni-comedes, y a las noches / en el

Concilio ni-ceno" (I wonder if I am mortal and if I eat and drink, because every day I need the philosophy of Nicomedes [you do not eat] and at night of the Nicene [I do not dine] Council) (224a). But Diego entertains no such worries because he is sure that he can always borrow more. When Rodrigo wonders how, since Diego already owes everyone, he marvels at his servant's ignorance of the economic system:

> ¡Qué poco sabes! No hay banco
> que esté más seguro y cierto
> que aquél que una vez prestó;
> pues por no perder aquello
> prestado, va dando más
> sobre su mismo dinero.
>
> (224b)

(How little you know! There is no bank as sure and certain as one which has once lent money; because so as not to lose what they have lent, they lend more against the same funds.)

Borrowing against further income, expansion of *vellón*, debasement of currency, and higher and higher premiums on silver led to disastrous consequences for the nation and its citizens. In times of stress, the government turned for loans to foreign bankers. The participation of foreign bankers in the crown's finances had a long history before Philip IV (see Domínguez Ortiz 1960, 85–147). While their support was indisputably helpful to the Crown, and often ruinous to the bankers, popular opinion held that they were, in part, responsible for Spain's terrible financial condition. Domínguez Oritiz (1960) quotes from the *Memorial de Hurtado de Alcocer* (1621):

> La primera sangría y más perjudicial que V. M. y estos Reynos han tenido es en los asientos con los estranjeros, en tanto daño del patrimonio real, se han hecho, pues le tienen consumido de suerte, que cuando vienen las flotas les está consignado lo que viene, y aun a veces lo del año siguiente, con que sacan en pasta y reales, no solo esto, sino a vueltas otras grandes sumas. (88)

(The first and most prejudicial blood letting that Your Majesty and these kingdoms have had is in the service contracts made with foreigners, which have caused so much harm to the royal patrimony; they have consumed it to the degree that when the silver fleets arrive, all they bring is already consigned to the foreigners, and even at times all that comes in the next year, so that they take away in raw silver and in reals, not only this, but in addition other great sums.)

Diego, a "foreigner" in Madrid, always confident of his abilities to wriggle out of any future debt, does not hesitate to borrow and simultaneously to prey on his friend, Juan. He comes looking for Diego because he owes a man eight hundred *reales* but only has four hundred at the moment. Since he believes Diego has four thousand, and since they are friends, he is sure of the loan. But he does not count of Diego's treachery. Diego says that it will take him six days to turn his letter of credit into ready cash and that right at the moment, he is terribly short of funds. So, he tells Juan, that if Juan gives him his four hundred, at the end of the week, he will return eight hundred. Juan believes him and readily complies.

But in the end, when Diego is caught kiting the bank, his *trazas* (schemes) come to ruin. In the final confrontation with Félix and Leonelo, and with Clara and Beatriz hiding and watching from the edge of the stage, Diego attempts to continue his double-identity ruse by not admitting who he is but yet declaring his nobility by appeal to the well-worn, and here certainly ironic, "Yo soy el que soy" (I am who I am) (223a). But his opponents will no longer let him rest on the circular appeal. Félix insists:

> Tengo causa
> siendo cualquiera persona
> de las dos que fingís, para
> hacer esto; y así quiero
> saber cuál sois.
>
> (232a)

(Because of whichever of the two people you pretend to be, I have cause to do this; and thus I demand to know which you are.)

Now trapped with his honor at risk, Diego must confess his doubling, "yo soy Don Diego / Osorio, y soy de Granada. / . . . / Vine de Granada aquí. / por disgustos que disfrazan / mi nombre: esta es la razón / por qué en la corte me llaman / comúnmente Don Dionís" (I am Diego Osorio, and I am from Granada. . . . I came here from Granada. Quarrels I had there made me change my name: this is the reason why in the court I am commonly known as Dionís) (232a). What he says, of course, is true, but as usual is not the whole truth.

Félix then challenges him directly, and Diego, appealing to his interpretation of masculine codes tells why he lied to the women, and in so doing, shows his true colors:

> porque un hombre principal
> puede mentir con las damas
> (que engañarlas con industria
> es más buen gusto que infamia,
> y los mayores señores
> lo suelen tener por gala);
> pero con los hombres no.
>
> (232a)

(because an important man can lie to ladies [because to deceive them cleverly is more good taste than infamy, and the greatest gentlemen often hold that charming]; but not to men.)

But Diego has lied to men as well and all throughout the play. Diego, in his speech, once more makes women the scapegoats for practices deemed unworthy by men but practices he engaged in indiscriminately.

In this "deflationary" move, Diego debases women, debases men, and debases himself. The women, the potential victims of Diego's self-aggrandizement, at that moment step forth to throw his deception back in his face. Beatriz gives her hand to Félix and says to Diego:

> castigo su ignorancia
> para que vea cuán poco
> le aprovecharon sus trazas.

(I punish your ignorance so that you may see how little your schemes got you.)

Diego holds out fleeting hope for Clara, "las esperanzas me quedan / de no haber perdido en Clara / la riqueza" (I still have hopes for not losing in Clara wealth) to which Leonelo responds "Yo, que estimo / más su virtud y su fama, / lo estorbaré" (I, who prize her virtue and fame more, will prevent it) (232b). Clara then steps out, giving her hand to Leonelo and saying, "Ved si el mentir con las damas / y engañarlas con ingenio / es más buen gusto que infamia" (See now if lying to ladies and cleverly deceiving them is more good taste than infamy) (233a). Diego's former friend, Juan, adds,

> Corrido estoy, ¡Vive Dios!,
> de considerar que haya
> valido yo sus engaños,
> siendo tantos, que me alcanzan
> a mí también. Hasta ahora
> no conocí mi ignorancia.
>
> (233a)

(I am embarassed, by God, to think that I have supported his many deceptions, which now affect me. Until now I did not recognize my errors.)

Diego then offers the lesson, "si en ellas [las trazas] halla / desengaños el que es cuerdo / mirando en mí castigadas / estas costumbres, porque / escarmentando en mis faltas, / perdonen las del autor" (if in them [the schemes] whoever is wise finds disabusal by seeing my punishment for such acts, let him learn from my experience, and pardon the author's errors) (233a).

Diego, like his identities, like the letter of credit, like the chain he offers Beatriz and the loans he promises his friend, when seen for what he really is cannot remain what he was. Not only does Diego spend the literal and metaphorical capital he has, he spends what he does not have, coining it, as it were, with abandon in the confidence that tomorrow he can recoup all. He courts two women, unwilling to settle for one since he invests each with a value the other lacks. Refusing to accept just one, he desires both and denies that he can fail, so well has he hedged his bets: "Cuando obre / esta pensión la fortuna, / y una pierda, otra me queda: / pues no es posible que pueda / de las dos faltarme una" (When the wheel of fortune turns, and I lose one, I will have the other one left: it is not possible to lose both) (219a). Rodrigo offers Diego material advice: marry Clara "que es la que dinero tiene" (who has money) (225b). Rodrigo then upbraids him for his refusal to choose and predicts his downfall, "Pues cásate con entrambas; / aunque yo tengo por cierto / que has de quedar con ninguna" (Well, marry both of them; I am sure that you will lose them both) (255b).

The signifying chain, emblematically, then links Diego's love, his worth, his desire, his love, his aspiration, and his "self." Transforming through language his "base" self into an object of value, into a

sign of his desire and "spontaneous" generosity, he reenacts the inflationary moves inherent in *vellón* coinage. Both the chain of signifiers
and *vellón* represent a promise to exchange a relatively valueless object for a more cherished one. In the play, the fake-gold chain he offers Beatriz, the inflated letter of credit, and Diego's identities, then,
function like speech in that they all represent what they are not,
much as a picture of food represents a satisfying meal.

Beatriz discovers that the chain is false when her suspicions are
alerted to the possibility of Dionís's false identity. Once the suspected
gap between signifier and signified is exposed, Diego's pyramid
scheme comes crashing down. His attempts to appeal to a presumed
value that undergirds and explains his deceptions (the "soy quien
soy" and the "this is how men treat women" appeal) are shown to be
as worthless and debasing as his deceptions since in advocating his
"original value," he defames the objects of his desire. The women de-
cry his deceptions as well as his appeal to original value and are
saved from ruin because they return to their first investment in the
form of Leonelo and Félix whose fidelity, honesty, love (and wealth)
turn out to be as good as gold.

Emblematic of Diego's efforts is the chain (*joya*) as a signifier in the
chain of signification. The chain is essentially worthless, "solo un
doblón me costó" (it only cost me a doubloon) but Diego raises its
value to one hundred *escudos,* to a sign of his love, to a sign that represents himself. The function of the sign in the chain of signification
has been taken up by Jacques-Alain Miller (1977–78). Miller says
that suture is the logic of the signifier; thus "suture names the relation of the subject to the chain of its discourse; . . . it figures there as
the element which is lacking, in the form of a stand-in, for, while
there lacking, it is not purely and simply absent" (25–26). Miller creates an analogy to the late nineteenth-century philosopher and pi-
oneer of modern logic, mathematical logic, and "analytical philosophy" Gottlob Frege and his *Grundlagen der Arithmetik* (see Frege
1985). Miller says that the concept of one (as the thing identical with
itself) cannot exist without the concept zero. Zero is the "number assigned to the concept 'not identical with itself'" (29). Zero then is described as both zero lack and zero number. Zero is simultaneously not
a number, not identical with itself, and a stand-in functioning as a
number, marking a place. Miller summarizes, "Our purpose has been
to recognize in the zero number the suturing stand-in for the lack"
(31). In parallel fashion, the subject tries to control language and yet
is controlled by it (parallel to Benveniste's (1971) subject of the
enounced/subject of the enunciation; see also Lacan (1981) on aph-

aninis). The pronoun "I," for example, like the zero number, traces both an absence and its suturing as presence.

The subject is sutured by language into the signifying chain, much as the zero number sutures the absence of the zero lack. The moment of suture, of access to the "I," is a point of pseudo-identification based on the assumption of a delusory mirror image.

Propelled by his own desires, Diego attempts to suture himself, as it were, into Madrid society through his words, through his creation of his two "new" selves each of which is and is not like his earlier self. His identities, then, function in a way parallel to zero number/zero lack. They are a stand-in for what is neither totally present or absent, but missing. Diego "theatrically" re-creates himself in Madrid, in the field of the Other, and thus displays what is most central to theater as that which "shows that it knows that it is showing" (B. Freedman 1991, 69).

If the suture is the logic of the signifier and a sign is anything that can be taken as substituting significantly for something else, and if all signs are arbitrary and gain "meaning" through culturally preexisting codes, we can posit that the monetary system, also part of cultural codes, and any monetary unit function as signs and obey the logic of the signifier. There is no natural relation, for example, between a dollar bill or a one hundred *peseta* coin and the loaf of bread it can be exchanged for. If gold or silver seem to have intrinsic value, they only do by convention, by their potential value as rare metals that can be reworked, for example, into jewelry. A gold coin can be melted down to a lump of gold and still have a value equal to what it was as a coin because of its commercial, industrial, or aesthetic value. In societies where gold and silver are unknown, other natural objects, shells or beads, for example, may function similarly. In other societies, cattle, sheep, reindeer, or hides may be used to measure worth. Money arises in relatively developed societies when the holding of other material goods becomes cumbersome.

In seventeenth-century Spain, the relative scarcity of precious metals led the government to issue coins of base metal (copper) so as to use the gold or silver they stood for in international exchange. *Vellón* coins were not used for such exchange but were for internal exchanges only. When the government arbitrarily stamps or restamps *vellón* coins, without an equal amount of silver or gold to back them up, "bad" money drives out "good" with an inevitable inflationary rise. The copper coin cannot be reduced to what it is (a piece of base metal) and still remain the thing it represents (the missing silver).

The *vellón* coin, then, functions in the monetary system as does the signifier in the linguistic system, the zero in the numerical system, and the subject in both language and ideology; it is a stand-in marking the place of lack.

Confidence in the monetary system rises and falls depending on the trust one has in the government or people who stand behind it. The *erario* (state banking) system as proposed by Olivares and Philip IV failed ultimately because the Cortes simply did not trust the king and his minister to keep their word. Lack of confidence in the banks or in the coins of the realm creates anxiety and inflation among merchants and consumers alike. When inflation occurs, people begin to suspect the sign value, the presumed "natural" relation, of the coin and its worth or content. Inflation to a large degree foregrounds the arbitrary, shifting relation between the coin and its value, between signifier and signified, sign and meaning.

In Calderón's *Hombre pobre todo es trazas* the interrelatedness of the word and the inflated and theatricalized self, the chain and the chain of signification can be connected to inflation and deflation, to the problems with *vellón* currency, and to financial and social debts as well. If Diego can be seen to inflate himself into what he is not and at the same time to have a potentially negative transforming effect on others and on their relationship, he can be seen as symptomatic of destructive and corrosive economic forces abroad during this period that could undermine personal, social, and financial security now and in the future. While his undoing through a "deflationary" return to the traditional restores order, his threatening and inflationary presence cannot be totally eliminated simply by exiling it.

Along with worries about inflation, deflation, and value came worries about debts. Hamilton's (1934) investigation of wages and prices from 1501 to 1650 show that real wages rose during the decades 1601–10 and 1611–20, but fell from then through 1650 (see his table 29, 278; table 30, 279; chart 19, 279). He notes that the "sluggish response of money wages and rapid adjustment of living costs to the depreciation of Castilian vellon money in 1622–27 caused real wages to drop more than 20 per cent" (281). He concludes that "recurrent increases in the tariff of the Castilian vellon money . . . swept away the advantages [caused by deflationary policies] in real money and forced workers down to the low level of subsistence experienced in the darkest days of the Price Revolution" (282). In *La dama duende*, it is no wonder that Cosme pilfers from his master when they are on the road and worries about his money. When left alone to unpack the suitcases after arriving in Madrid, the first thing he does is search out the sack wherein he guards what he has been able to filch during the journey:

> Hacienda mía,
> ven acá; que yo quiero
> visitarte primero;
> porque ver determino
> cuánto habemos sisado en el camino;
> que, como en las posadas
> no se hilan las cuentas tan delgadas
> como en casa, que vive en sus porfías
> la cuenta, y la razón por lacerías,
> hay mayor aparejo de provecho
> para meter la mano, no en el pecho,
> sino en la bolsa ajena.
> (*Abre una maleta y saca un bolsín*)
> Hallé la propia; buena está y rebuena,
> pues aquesta jornada
> subió doncella, y se apeó preñada
>
> (246a)

(Come here, my fortune, for I would visit with you first; because I am determined to see how much we have pilfered on the road; because, since in inns they do not keep such tight accounts as at home, where accounts are stubborn and a cause for poverty. There is a greater possibility for profit by putting your hand in another's pocket than by being honest. (*He opens the suitcase and takes out a small purse*) I found what's mine; it's good and very good, on this journey it mounted up a virgin and dismounted pregnant.)

He leaves briefly to visit a tavern and upon his return, finds his room in such disarray that it reminds him of the "plazuela de la Cebada" (Cebada Plaza) (247b). Cosme trembles as he searches for his purse. Opening it, he is positively distraught to see his coins turned to coal (248a).

While he was out, Angela and Isabel entered the room and systematically went through the visitors' bags. As Angela writes Manuel a note, Isabel opens the servant's case. Immediately she finds the money and the discovery prompts a brief statement on the value of monetary units and their relation to class structure:

Esto es dinero:
cuartazos son insolentes,
que en la república donde
son los príncipes y reyes
las doblas y patacones,
ellos son la común plebe
(247b)

(This is money: they are insolent copper (*vellón*) coins, for in the republic where gold coins and silver coins are princes and kings, they are the common folk.)

Then she plays her joke on poor Cosme substituting coal for coins. Cosme's distress when he sees the "worthless" coal where the "valuable" coins once were may be seen as a metaphorical displacement of the genuine distress felt in 1628—as Lope showed in his letter to the duke of Sessa—when the government devalued the *vellón* currency by half of its face value and did not indemnify holders.[2]

La dama duende, written or rewritten in 1629 after the drastic deflationary moves shows characters concerned with their economic situation and with a more widespread system of indebtedness. Characters in the play are linked in a chain of debt, financial, social, and personal, that ties them to each other even when they might wish that such associations were looser or even nonexistent. I shall begin looking at the financial indebtedness and the financial problems of the character; I shall then move toward a broader structure of indebtedness in which they are all enmeshed.

In Manuel's second speech he recounts his long and close personal relation with his future host, Don Juan de Toledo. Not only were they fellow students but companions in arms as well serving under the duke of Feria in the Italian campaign (238a). When Juan was wounded, Manuel recounts, "le curé en mi cama mesma" (I tended to him in my own bed); thus, he concludes, "La vida, después de Dios, / me *debe*" (His life, after God, he owes me) (239a; my emphasis). But their friendship gave rise to another more material debt, made ob-

2. Margaret Greer reaches the same conclusion in her unpublished "The (Self) Representation of Control in *La dama duende,*" which she so generously sent me. She says, "It was not only Cosme who suddenly found his valued *cuartazos* turned to charcoal. In the wake of such a devaluation, Isabel's comments on the worthlessness of the *cuartazo* in the hierarchy of money (863–68) would presumably have had special resonances for an audience of 1629" (14). In *En Madrid y en una casa,* Majuelo echos Cosme's fears, "Miedo / que se nos vuelva carbón / toda esta doblonación" (1268b).

vious when Manuel continues his narrative, "dejo otras *deudas* / de menores intereses, / que entre nobles es bajeza / referirlas" (I leave aside other debts of lesser interest, which among nobles it is mean to mention) (239a; my emphasis). Manuel may wish to forget the financial debt because it would be utterly noble to do so, but apparently he cannot since he refers to it in his exchange with Cosme. Angela, the young, attractive widow, now lives in her brothers' house because her husband died "*debiendo* al Rey / grande cantidad de hacienda" (owing the king a large amount of money) (241b; my emphasis) and she is in Madrid "de secreto, donde intenta, / escondida y retirada, / componer mejor sus *deudas*" (secretly, where she attempts, hidden and withdrawn, better to put her debts in order) (241b/42a; my emphasis). Luis as well is aware of his financially dependent position. In the play, he is a marginalized character, a *segundón* (second-born male child) with, as far as can be told, "ni oficio ni beneficio" (neither income nor occupation). Both Angela and Luis owe their brother, and their debt entails both repressed feelings of anger and an outward show of subservience. Their brother may be a pain, Angela confesses to Luis, but "Al fin sufrirle es mejor; / que es nuestro hermano mayor, / y comemos de alimentos" (finally it is better to suffer him, because he is our older brother, and we eat from his table) (243b). Covarrubias (1943), under *alimentos* (foodstuffs, allowance) states "Mándanse dar alimentos a los hijos quando el mayor se ha llevado toda la hazienda por razón de ser mayorazgo" (Allowances/sustenance, are bequeathed to children when the oldest, because of primogeniture, has taken/inherited all the property) (90).

Indebtedness, and not just economic indebtedness, binds all relations in this play. If Juan owes his life and money to Manuel, Manuel in turn will owe Juan for his hospitality. Manuel owes a debt to the unknown woman he encounters as the play opens; namely, intervention on her behalf, because of the "chivalric code" he upholds, whereby he, as noble, must protect and defend women. After the duel near the end of the play, Luis owes Manuel a debt of gratitude and courtesy when he allows Luis to search out another sword after his breaks during their fight. Angela, of course, owes Manuel for his initial intervention, and at the end of the play for saving her life. Even the king is involved in indebtedness. Both Manuel and Juan became soldiers in the king's service and now, Manuel states, the king rewards him with a government post, "Su magestad / con este gobierno premia / mis servicios" (His Majesty with this governorship rewards me for my services) (239a).

Besides the acknowledged debts, there are yet others that go un-

spoken or that, when spoken about, arouse feelings of anger or humil-
iation. Manuel carries in his bag a picture of an unidentified woman,
along with a number of her love letters. At the end of the play, Manuel ignores that debt when he agrees to marry Angela. Angela's husband's premature death accidentally breaks the marriage bond. His
unpaid debt to her, he of course can never retrieve; repayment must
be sought elsewhere. And, as mentioned, both Angela and Luis owe
their older brother.

The failure to acknowledge and repay fully the debts one has, creates a sense of guilt because of the concomitant inability to fulfill
one's obligations (B. Freedman 1991, 93, passim). Neither the play
nor any character in it owns up to their debts entirely and thus "a
sense of guilt moves" through the text from character to character
"like a signifier dislodged from its signified" (B. Freedman 1991, 93),
splitting the characters as they avoid acknowledging what they
know.

To avoid knowing what one knows might serve as a layman's definition of repression. Repression is a defense mechanism whereby an
idea or wish is kept out of consciousness because it is unacceptable to
the ego (because maladaptive) or to the superego (because offensive to
moral precepts). Said another way, when an idea or wish associated
with strong emotions threatens seriously to lower self-esteem, or to
conflict with deeply held values, or to promote anxiety, the ego seeks
to remove that threat from consciousness. That repressed material,
however, does not just disappear; rather it may return and gain conscious expression in various disguises (for example, in parapraxis or
in neurotic symptoms). People, or here, characters may then project
their negative feelings; projection is a defense mechanism by which
persons unaware of their own antisocial impulses attribute them to
others.

Luis, for example, is a marginalized character, a *segundón,* living
off his older brother because, in part, of an accident of birth. He re-
presses the anger and guilt he feels transforming them and projecting
them outward in arrogant, thoughtless, precipitous, and dangerous
acts. At every step, furthermore, he tries to usurp his brother's place.
He attempts to court his brother's beloved, Beatriz, only to be continually frustrated. When his servant, Rodrigo, says that it is because of
jealousy that Luis feels angry, Luis says no, not because of Juan's
success with Beatriz, rather, "es que sea / mi hermano tan poco at-
ento, / que llevar a casa quiera / un hombre mozo, teniendo, / Rodrigo,
una hermana bella, / viuda y moza . . . [en casa] / tan de secreto" (it is
that my brother is so inattentive as to bring into the house an unmar-

ried young man, Rodrigo, while his beautiful, young, widowed sister lives here so secretly) (241b). Rejected as a lover, he then usurps the role of his sister's protector, and thus of the family's honor, and in the final scene, states his role quite clearly, "Esa mujer es mi hermana; / no la ha de llevar ninguno / a mis ojos de su casa / sin ser su marido" (That woman is my sister; no one will take her from my sight, from her house unless he is her husband) (270b), acting now as fraternal guardian. Luis's anger, frustration, and guilt over his secondary, marginalized place in the family structure leads to, on the one hand, violent, arrogant action, and on the other, to servile, grudging groveling.

Each of the characters is guilty and equally split. Juan is both substitute father and single lover; Angela is (bereaved?) widow, cloistered sister, and flirtatious thrill-seeker; Manuel, having been both student and soldier, is now serious pretender to a government office and a "Don Quijote" (241b) as Cosme names him or "El caballero de la Dama Duende" (the Knight of the Phantom Lady) (250b) as he dubs himself. In general terms, the play, and the society in which it is always enmeshed, splits the male subject into husband/bachelor, businessman/poet, sinner/exorcist, master/servant (after B. Freedman 1991, 86), as it shows characters attempting to conform to shifting requirements; as, for example, when Manuel tries to draw a line between honor and pleasure: "uno importa al honor / de mi casa y de mi aumento, / y otro solamente a un gusto" (one is important to my honor and to the promotion of my lineage, and the other only to a whim) (257a). The female subject is split into angel (Angela), nun (cloistered in her small cell dressed in black), wife/widow (here, *viuda recatada*) (concealed widow) and devil (*duende, demonio*) (phantom, devil); courtesan (*una tapada / a quien todos celebraron*) (a veiled woman celebrated by all) and eligible woman (*bella, moza*) (pretty, young) (after B. Freedman 1991, 86).

Angela is always defining and redefining herself as others also try to define and delimit her. For Manuel she is an unknown married woman in distress, Luis's *dama* (lady) not Luis's *dama,* something supernatural, a woman, a high noble, Juan and Luis's sister, and finally Manuel's bride. For Luis, she is a danger, a long-suffering sister, a wanton woman, and finally Manuel's bride. Angela, as the play opens, is no longer just what she was. She is still Juan and Luis's sister, but that role grates because she was married and is now a widow. As a married woman, she left her brothers' house, went to another part of Spain, set up and ran a household, and had sexual and social experiences. Now returned to the Madrid home, she finds herself confined, dressed in mourning, "con dos hermanos casada" (married to two brothers) (242b) but without any of the limited freedoms she enjoyed when married. She must play the role of indebted sister, of contrite widow; when Luis asks her how she spent her day, she responds "En casa me he estado / entretenida en llorar" (I have been at home entertaining myself by weeping) (243b). These roles, these debts chafe so Angela leaves the house whenever she can, dons other clothes and heads for the Plaza de Palacio where, as Luis describes her, she is "una tapada, / a quien todos celebraron" (a veiled lady, celebrated by all) (243a). She later becomes a woman driven by curiosity, and then by jealousy, a *duende* (phantom) in her own rooms, a noblewoman, etc.

When Manuel visits "the noble woman" he employs a series of traditional metaphors to describe her: *aurora, alba, sol, día* (aurora, dawn, sun, day). In her response, she denies each of the epithets in turn:

> No soy alba, pues la risa
> me falta en contento tanto;
> ni aurora, pues que mi llanto
> de mi dolor no os avisa;
> ni soy sol, pues no divisa
> mi luz la verdad que adoro,
> y así lo que soy ignoro. . . .
> Y así os ruego que digáis
> señor Don Manuel, de mí
> que una mujer soy y fui . . .
> (264a)

(I am not dawn for I lack its contented smile; nor aurora, as my suffering tears should make clear to you; I am not the sun, because my light does not herald the truth I adore, and so I do not know what I am. . . . Thus I beg you Sir Manuel that you say of me that I have been and am a woman.)

Here, she rejects his poetic characterizing, presents herself as an enigma, and then asks him to see her as a woman. Yet to see her as a woman is not so simple as it might seem since "woman" includes all of the many definitions she, he, and others have brought to bear upon her; thus her "definition" instead of offering closure only opens the question of who and what she is once again.

A woman or a man is enmeshed in a web of relations, in a web of social, cultural, economic debts always. "Being oneself," Terry Eagleton (1986) says, "involves a degree of play-acting" (13); it involves a relational shifting of attitudes, behaviors, speech, desire, and repression. The characters in *La dama duende* slide between desire and guilt, affirm and disallow what they know, and project their anxieties in vain attempts to conform to their always already socially imposed roles only to contradict the requirements of those roles as impulse breaks the shackles of imperative. The result is an ever more confused and complicated, contradictory set of situations and circumstances that provoke the characters to theatrical ordering and reordering of themselves and their debts; each reordering, however, only produces more dangerous confusion until suddenly marriages occur and the metaphorical curtain falls.

Angela and Manuel seem to offer, near the end of the play, two interpretations of identity and, with those and the subsequent marriage, the possibility of stability. Angela once more redefines herself now as the knowledgeable, controlling subject of her desires and goals as she says to Manuel: "Mi intento fue el quererte, / mi fin amarte, / mi temor perderte" (My goal was to love you, my end to love you, my fear, to lose you) (271b) etc. In addition, she says she is conscious of her intentions and the required steps she has taken to bring them about, "Por haberte querido, / fingida sombra de mi casa he sido; / por haberte estimado, / sepulcro vivo fui de mi cuidado" (For having loved you, I have been the pretend shade of my house; for having esteemed you, I have been a living tomb of my worries) (217b). If Angela holds herself the unified subject of emotions, desires, intents, means, and ends and invites Manuel to enter yet another web of debts, "Mi intento fue . . . / . . . / persuadirte / que mi daño repares, / que me valgas, me ayudes y me ampares" (My goal was to persuade you to repair any harm I have caused, to stand up for me, to help me and to protect me) (271b), Manuel, on the other hand, after reviewing his immediate problems, offers himself dutifully as socially indebted and split: Angela is his friend's sister, and if he takes her out of there, "he sido / traidor, y que a su casa he ofendido" (I have been a traitor, and I have offended her family); on the other hand, if he does not help her, "si la dejo, villano, / si la guardo, mal huésped" (if I abandon her, villainous, if I protect her, an evil guest) (271b). Thus, given his socially produced dilemma, he can only respond with the socially correct move, marry her, not out of love, but rather "Para cumplir mejor / con la *obligación* jurada" (to better fulfill my sworn obligation) (271b; my emphasis).

Neither Angela, purported subject of her desires, nor Manuel, purported subject of his social understanding, originally sought the marriage, but in the play, that does not matter. It does not matter because it is not pertinent to comedy's sense of triumph. That they do not really know each other, that they hide things from each other even in the last scene, that each holds out to the other as well as to himself or herself only a very partial picture of who and what they are does not matter to the web they continue to spin (see B. Freedman 1991, 103). Nonetheless, the audience could see the debts, splits, deferrals, differences, and unresolved conflicts to glimpse that the supposed smooth unity is replete with cracks and rifts. After all, it is no coincidence that the majority of the play's action takes place, literally, in a house divided.

By following Angela's model of how she sees herself, one could see the play as the impossibility of self-presence through debt relations by raising the question of whether the place one occupies as subject of the signifier is ever the same as the place one occupies as subject of the signified. Can Angela ever name herself correctly? During the game she invents she insightfully states that "un enigma a ser me ofrezco / que ni soy lo que parezco / ni parezco lo que soy" (I offer myself as an enigma, for I am not what I seem, nor do I seem what I am) (264a); at the end of the play, does she really say much more? Read thus, the play would posit misrecognition not just as necessary for this play, but as the essential condition of this comedy and perhaps of subjectivity itself. Being would then be seen as a theatrical process of indebtedness, of dispersal and failed recuperation such that no sooner do characters say what they are than do they split yet again (parallel to suddenly deflated or inflated, restamped coins). This play and theater itself would be a model wherein the battle between representation and presence is always staged and comedy would be that theatrical subset where misrecognition is a precondition and where error is truth (after B. Freedman 1991, 109).

If we attend to Manuel's attempted self-definition, we might want to foreground the role of social, cultural, and historical pressures as formative of the self and perhaps read the play through Louis Althusser's notions of ideology. Upon birth, perhaps even prior to birth, certain roles and debt relations are instantaneously imposed upon people, a fact the play emphasizes at the very beginning through references to the birth of Prince Baltasar Carlos and the celebrations in his honor. If one is born first son or second, noble or non-noble, rich or poor, male or female, in this society, certain things instantly obtain. Ideology interpellates individuals as subjects because part of ideology's function is to define and constitute people as subjects. Certain roles, male, female, son, daughter, student, soldier, husband, wife, bureaucrat, *mayorazgo, segundón* (first-born son, second-born son) widow, and so forth, preexist the subject. What we see in the play is a conflict, then, between the assigned, limited, and limiting social role and the individual who often chafingly and frustratedly, occupies that role. The play in its use of character, language, and situation would offer a model through which they live and define themselves. Theater, then, would be an important discourse within an ideological world because it recognizes and attempts to present conflicts, thereby discursively producing knowledge.

Though psychological and ideological analyses approach the subject from different angles, they converge on the recognition of the debt and division that mark the subject. From an ideological stance, the subject is produced by historical and cultural processes, caught in a web of relations that define and divide. For both Freud, Lacan, and others, division, loss, differentiation are prices to be paid for becoming a subject in the world. *La dama duende* shows that no one is a free master of himself or herself, that all are divided and indebted, and thus that any supposed master discourse is imperfect. The unsought marriage that caps the play ironically repeats the problems illustrated by the situations and action of the play, because it raises the question of how the old and new debt relations will play out, of whether in marriage Manuel and Angela will find self-determination within self-limitation, whether by this marriage the characters are freed and fulfilled or framed and tamed?

Debt, inflation, deflation, and the value of monetary units were not just passing concerns for the nation, the leaders, the nobility, and the commonfolk throughout the 1620s. "Circumstances obliged Philip IV," Hamilton (1934) reports, "to continue the inflationary policy initiated by his predecessor. In two respects his reign witnessed an increase in monetary disorder: first, debasement was more flagrant; and, second, instability was heightened by deflation as well as inflation" (80). Such instability could not pass unnoticed by the dramatists of this period; in many of their plays, characters comment on their own economic condition as well as on that of others and on the nation's as well.[3] As Tomasa says in the opening scene of *La huerta de*

---

3. Historians have divided into two camps on the issue of how Spain's economic woes affected the nobility. Charles Jago (1982) sums up one view:

> The most dissolute nobles squandered their patrimony; they succumbed under the weight of debt, and they never awoke to the dawning of the capitalist ethos. They defied the possibility of their political displacement before the springing up

Juan Fernández, "¿qué perdición no se aguarda / de nuestra pobre Castilla?" (what ruination does not await our poor Castile?) (lines 49–50).

As the characters in these plays deal with their economic situation, they do so within a broader system of debts and responsibilities that extend outward from the individual to encompass the entire society. In the old feudal system, those debts and responsibilities were hierarchized, ordered, dependent on a tight net that extended downward from the king to the lowest beggar and back upward as well. As that system cracks, as the relations among power, social status, land, and wealth begin to crumble the new men and women emerge in the forms of mercantalists, merchants, owners, entrepreneurs, bureau-

---

of an educated bourgeois elite that forcefully took away their positions, and before the growing force and attraction of centralized governmental institutions. Under these circumstances, even the category of aristocracy decayed. An uncontrolled inflation of honors undermined the exclusivity of their estate, new concepts of social worth that emanated from the Renaissance threatened traditional distinctions based on lineage and military service, and empoverished monarchs put in doubt long standing noble privileges and exemptions. (248)

and later presents the opposing side:

Seventeenth-century Castile underwent a "nobiliary reaction" on a large scale. Attending to the process of capital accumulation, it was argued that liquid capital in the form of precious metals and annuity income acquired during the sixteenth century were destroyed by the massive gush of silver used to finance Spanish participation in the Thirty Years' War, and by the forced reduction of interest payments on individual or corporate bonds, and state bonds which decreased their value. Faced with the loss of economic importance from these sources of liquid capital, land once again became the best stable refuge, thereby creating the conditions that led to a "nobiliary reaction" since it was the nobles who controlled the greatest part of the land. "And their forceful return, favored by the decay of royal power, constitutes a historical certainty." José Antonio Maravall arrives at the same conclusion though through a slightly different approach. In his effort to describe the essence of "Baroque culture" that developed in Spain during the long period of economic and social crises between 1605 and 1650, he analyses the fundamental character of what he calls "Baroque absolutism." Seventeenth-century monarchs, he maintains, in their defensive reaction before the parallel threats brought about by growing social mobility and by popular discontent, strove to reaffirm the foundations of the dominant social hierarchy. So completely did they identify with seigniorial interests and with a social and political system founded on land-based wealth that they naturally encouraged an aristocratic renaissance. (249–50)

While there is little doubt that by the middle of Charles II's reign, the nobility was firmly entrenched in powerful positions, popular discontent made itself felt throughout the entire period of Philip IV's reign. Tension and conflict, if not outright crisis, then are constants in the economic, political, and social spheres of seventeenth-century Spain.

crats, itinerant salespeople, even theater-company managers, actors and actresses. That is to say, as the system moves from iconic relation to the relation of the sign—nobility does not now necessarily entail land ownership, wealth does not necessarily equal noblity, and vice versa—an emergent dynamism makes itself felt. Such fluidity tends to loosen the bonds that held the people together under the older system. In the plays, women and men begin to seek that which they could not on their own before. Women look for their own husbands without or against their family's wishes. Men violate accepted social codes in order to fulfill their desires. Such overreaching is not always attributable to greed alone, but is symptomatic of changes occurring in Spain.

Characters act, however, not in complete disregard of their debts, of the ties that bind; thus their sense of anxiety, crisis, and guilt. They seek a means of unifying their actions, words, desires, and self-concepts with the older system of values that still hangs on in the society even if that system is more a nostalgic illusion than a current reality. Characters are alternately active and passive, rebellious and submissive. The marriages that end the comedies project a return to the past; yet as the characters move along the paths that lead to the final curtain, some sense possibilities they might not have before. The characters at the end of the plays are not just as they were when the plays began. Though they enter into a "new" web of debts, of social, cultural, and personal relations through their marriages, the experiences that eventually led them there may have had effects on them, and on the audience who saw the plays, that are difficult to measure. The experience of "another way of seeing" may be enough to drive some strongly back into the comforting arms of traditional values, but others may not go so willingly.

4

COMEDY AND
LEGAL MATTERS

Characters in several of the comedies come to Madrid, some for love, some for marriage (not always the same thing as love), some for revenge, some for money, some for position, and yet others come to attend to legal matters sometimes involving one or more of the other reasons just mentioned. Don Duarte answers Don Fernando's "why are you once again in Madrid?" with "Pleitos que no he concluido / me vuelven acá" (Unfinished lawsuits bring me back here) (*Por el sótano y el torno* 555a) and later we hear Fernando declare, "De Aragón volví a Madrid, / necesitado de pleitos; / fáciles al comenzarlos / y al concluirlos eternos" (I returned from Aragon to Madrid because of lawsuits; they are easy to start but drag on eternally) (562b). Don Baltasar was in Madrid at his father's insistence, "Manda que asista en la corte / Para que pleitos concluya" (He orders me to be in the court to bring some lawsuits to an end) (*Desde Toledo a Madrid* 488c). Angela, *la dama duende* (the phantom lady), lives in her brothers' house in Madrid trying to untangle the legal problems her husband's death created. And Don Juan pretends to have legal business to facilitate his "return" from Flanders, "una pretensión mía, / causa de pleitos muy grandes / que hoy a la corte me han vuelto" (an aspiration of mine, cause of huge lawsuits, has brought me back to the court today) (*El astrólogo fingido* 153b).

Characters' confidence in the courts and the legal system range from Violante's utter trust, "En Madrid hay tribunales / Para todos" (In Madrid there are courts for everyone) (*La villana de Vallecas* 47c); to Inés's pessimism (*El examen de maridos*). When her advisor Beltrán says that a particular suitor's case is a good one, "Y dicen que con derecho; / que sus letrados lo afirman" (And they say his cause is just, his attorneys affirm it), she says, "Ellos, ¿cuándo dicen menos?" (When do they ever say anything else?)—thereby showing that popular opinion about lawyers has not changed much over the centuries—and refuses to allow the man to court her further (360). Sebastián demonstrates outright cynicism when he plans to use the courts to break up Magdalena and Melchor by swearing that she promised to marry him, Sebastián, first. When his sister asks where he will find witnesses for such a claim, he says "Tiene en sus calles / Todos los vicios Madrid. / . . . / Siendo así, ¡bueno sería / Que aquí el interés no venda / Testigos falsos" (Madrid holds all vices in its streets. . . . That being the case, it would be amazing if you couldn't buy false witnesses) (*La celosa de sí misma* 139a/b).

Tirso, as previewed in an earlier chapter, weaves two legal matters into the love plots in *La huerta de Juan Fernández*. The Conde de Valencia del Po, lacking male offspring, named his daughter, Laura, his principal heir, but her uncle, Alejandro Malatesta, alleged that the county belonged to him "por la línea de varón" (though the patrilineal line) (line 424) and took it by force. Laura comes to Madrid seeking legal redress, "En Madrid me tienen pleitos / de parientes" (Lawsuits against relatives have me in Madrid) (406–7), where she is confident of a just outcome, "Sentencia espero en favor, / que alentada de parientes, / y segura en mi derecho, / con los jueces solicito" (I await a favorable judgment that, encouraged by relatives, and sure of my rights, I solicit from the judges) (466–69). Her uncle, meantime, hedging his bets, offers to reconcile the dispute by means of an interfamilial marriage. Laura reports that he wants

> . . . que dé la mano a un hijo,
> que afirma llegará presto
> a esta corte; mas yo digo,
> puesto que no le conozco,
> que si pleitos dan maridos

de tan mal casamentero
poca paz me prognostico
(475–81)

(me to give my hand to a son of his who he affirms will arrive
shortly at court; but I say, since I do not know him, that if
lawsuits offer husbands, from such a poor marriage broker I
can expect little peace.)

Alejandro's son, the Conde Galeazo, comes to Madrid to try to bring
the marriage about. He thinks that the legal system is much less just
and impartial than does Laura:

Mal su justicia asegura
quien en pleitos ignora
que mujer competidora
se ampara de su hermosura
. . . .
Llora, encarece y intima,
la belleza es eficacia
que enamorando lastima;
y en fin, como nacen dellas
los jueces templan cuidados;
que no hay tales abogados
como son lágrimas bellas.
(1270–73, 1278–84)

(Whoever involved in lawsuits will assure himself an unjust
outcome if he ignores the fact that a female competitor will use
her beauty. She cries, she urges, she becomes intimate, beauty
is efficacy because inspiring love can harm; and finally, since
judges are of woman born, they temper their thoughts; for
there are no lawyers as good as lovely tears.)

A second legal matter in that play involves Petronila and Hernando. He was taken in by his cousin, Petronila's mother, and for her
help, he promised to marry Petronila after he returned from Italy.
When he returned, he has forgotten his promise since he is now in
love with Laura. Petronila, however, tracks him down, reminds him
of his obligations, his broken promises, and the value of keeping his
word.

So thoroughly do legal problems permeate the play that characters express their love and describe their surroundings invoking a legalistic vocabulary. For example, Hernando, speaking to Laura, says of his love and of the gardens wherein he works:

> Permitid, Laura mía
> que mis sabrosos males,
> destas flores haciendo tribunales,
> sitial y trono desta fuente fría,
> formen de vos querellas,
> y os digan mis agravios,
> vos la acusada, los testigos ellas.
> (237–43)

(My Laura, permit my pleasant sufferings, making these flowers tribunals and a seat of honor or throne of this fountain, to shape my complaints about you, to tell you of my injuries, you as the accused, they the witnesses.)

When Laura believes that Petronila, wearing her masculine disguise, is the Conde Galeazo, she says, "Pues, conde, acabóse el pleito: / sentencia es este abrazo" (Well, Count, the lawsuit is over: the sentence is this embrace) (2337–38).

Laura wins her lawsuit but the play ends with compromise as Petronila marries Hernando and Laura marries her cousin, to whom she says:

> . . . y pues salí
> en el pleito vencedora,
> dándole la mano agora
> verá que hay valor en mí
> para pleitar estados
> y amor para restaurar
> pérdidas que han de premiar
> sus amorosos cuidados.
> (3055–62)

(and since I was victorious in the lawsuit, I now give him my hand so that you will see how worthy I am to sue for estates, and how loving as I restore losses that reward your loving concerns.)

While the lawsuit establishes her rights, her wisdom, and her strength, the compromise that sustains the family was, from many people's perspective—as I shall later show—the greater victory. If love is war, as Calderón says and as Robert ter Horst correctly asserts (see "Amor es guerra," 5–68, in ter Horst 1982), so too is a lawsuit:

> pelean los letrados y oficiales,
> hacen campo de guerra tribunales,
> [ejércitos testigos]
> y litigan los nobles como amigos.
>   (306–9)

(lawyers and officials fight, they make a battleground of the courts, [and armies of witnesses], and nobles litigate as friends.)

Despite the conflicts, the lawsuit in *La huerta de Juan Fernández* was civil (pun intended), but not all are.

As with many of the characters, all of the dramatists had personal experience with the legal system, but perhaps no one knew its dangers and its dodges better than Lope. In 1582, Lope falls in love with Elena Osorio, daughter of Jerónimo Velázquez, director of a popular theatrical company in Madrid. But in 1576, Elena had married Cristóbal Calderón, an actor. Since Cristóbal Calderón was frequently absent from the capital, and since Jerónimo Velázquez saw that his daughter's relationship with the famous dramatist might well prove profitable—and in fact Lope soon began to write exclusively for Velázquez's company—the affair prospered for about five years.

In 1587, however, Lope went to Seville to visit an uncle; upon his return he found Elena cool if not cold to his advances. In Lope's absence, Elena fell in love with Francisco Perrenot (count of Cantecroix, nephew of Cardinal Granvela), and Francisco with her. Lope, hurt and angry, as we can see in his three *pastor/manso* (shepherd/bellwether) sonnets, turns his attention, like a character in one of his plays, to another woman, Isabel de Urbina, perhaps to make Elena jealous. He then turns his literary talents over to Porres's theatrical company, Velázquez's rival, and finally turns to more personal vengeance. He starts writing scurrilous verses against Elena and her family. In the following example, *la capitana* (the captain) is Elena, *el alférez* (ensign) is Juana de Rivera, Elena's cousin, and *el cabo* (corporal), Anilla Velázquez, is Ana, Elena's mother:

> Los que algún tiempo tuvistes
> noticia de Lavapiés [where Elena lived]
> de hoy más, sabed que su calle
> no lava, que sucia es;
> que en ella hay tres damas
> que, a ser cuatro como tres,
> pudieran tales columnas
> hacer un burdel francés.
> La capitana de todas,
> hija de la sabia Inés . . .
> El alférez, doña Juana, . . .
> el sobrenombre Rivera:
> un linaje montañés
> tan antigua, que se acuerda
> de aquel profeta Moisés.
> Es puta de dos a cuatro
> y a mí me dijo un inglés
> que la vio sus blancas piernas
> por dos varas delantés.
> El cabo de escuadra honrada
> Anilla Velázquez es,
> antes puta que nacida,
> como lo sabe el marqués . . .
>   (Astrana Marín 1935, 100)

(Those of you who once heard of Lavapiés [literally "wash feet," the neighborhood where Elena lived], from today forth, understand that her street does not wash, it is filthy; on it there are three ladies who, if they were four, could serve as columns to build a French whorehouse. The captain of them all, is the daughter of the astute Inés. . . . The ensign, Juana, . . . whose name is Rivera: from the mountains she hails with a lineage so old that it recalls that prophet Moses. She is a well-known whore, and an Englishman told me that he saw her white legs all the way up her thighs. The corporal of this honored squadron is Anilla Velasquez, a whore before she was born, as the Marquis knows well . . .)

Not content to attack just the women, Lope also composes nasty poems about Granvela, about Elena's brother, Damián Velázquez, "Licenciado, dotor o cazalegas" (University graduate, doctor, or ambulance chaser) (Astrana Marín 1935, 102), and about her father, "Un

solador se ha vuelto caballero" (A floorer who has become a gentleman) (105). But Lope had picked on a well-placed and powerful man
in Francisco Perrenot, and Elena's brother held a law degree. On 29
December 1587, as Lope attends a play in the Cruz theater, he is
arrested for libel.

Lope's accusers marshaled their witnesses well, whereas in his own
testimony, Lope contradicted himself and failed to undermine his accusers (108). As witnesses against the poet grew in number and in the
specificity of their testimony, Lope's fate was sealed: guilty as
charged. He was sentenced to four years' exile from Madrid, two from
Castille. If he violated the sentence once, the punishment would be
doubled; twice, and he would be executed. Lope married Isabel and
the two moved to Valencia.

Years later, in 1616, back in Madrid, older and perhaps wiser, a
priest but as amorous as ever, Lope met Marta de Nevares and was
instantly taken with the actress's beauty, voice, and intelligence. But
as that master of malapropisms, Yogi Berra, said, it was *déjà vu* all
over again: the twenty-six-year-old Marta, like Elena before her, was
married. At the tender age of thirteen, she was wed to Roque Hernández, but unlike Cristóbal Calderón, Roque was no itinerant actor;
rather, he was a hard-nosed businessman not about to allow his in-
come-producing wife easily out of her marital contract. Lope pursued,
Marta at first demurred, then accepted, then had Lope's child, Antonia Clara, whom Roque wound up "recognizing" as his legitimate
daughter. More discreet now, Lope this time kept his public pro-
nouncements quiet, though he did write constantly to Marta and to
the duke of Sessa. In his letters to the latter, Lope recorded his fears
and boasts, his depressions and joys, and his cynicism. After the bap-
tism of Antonia Clara, Lope writes "Grandes cosas hay estos días: no
se puede escribir; pero pudiese hablar, y para todo veré esta tarde al
caer el sol a Vuestra Excelencia, y aun creo llevaré conmigo al padre
putativo de la niña, que iba a decir al puto" (There are great things
these days: they cannot be written; but they can be spoken of, and I
will see Your Excellency about it all this afternoon at sunset, and I
even believe that I will bring with me the putative father of the child,
I almost said the cuckold) (Astrana Marín 1935, 253).

Lope and Marta turned to the courts where she accused Roque of
abuse and demanded a divorce, claiming that she was forced to marry
him against her will. After much turbulence and tribulation—Roque
tried to kidnap the child to force Marta's return—the couple separated in 1618 and Marta won her suit. Celebrating victory, Lope
crowed:

Señor, hoy acabaré de escribir estas cartas; que doy palabra a vuestra excelencia, a fe de criado suyo, que con la definitiva de el pleito de Amarilis ni he comido, ni sabido si estaba en mí o en el proceso. Mucho he pasado. Doy gracias a Dios que se ha lucido, pues tuvimos sentencia en favor, y la mandan amparar en su dote, dando la fuerza por bien probada. (Lope de Vega, n.d., no. 408, 62)

(Sir, today I shall finish writing these letters; and I swear to Your Excellency, as a loyal servant, until the final decision in Amarilis's lawsuit, I have not eaten, nor known what I was doing, nor known how the trial might come out. I have gone through a lot. I thank God that it has come out well, since we have a favorable decision, and they have ordered that her dowry be protected, since force was proven.)

Then he cynically laughs:

Ríome mucho de que una mujer pruebe bofetones y coces para decir que su marido la forzó a firmar escrituras. (62)

(I laugh a lot at the thought that a woman can prove punches and kicks to say that her husband forced her to sign a marriage contract.)

He ends, however, fearing the next step, Roque's inevitable appeal:

Resta ahora la apelación del Consejo por la parte contraria, donde hay que temer, y ejemplos cada día; para su remedio será importantísimo el favor de vuestra excelencia: desde aquí se dé por implorado, étcetera. (62)

(The appeal to the Consejo by the defendant is next and it is to be feared given what one sees every day; for a successful outcome Your Excellency's favor will be most important; and herein I implore you to help, etc.)

But before the appeals could be heard and decided, Roque died. Lope, in what may qualify as one of his most un-Christian and uncharitable moments, wrote to Marta in the dedication of *La viuda valenciana*:

¡Bien haya la muerte! No sé quién está mal con ella, pues lo
que no pudiera remediar física humana, acabó ella en cinco
días con una purga sin tiempo, dos sangrías anticipadas y tener
el médico más afición a su libertad de vuesa merced que a la
vida de su marido. (Astrana Marín 1935, 255).

(Praised be death! I do not know who is against it, what human
agency could not remedy, death did in five days with a tardy
purge and two early bloodlettings and with a doctor more interested in your freedom than in your husband's life.)

Lope's involvement with the legal system, while surely lurid, was
anything but an isolated case. In the early seventeenth century, Baltasar Alamos de Barrientos "calculated that at least three-quarters of
Castile's population was in the habit of litigating. Although undoubtedly inflated, this estimate suggests the degree to which an educated
Castilian was ready to believe that he lived in a society in which
lawsuits were familiar to everyone, rich and poor alike" (Kagan 1981,
10).
   The Spanish legal system, by the sixteenth and seventeenth centuries, was a maze of laws and *fueros,* as the two huge volumes containing "over four thousand royal laws, edicts, pragmáticas, and provi-
sions" (Kagan 1981, 26) called the *Nueva recopilación de todas las
leyes de Castilla* proves. The collection was published in 1569 and
supplemented in 1592 and 1598. Finding one's way through the labyrinth required the services of *abogados* (advocates), *procuradores* (attorneys), and *solicitadores* (solicitors), and it required a great deal
of money. The duke of Medinaceli, Kagan reports, "had agents in
Granada, Valladolid, and Madrid as well as a regular council com-
posed of law graduates to help administer his estates and supervise
his many lawsuits" (11). The count of Rivadivia declared, in 1634,
"that he owed 487,500 mrs. to his advocates, attorneys, and solicitors"
(15).
   Castile, by comparison, was a litigious place. At the end of the sixteenth century, "the royal chancillería of Valladolid, which had ap-
proximately four million people living within its jurisdiction, received
as many as six or seven thousand new cases a year. . . . In contrast,
the Court of Chancery during the reign of Elizabeth I (1558–1603)
was the largest of England's five central courts, yet it received only
about five hundred new cases a year from a county with a population
of well over four million" (Kagan 1981, 16).
   Besides the high costs of litigation, litigants often needed the pa-

tience of Job. In the lower tribunals, justice was relatively swift as cases were settled in less than a year (Kagan 1981, 43), but the higher up the case started or rose on appeal, the slower the wheels of justice ground. The average case in the higher courts "required between two and three years, although three percent, most of these complex inheritance disputes, dragged on for ten years or more. Dispatch of cases in the Royal Council of Castile, which was accustomed to heavy cases of major importance, was somewhat slower. Its records contain numerous examples of lawsuits lasting a lifetime" (43). Even the powerful complained. The count-duke of Olivares had a lawsuit against the duke of Medina-Sidonia about which the former laments that it has been "'more than ten months since my lawsuit was last seen; . . . had I known this before, I would not have continued with the suit . . . even though my children might have died of hunger'" (cited by Kagan 1981, 42).[1]

When Philip IV and Olivares came to power there was substantial corruption afoot and little being done to correct it. During the reign of Charles I and Philip II, those kings used the *visita,* or judicial inquest, to keep abreast of legal officials. Under Philip III, *visitas* were kept to a minimum not only because of the expenses involved but also because of the king's apparent lack of interest in judicial affairs. Kagan (1981) studies the *visitas* (198–209) and notes that:

> The only visitations ordered by Philip III took place in the New World when in 1602 the audiencias of Santo Domingo and Mexico received a visitador real. Philip, however, did suspend Lic. Lorenzo Texada, an alcalde de hijosdalgo at the chancellería of Valladolid for "favoritism." Apparently Texada had served as judge in a suit concerning nobles of his own family. In 1614, he was suspended from office for six years, but in 1616, with Philip's help, he was back on the job (199 n. 134).

Under Olivares's reform policies, efforts began to reduce the corruption and streamline the justice system so as to make it better mirror the king's will. "In less than a year," Kagan (1981) says, "sixteen oidores had been dismissed and two others temporarily suspended, tough measures, but ones that were meant to serve as a sign to the whole of the royal bureaucracy that the new regime would not toler-

---

1. Kagan (1981) says that the case was pending before the Royal Council of Castile in 1622 and that Olivares writes his letter in 1623. According to the *Noticias de Madrid,* Olivares won his suit on 27 January 1624; see Kagan (1981), 89.

ate the corruption and laxity characteristic of the previous reign" (200). But the tough measures were short-lived.

In 1632, Jerónimo Cevallos in his *Arte real para el buen gobierno de los reyes y príncipes y de sus vasallos* (Royal art for the good guidance of kings and princes and their vassals) calls judges "meat-eating wolves, living off the blood of lambs" (cited by Kagan 1981, 203). In 1624, a royal visitor says of the Sevillan judge, Sancho Hurtado de la Puente, he is no better than "'a public thief . . . who sells justice [by means of] many illicit pacts and contracts'" (cited by Kagan 1981, 203). Olivares, in the Gran Memorial of 1624, urges Philip to stem corruption and punish misconduct in judicial officials, or else royal justice will lose face:

> Conviene ocupar estos oficios las personas de mayores es-
> peranzas y mayor virtud propia que se hallare y irlos ascen-
> diendo conforme dieren la cuenta en los menores corregi-
> mientos. Algunos tiene V. Mjd. buenos, pero no muchos. . . .
> [Del] no haber justicia hace el no haber buenos corregidores,
> porque ellos introducen a sus criados por ministros, y el criado
> en confianza de su amo trata de hurtar y hacer dinero, el cor-
> regidor no le castiga porque le puso allí, los otros con este
> ejemplo hacen lo mismo, y como no puede castigar a los unos y
> dejar a los otros se disimula con todos. Los regidores hacen lo
> que quieren usurpando a los pobres sus haciendas, atropellán-
> dolos y vejándolos . . . como hacen todos, no viendo castigos
> ejemplares en los que proceden así . . . no se ha visto cabeza
> cortada de corregidor, alcalde, ni ministro de ahí arriba, con lo
> cual no puede haber escarmiento ni justicia donde falta (Elliot
> and de la Peña 1978, 1:64–65).

> (It is necessary to fill these posts with the people of greatest
> confidence and greatest personal virtue you can find and pro-
> mote them as they account themselves well in minor judg-
> ments. Your Majesty has some good ones, but not many. . . .
> From lack of justice there is a lack of good corregidors, because
> they install their servants as ministers, and the servant who
> has his master's confidence tries to steal and make money, and
> the corregidor does not punish him because he put him in that
> position, and others following this example do the same thing,
> and since one cannot punish some and not punish others, one
> looks the other way with all. Councilmen do what they want,
> usurping poor people's property, running roughshod over them,

vexing them . . . as they all do, with no visible exemplary punishment for those who proceed thus . . . not one corregidor's,
mayor's, or minister's, or anyone higher's head has been
chopped off, and given that, there can be no justice nor any
lesson to others.)

However, recognizing the problem and taking sustained and effective
action do not necessarily go hand in hand. In 1629, Olivares "wrote
secretly to Philip to tell him that 'the ambition of the ministers is
without measure.'" He added that as a result of the Crown's failure to
punish corruption within the judiciary, justice was "'in almost total
abandon,'" (Kagan 1981, 206).

By that date, the king's and the chief minister's main attention had
been diverted by the war in Flanders, the *vellón* (copper coin) problems, the failure of the *erarios* (state deposit bank) plan, and the
Mantuan affair. That is to say that international affairs and national
financial problems took up more and more time and energy. "In essence," Kagan summarizes, "the rey justiciero of the sixteenth century was forced, by necessity, to become the rey financiero, a monarch
preoccupied with providing the wherewithal to sustain Castile's vast
military effort" (207). The result was that in the justice system lawyers gained control over the royal judiciary by default (see Kagan
1981, 207–9).

In 1621, only a short time after the case involving Marta, Lope, and
Roque Hernández, Lope wrote *Amor, pleito y desafío*. The plot of this
play is somewhat confusing, in part because the two main male characters share the same first name, Juan. There are two love triangles,
one involving Juan Padilla, Beatriz, and Juan de Aragón and another
with Beatriz, Juan Padilla, and Ana. Beatriz's father, Alvaro de
Rojas, rejects his daughter's desire to marry Juan Padilla because,
though noble by birth and valiant in his soldierly service to King
Alfonso XI, Juan Padilla is not only from a poor family, but the third
male child to boot. The wealthy, but avaricious, petulant, and both
socially and politically ambitious father wants Beatriz to marry Juan
de Aragón because he is noble, rich, and the king's favorite. Sometime before the play's action begins, Juan Padilla had courted his
cousin, Ana, who now steams and schemes over his love for her
friend, Beatriz.

Laced into the two love triangles is a secondary plot involving the
rising or falling fortunes of the the two principal male characters. As
the play opens, Juan de Aragón enjoys an apparently merited reputation as first among the king's nobles, whereas Juan Padilla, though a

good soldier, remains in the shadows. This secondary plot traces Juan de Aragón's fall from grace and Juan Padilla's rise. Those two plots spawn numerous subplots as the action moves from love to litigation. Juan Padilla's and Beatriz's love comes up against powerful opposition. Not only does her father disapprove, but Juan de Aragón also loves Beatriz. Juan Padilla is ignorant of his rival's feelings; therefore when Juan Padilla's servant, Martín, recommends asking, "Don Juan de Aragón, que priva / Con el Rey" (Juan de Aragón who is the king's favorite) (11) to intervene with the king on his master's behalf in asking for Beatriz's hand, Juan Padilla readily agrees. Juan de Aragón, Martín assures, "Tiene . . . / Justa fama y opinión. / No puedes hombre buscar / De mayor satisfacción; / Es gallardo caballero" (has . . . well-deserved fame and renown. You cannot find another man of greater confidence; he is a gallant gentleman) (12). Juan Padilla gladly chooses him as his advocate.

But Juan de Aragón proves a slippery agent: after listening to Juan de Padilla's request, he ambiguously replies, "Yo os he entendido ya" (I have understood you) (14). In his subsequent monologue, Juan de Aragón explains his response: I love Beatriz, Juan Padilla came to me asking my intercession with the king, I was in a difficult situation, thus my response, "No me obligué ni la palabra he dado, / Sólo le respondí, 'yo os he entendido,' / Con que ni la quebré ni me he obligado / A cumplir lo que á nadie he prometido" (I neither committed myself nor gave my word, I only responded with 'I have understood you,' so I neither broke my word nor have I committed myself to fulfill what I never promised) (14). After that sly, legalistic rationalizing, Juan de Aragón begins to push his own case. He admits to himself that Juan Padilla has perhaps beaten him to the punch, "¡Ay Dios! si tiene la licencia della / Navego en vano, moriré á la orilla," (Oh God! If he has permission for it, I navigate in vain and will die on the shore) but then quickly amends, "Pero si tengo la del Rey, que espero, / Cayó la suerte en Aragón primero" (but if I have the king's [permission], as I expect, then luck has fallen to Aragon first) (15), thereby linking the love problems with the rising or falling influence subplot.

Juan de Aragón asks Alfonso for Beatriz's hand, and the king, ignorant of prior events, calls Alvaro to his side and tells him, "Dale a don Juan tu Beatriz" (Give Beatriz to Juan) (17). Since earlier Alvaro had agreed to let Juan Padilla present his case to the king, in the confidence that the monarch would reject his petition on grounds of the financial imbalance between the two families, and now misinterpreting which Juan the king refers to, Alvaro launches into a series of whining complaints about Juan's poverty. The king turns to Juan de Aragón and asks him if he is poor, and Alvaro suddenly and happily realizes that it is to this Juan that his sovereign has promised Beatriz. That cleared up, the king remembers Juan Padilla's long and faithful service and tells Juan de Aragón to have Juan Padilla accompany the king to Compostela because "le quiero hacer merced" (I want to honor him) (18).

When Juan Padilla comes to see Juan de Aragón, the latter does not directly refer to the former's suit, but says that the king wishes to honor him and that the king "dió también / A don Alvaro en respuesta / que aceptaba el memorial" (also gave Alvaro his reply that he accepted the petition) (19). He does not say, however, whose petition. Juan Padilla and Martín are thrilled and grateful. Juan Padilla wants to give Beatriz a gift but lacks the funds, so Martín suggests that since Juan de Aragón has been so helpful, "Dile tu mucha pobreza / Que no hará mucho si agora / Dos mil ducados te presta" (Tell him of your great poverty, and it would not be surprising if now he loans you two thousand ducats) (23).

Meanwhile Ana has heard that "Juan" has successfully asked the king for permission to marry Beatriz. Burning with jealousy, since she assumes that the Juan who will marry Beatriz is Juan Padilla, she swears to interrupt the marriage legally, "Que me quiero levantar / Un testimonio" (I want to make an accusation) (24) even if it means her loss of face and a public scandal. She calls on Alvaro to intervene on her behalf, subtly suggesting in her narrative that she and Juan Padilla consummated their love. In that story, she casts Juan Padilla as a latter-day Calisto and herself as Melibea: "Concertamos los dos que en una huerta, / Saltando las paredes de mi casa, / Entrase cierta noche" (We two arranged to meet in a garden; he would come in one night leaping over the walls around my house) (28) as she continues embellishing the scene with murmuring waters and aromatic flowers. When Alvaro tells her that she too has been confused by the shared name, Juan, and that Beatriz will marry Juan de Aragón, not Juan Padilla, Ana is mortified by her unnecessarily suggestive testimony. She quickly recants, "Hice este agravio á mi honor, / Celosa y desesperada, / Que no él de noche me vió, / Ni en tal huerta me ha burlado" (Out of jealousy and desperation I injured by honor, for he never saw me at night nor in any such garden did he seduce me) (30).

Juan Padilla bids loving goodby to Beatriz as does Martín to Leonor, Beatriz's maid, and they leave to accompany the king. Alvaro enters, congratulates his daughter, and invites Juan de Aragón in.

Beatriz, aghast, rejects him, to Alvaro's disgust. Her father states that with the king as go-between, Beatriz now has no choice in the matter.

When Juan and Martín return from their trip, Leonor tells them that Beatriz has been forced to accept Juan de Aragón's hand. Juan Padilla crudely asks, "¿Gozóla?" (Has he had sex with her?) (43), and Leonor recounts Beatriz's heroic and ongoing resistance: though she has been forced to accept the proposal, she has defended herself against any further action. Adding to Juan Padilla's depression, Ana enters and asks the "capitán gallardo" (gallant captain) for an embrace (44). Unable to contain himself, Juan Padilla responds with crude insults (44–45). Beatriz enters, explains the situation to Juan Padilla, and he threatens to kill Juan de Aragón. Beatriz, coolheaded, reminds Juan Padilla of how well-placed his rival is and tells him, no, "Pues con la espada es perderme, / Y con la pluma es ganarme" (You will lose me with the sword, whereas with the pen will you win me) (48); that is, we must now proceed by lawsuit. Ana overhears and promises to seek redress in the courts too.

Alvaro comes in to tell Beatriz that Juan de Aragón has returned since after she rejected him, he joined the king on his journey. Beatriz, insisting that Juan Padilla is her true husband, retires. Juan de Aragón enters to Alvaro's fond greeting, and they send a servant to fetch Beatriz. The servant returns with the news that she has left the house in a carriage surrounded by a group of men, namely, "notarios, y entre ellos / Pienso que iba un alguacil" (notaries, and among them I believe went a bailiff) (52). The legal battle has been joined. Though disheartened, Juan de Aragón remains convinced that his position, his wealth, and the king's favor will guarantee a decision in his favor. Sancho, his servant, agrees since "Favor y dineros son / Pies y manos de los pleitos" (Favor and money are the feet and hands of lawsuits) (53).

Juan Padilla speaks to the king recounting his past service and informing the monarch of the impending lawsuit and its causes. Juan de Aragón enters and says that he promised Juan Padilla nothing; moreover, he adds that since "Guerra es amor" (Love is war) (58), he just used a clever strategy to win. The king grants permission for the lawsuits to proceed, but Juan Padilla worries aloud that his lack of funds will work against his case: "Pienso / Que le perderé, señor, / Porque soy pobre y no tengo / Dinero para seguirle, / Que son menester dineros" (I believe that I will lose, sir, because I am poor and I have no money to pursue it, and money is necessary) (58). The king addresses Juan's problems and redresses his past forgetfulness: he makes Juan a knight with an income of six thousand ducats (58). Juan de Aragón, observing the king's actions, begins to wonder if his star is waning.

Ana and Alvaro console each other and Alvaro tells her of his plan. He will remarry; "que aún tiene bríos" (he still has vigor) (67), he assures her. He will produce an heir and cut off Beatriz and Juan Padilla. Ana adds to the plan, "Mas si queréis fingir el casamiento, / . . . / Publicad que os queréis casar conmigo, / Que yo diré lo mismo" (Well, if you want to feign a marriage. . . . Announce that you want to marry me, and I will say the same) (67), with which stratagem she hopes to make Juan Padilla both angry and jealous. She advises her elderly gallant, who animatedly declares his delight—"Yo voy contento, / Y lo fuera mejor si verdad fuera" (I leave happy, and I would be more so if it were true) (68)—to publicly ask the king for permission to marry her.

When Juan Padilla arrives, Martín advises him to be nice to Ana since they are already involved in a lawsuit and they need no more enemies. Martín, speaking for his reluctant master, says that he has no interest in Beatriz since she proved ungrateful and is promised to Juan de Aragón. As Juan seconds Martín's lie, Beatriz enters, overhears, and fumes. Juan Padilla swears that it was all a deception and despite her anger, she, Leonor, and the two men agree to work to block Alvaro's remarriage. But how? Beatriz wonders. With another lawsuit of course, Martín responds. He proposes that Leonor swear that Alvaro promised to marry her. To back up her claim, Martín will prove that Leonor is noble and that her petition is true.

The final act opens with the news that the first judgment has been in favor of Juan Padilla and Beatriz. Juan de Aragón and Ana join forces to get the former back in the king's graces and to get Ana out of her announced marriage to Alvaro, out of "la locura / Y desigual casamiento / Que con don Alvaro intento" (the madness and misalliance that I have planned with Alvaro) (78). To her surprise, the old man's intentions have proved more serious than she imagined, "Don Alvaro . . . procura / Su venganza á costa mía, / Pues me sepultaba un viejo" (Alvaro seeks his vengeance at my expense, for an old man is burying me) (78). Juan de Aragón tells Juan Padilla that the lawsuits can be dropped because he will marry Ana. Emphasizing the reversal of fortunes, Juan de Aragón now asks Juan Padilla to speak to the king on his behalf. He agrees only after chastizing Juan de Aragón for his earlier actions.

The king and his advisers converse about what virtues a nobleman should possess and all defer to the king's "Amor, pleito y desafío" (love, lawsuit, and duel) (86). Juan Padilla presents Juan de Aragón's request and the king agrees. Juan de Aragón enters and asks permission to return to his homeland, which the king grants.

Martín counsels Leonor about her upcoming testimony (89–92); Juan Padilla and Beatriz mend fences; and a servant enters with the news that Juan de Aragón has challenged Juan Padilla to a duel at the border between Castile and Aragon. The latter seeks the king's permission to go; the king grants his request; he then sends a party to arrest Juan de Aragón for breaking his order against fighting while the lawsuits were in progress. As the cast unites, Juan de Aragón says that he did not break the king's order since the lawsuits were effectively terminated, because he is marrying Ana and thus no appeals will be filed. Juan Padilla forgives Juan de Aragón; the king makes Juan Padilla a count; and with Alvaro's blessing Juan and Beatriz marry as do Juan de Aragón and Ana, Martín and Leonor.

The labyrinthine play with its plots and counterplots, suits and countersuits, may be analogous to the involuted legal system and shows that Lope was well aware of how lawsuits worked, how expensive they were, how complicated they could become, and how one suit often spawned others. Kagan (1981) points out that legal redress was not just in the purview of the nobility, but of commoners as well who were knowledgeable about the courts and quick to use them. Writing on the *fiel del juzgado* in the Toledo area, Kagan states that *labradores,* who constituted 10 to 15% of the local population, "figured prominently in the fiel's court, as both plaintiffs and defendants" (87). Lope could expect therefore any member of his audience to appreciate the legal atmosphere in his play. Kagan also shows how countersuit and appeal, both of which figure in Lope's play, were entered into "to force one's opponent either to abandon his case or to agree to a compromise out of court" (84). It seems clear, then, that Lope focuses this play on legal matters not only because of his own firsthand experience, but because of the litigious contexts of the period.

The character who best knows how to navigate the legal waters to advantage is Martín. He designs the plan to block Alvaro's marriage to Ana and thus to preserve Beatriz's inheritance. He acts, of course, out of personal interest: if his master's wife inherits Alvaro's wealth, he and she, and along with them, Martín and his beloved Leonor, will all prosper. Should Alvaro remarry, their future looks bleak. But how, Beatriz wonders, can they block the marriage since Alvaro is a widower and has the right to marry? The streetwise counselor, Martín, offers a two-pronged plan. First they will prove Leonor worthy to marry Alvaro, "probar que es hija de algo, / Y que viene su abolengo /

Del conde Fernán González" (prove that she is noble and that her ancestry goes back to count Fernán González) (75). To bring this about, Martín will hire "veinte testigos falsos" (twenty false witnesses) (75). When Juan Padilla innocently questions, "¿Falsos hay?" (Are there false ones?) Martín, and no doubt with him the audience responds, "Bueno es eso" (That's a good one) (75).

One of the areas where the *Chancellería* took special responsibility, Kagan (1981) states, was with *pleitos de hidalguía* (lawsuits about nobility) since such suits had social, economic, and political importance. Nobles, after all, were exempt from certain taxes and were expected to marry within their class. "As one might expect," Kagan reports, "considerable corruption was involved in these pleitos de hidalguía" (121). Not only did petitioners enter false patents, but more often "would-be nobles produced friends and relatives to testify on their behalf, and others were willing to pay local vecinos [some, apparently, semiprofessional witnesses] who would testify to their nobility" (121). Kagan cites Francisco de Castillo who, in 1592, writing about a specific case, says "all of the witnesses who took part are accustomed to give testimony in hidalguía cases for money . . . ; most are drunks and poor beggars" (121). Therefore, Martín's plan is more a reflection of reality than a comic device invented by the dramatist.

While the legal archives, Kagan says, can offer some small picture of how actual court proceedings moved, Lope paints a vivid, large canvas, especially in the scenes where Martín coaches Leonor on how to lie on the stand. He tells her not to get flustered when she sees the judge, but when he takes the judge's part in the mock trial he represents, Leonor is unnerved. "Haz cuenta que soy juez" (pretend that I am the judge) he tells her. "Pues no te pongas tan grave / Que el ánimo se me acabe, / Y me turbe alguna vez" (Well, don't look so serious because I will lose heart and get flustered again), she responds. Martín begins his examination of the litigant. What happened? he wants to know and Leonor begins:

> Señor, mis padres, que fueron
> Tan principales hidalgos,
> Que por la línea de varón,
> Descienden de Arias Gonzalo.
> Me trujeron á criar
> A su casa en tiernos años
> De Alvaro de Rojas.
>
> (90)

(Sir, my parents were such high nobles that in patrilineal line they descend from Arias Gonzalo. In my tender years, they brought me to nurse in Alvaro de Rojas's house.)

Martín interrupts, declaring that her testimony is all wrong and leaping on her word choice:

> ¿A criar dices que entraste?
> Pues si crías, ¿no está claro
> Que has parido, y que no puedes
> Pedir el doncellicato?
>
> (90)

(You say you came to nurse? Well if you are nursing, isn't it clear that you've already given birth and that you cannot claim virginity?)

Beatriz amends, "A criarme con Beatriz" (To nurse with Beatriz) (90), but then apparently pauses and gets upset because Martín prompts her, "Adelante y sin turbaros" (Go ahead and without getting flustered) (90).

She recounts how Alvaro entered her bedroom one night, grabbed her by the arms, and how she resisted. Martín interrupts once again coaching her at this dramatic moment in her testimony, "Llora agora" (Cry now) (90). Feigning tears, Leonor continues, but Martín breaks in once more to refine her gestures and to suggest just the right wording:

> Tápate los ojos
> Con el delantal, llorando,
> Y di ansí, mírame acá;
> En fin, el cruel tirano
> Me rindió, venció, violó.
>
> (91)

(Cover your eyes with your apron, crying. And speak thus, look at me; in short, the cruel tyrant overcame me, conquered me, raped me.)

Martín next takes the role of *escribano* (scribe), the person who prepares written testimony, the battery of briefs and notarized proofs required to file suit (for more on this and other roles, see Kagan's [1981] chapter "In the Cretan Labyrinth" 21–78). He advises her to lie about her age and recounts, as an example, a story about a seventy-year-old woman who swore she was thirty-four and that a young man raped her. In the example, Martín plays with legal language:

> Dijo que estando rezando,
> En su aposento una noche
> . . . .
> Entró el dicho y a la dicha
> Asió de los dichos brazos,
> Y con los dichos amores,
> El dicho doncellicato
> Desapareció de allí,
> La dicha sin él quedando,
> Y el dicho se fué.
>
> (91)

(She said that while she was in her room praying one night . . . the said [man] entered and opportunely seized the said arms, and with the said love the said virginity disappeared. The said [woman] was then left without him as the said [man] left.)

When Leonor expresses awe at "tantos dichos" (so many saids), Martín says "Son los tantos / Del juego de los procesos" (They are the so many of trial's games) (91–92). He calls on "esta confesante" (this one making a declaration) to continue, but Leonor has no idea he is speaking to her. When he exasperatedly clarifies, "Tú, Leonor, está en el caso: / Esta que declara dijo" (You, Leonor, pay attention: the one who is declaring said . . .) (92), poor Leonor still does not understand that he speaks to her. At the end of his rope, Martín declares, "Eres un mármol" (You are as thick as a brick) (92). He prompts her to testify if she has had any strange cravings lately or if she has felt any "Bulto ó hinchazón" (swelling or distention) (92), but before she can make up an answer, their masters enter and the scene closes.

Here we get some powerful insight into court proceedings, client-lawyer relations, witness coaching, legalistic language, and uses and abuses of both oral and written testimony. We see how judges' demeanor can intimidate witnesses and how they must prepare for the legal ordeal. We see how adept a lawyer can be at seizing upon a word carelessly used and turning it swiftly against a witness. We sense how prepared one must be, especially if she or he is to testify falsely. Lope's play, in many ways, offers a more vivid picture of court proceedings than do the archives.

Let me now turn back to Lope's two legal adventures I mentioned earlier. In the Elena Osorio case, Lope shot his mouth off, was caught in contradictory testimony, and was unprepared for the witnesses and evidence brought against him. In the later Marta de Nevares case, Lope held his tongue while Marta convinced the judges of Roque's alleged mistreatment. Lope then states how it amused him that a woman could prove being mistreated and being forced to sign a marriage contract. But, with the Martín/Leonor scenes in mind, we should remember that Marta was an accomplished actress and, obviously, Lope was a masterly scriptwriter. While we could never absolutely prove that the two colluded to produce a well-coached, well-scripted, false testimony, we might have to wonder, nonetheless, just how much of the scene in *Amor, pleito y desafío* was a product of Lope's rich imagination, and how much may have sprung from personal experience. Be that as it may, Lope surely appeals to the contemporary audience's beliefs and knowledge about legal proceedings and some of the shenanigans that can go on in trials.

One more scene merits attention though at first blush it seems to deal more with a discussion of noble virtues than with litigiousness. At one point in the play, the king, the Conde de Haro, Don Enrique, Don Pedro, and Juan Padilla discuss what qualities a noble should possess. The Conde de Haro says that such values can be reduced to two, "el consejo y la espada" (council and the sword) (85); that is to say, defend the kingdom and offer good advice and wise judgment when called upon to do so. Enrique recommends loyalty and the capacity to keep secrets; requirements, it would seem, for counsellors such as he who are privy to state matters. Pedro proposes "ser afable, / Humilde y comunicable / En la fortuna mayor" (to be affable, humble, and sharing in great fortune) (85), that is to say, good social manners. Juan Padilla adds temperance and patience, for these are the values by which God judges men. Martín uninvitedly adds his voice to the conversation promoting generosity.

The virtues these men proclaim, then, are valor, wisdom, service, loyalty, generosity, humility, temperance, a combination of some of the cardinal virtues and traditional values. The king listens patiently and then says that what they have proposed is all well and good, but he did not have such a philosophic response in mind, "no fué mi intento llegar / A virtudes generosas" (it was not my intent to reach such liberal virtues) (86); rather he sought more practical and immediate qualities. When his nobles wonder what the values are, Alfonso responds, "Amor, pleito y desafío" (love, lawsuits, and duel) (86). While Lope is obviously using the king as a mouthpiece to underscore the title of his play, the fact remains that Alfonso stresses the practical over the abstract, and central—literally—to those values is *pleito*.

Golden Age Castillian society has regularly been presented as hierarchical, rigidly ordered, and estate-dominated, and there is little doubt that allegiance to class and caste was the norm. But it is also true that this society was, as Kagan (1981) states, "an amalgam of hundreds of small corporate groups and communities held together only loosely by common economic circumstances, legal privileges, and shared allegiances to the Church and the Spanish crown" (18). Perhaps more important on a day-to-day basis than the general alliances to God and country were those close personal ties to family, both immediate and extended, to parish, guild, village, region, and confraternity where loyalty and fraternity mark each member. While each small group was more than prepared to defend its interests against encroachment from "outsiders," solidarity and fidelity among comrades was required. When disputes arose within these communities, "compromise was the ideal, and an arbitrated settlement within the confines of the community was the prefered mechanism for ending disputes. In contrast, lawsuits . . . were thought to disrupt normal workings of the community" (18).

Represented in *Amor, pleito y desafío* is the microsociety that surrounds the king, a microsociety teetering on the edge of entropy. In the play, lawsuits arise and multiply among members of this small group wherein cohesion would be the sought-for and expected characteristic, and in which dissension and legal squabbling would not only be unseemly, but fractious. In the play, noble sues noble, a well-placed man expects a favorable outcome because of his political position, daughter sues father, maid sues master.

Among the reasons that lawsuits were despised by many in this period was that they were considered un-Christian. Juan de Mariana likens them to the unjust oppression of the weak by the strong. Alamos de Barrientos "writing early in the seventeenth century, went even further: he classified lawsuits along with crime, vice, and luxury as 'public evils' fomented by human envy and greed that ought to be eradicated from Castile" (Kagan 1981, 17). The notion that lawsuits were anti-Christian came, as Kagan reminds us, from Saint Augustine's "condemnation of this particular legal instrument as a symbol of discord in the earthly city. The lawsuit epitomized man's inherent sinfulness and served as proof positive of his lack of good will, justice, and simple Christian charity" (18). Popular sentiment against lawyers, scribes, and other court functionaries was legend as proverbial expressions and many poems attest.

Lawsuits against close relatives or against members of what should be a tight-knit group were tantamount to war. With such suits, the covenants that held the community together shattered while affiliation, courtesy, cooperation, and respect were replaced by contentiousness, intrigue, and insolence. Many longed for a return to some utopian age of peace and civility wherein the ordered society would once again reign, but the proliferation of lawsuits signaled the end of such dreams. As Kagan observes, "[T]he tide of litigation was symptomatic of a society in which the traditional bonds of loyalty and fraternity were weakening as a result of the numerous changes—demographic, economic, social, legal, and political—that rapid growth and development . . . had engendered" (20).

In *Amor, pleito y desafío,* the king stands curiously aloof from the lawsuits as his nobles go at one another with a vengeance. He acquiesces to their suits, demonstrates only passing curiosity at their progress, and remains ignorant of their outcome. When he does intervene by arresting Juan de Aragón for treason, he discovers that his actions may not hold up because of a legal technicality. As Juan Padilla and Juan de Aragón argue out their positions before him, it is only through Juan Padilla's "noble generosity" that the projected *desafío* (duel) is rendered null. To the king's offer, "yo tomo en mi palabra / Real, el honor de entrambos" (I take the honor of both under the protection of my royal word) (114), Juan Padilla tells the king, "Dalde á don Juan [de Aragón], pues se casa / Con mi prima [Ana], gran señor, / El título que me daban / Esas manos generosas" (Give Juan [de Aragón], since he is marrying my cousin [Ana], noble lord, the title that your generous hands were giving me) (115). Yet this is the same man who just a few scenes before quietly and ungenerously acquiesced to Martín's projected lawsuit against his future father-in-law, a lawsuit replete with false accusations, false testimony, and false witnesses. This play, then, may stand as both a moralistic message on how far society has fallen and as a telling comment about what one has to know how to do in order to survive in the "modern" world. In any case, *Amor, pleito y desafío,* with "lawsuit" as central, is a sign of the times.

5

Comedy and the Self

In 1957, Alexander A. Parker published what may be the single best-known piece on Golden Age theater, *The Approach to the Spanish Drama of the Golden Age.* At the close, he summarizes the five principles that govern all Spanish *comedia:*

> (1) the primacy of action over character drawing; (2) the primacy of theme over action, with the consequent irrelevance of realistic verisimilitude; (3) dramatic unity in the theme and not in the action; (4) the subordination of theme to moral purpose through the principle of poetic justice . . . ; (5) the elucidation of moral purpose by means of dramatic causality. (27)

Parker insists that character is of least interest in *comedia:*

> The generic characteristic of the Spanish drama is, of course, the fact that it is essentially a drama of action and not of characterization. It does not set out to portray rounded and com-

plete characters. . . . This does not mean that characters are unimportant. What it does mean is that since the dramatists are out to present, within a strict limitation of time, an action that is full of incident, they generally have no time to elaborate their characters, and must confine characterization to brief touches. They left it to the audience and the actors to fill in, from these brief hints and touches, the psychology of the characters. (3–4)

The lowering of expectations about character responds to a series of conditions. In the mid-1950s, New Criticism was the theory of choice. As we all know, the New Critics attempted to free a work from entangling alliances with authors, history, politics, economics, sociology, and the rest in the belief that by so doing the work could be studied in terms of its own coherent structures and unities, which, in turn, could teach across time the great moral lessons of human existence to any sensitive and well-trained reader. Since characters in the plays are frequently enmeshed in the linguistic, social, cultural, economic, and legal doings of their time and place—referring as they do to geographical place, current events, streets, buildings, people, style, debt, lawsuits, and so forth—it was politic in a New Critical approach to diminish interest in such matters.

Moreover, implicit in Parker's approach is a reevaluation, through inverted comparison, of Spanish drama. Spanish drama is different; different, that is, from Shakespearean drama and from realistic drama as well. He says that by comparing *comedia* with the latter, "This tendency to associate significance with realism—a tendency we owe to the eighteenth and nineteenth centuries—is something we must abandon if we are to understand the Spanish drama" (6). Spanish drama is different and part of that difference lies in its indifference to realistic action and character drawing. In Shakespearean drama, traditionally speaking, the towering, "rounded" figures of Lear, Macbeth, Hamlet, and others are among the greatest accomplishments. In Spanish drama, Parker replies, what counts more is the elucidation of great moral principles because Shakespeare's drama is Reformation/Protestant drama, Spain's is Counter-reformation/Catholic. In the former, focus falls on individual responsibility; in the latter, on shared values and shared responsibility. In the former, individual character is magnified; in the latter, group beliefs are prominent (see his comments on *Romeo and Juliet* 9–10).

I am not going to argue against Parker's position; to some degree he was right. The characters in *comedia* are not "rounded and complete"—but then I do not think that Prospero is either. On the other hand, I do not believe them to be mere papier-mâché mouthpieces for an overarching moral message. The main characters are rarely of a single piece, rarely simply products; rather, they are characters in process. They have conflicting opinions about the situations they find themselves in, and regularly express "rebellious" attitudes toward what may be termed received social or cultural imperatives. Often they go against their father's or society's wishes; they do not automatically or unquestioningly accept the role others would cast them in. In a word, many resist.

It would be utterly silly to see *comedia*'s characters as flesh-and-blood human beings, but then the chances of running into Perdita near Bohemia's coast are quite slim too. While I do think that the dramatists give the audience more than "brief touches" around which they are supposed to construe a psychology, I must note here my agreement with Parker about the active and constitutive role played by the actors and the audience in amplifying the concept of character. This seems to be one of the few times that Parker refers to the material conditions of theater. The choice of an actor or an actress to represent a character would add immeasurably to the written text. The actor or actress has physical presence, bodily form, speech characteristics including tone, intonation, accent, and timbre which, along with costume, gesture, and movement, could automatically modify whatever mental image one might form simply by reading a text. In fact, the "right" or "wrong" actor or actress could make or break a play. Tirso, for example, complains loudly about the debut in Toledo of his *Don Gil de las calzas verdes*,[1] and the reaction caused by the actress in the lead role. In *Los cigarrales de Toledo,* Don Melchor, while listing the causes of a play's poor reception says:

> La segunda causa de perderse una comedia es lo mal que le entalla el papel el representante. ¿Quién ha de sufrir, por extremada que sea, ver que habiéndose su dueño desvelado en pintar una dama hermosa, muchacha, y con tan gallarda talle que vestida de hombre persuada y enamore a la más melindrosa de la Corte, salga a hacer esta figura una del infi-

---

1. Gordon Minter (Tirso 1991), in his introduction to his edition and translation, says, "It was a flop. How could it have been otherwise, Tirso laments, when Valdés [the actor-manager of the rep company] had cast his overweight middle-aged wife as the quicksilver young Doña Juana, who masquerades in drag as the dashing young lover Don Gil" (15).

erno, con más carnes que un antruejo, más años que un solar de
la montaña y más arrugas que una carga de repollos, y que se
enamore la otra y le diga: "¡ay, qué don Gilito de perlas! ¡Es un
brinco, un dix, un juguete del amor . . . !" (340)

(The second cause for a comedy's failure is for an actor not to be
suited for the role. Who would put up with seeing a lover take
great pains in portraying a beautiful, young lady with an elegant shape, and who, dressed as a man, could convince and
enamour the most finicky woman in the court, and then the
person who comes out in the role is hellish, fatter than a Carnival clown, older than an ancestral home in the mountains, and
more wrinkled than a load of cabbages, and then to have a lady
fall in love with her and say, "Oh, what an exquisite little Gil!
He is a jewel, an adornment, a love toy.)

The relations between characters and their circumstances are complex, and parallel, insofar as the plays' brevity permits, the relations
between an individual and her or his circumstances. These plays present the social self enmeshed in personal circumstances involving
love, hate, marriage, fathers and children, as well as economics, politics, class, law, duty and desire, and many of the material circumstances of life without any one of these being the character's sole preoccupation. Many of these matters enter the warp and woof of the
play as hints that audience members can use to fill in the character,
as Parker said, but to fill in around the character as well, to catch a
glimpse of her or his world and compare or contrast that world with
their own. The plays show the characters reacting to their circumstances, and since those circumstances overlap to some degree with
the audience's circumstances (the play may take place in and require
a working knowledge of Madrid; the play may concern relations between men, between women, and between men and women; the play
may show men seeking position and advancement in the court, and so
forth), the audience may look at how those characters imaginatively
solve their problems and then compare what they did to what they
might do. In many of the comedies, that is exactly what moralists
feared.

Before turning to particular characters in particular works, I shall
briefly review what some writers have said about "the self." It is not
an easy matter to discuss the subject or individual or person since all
these terms are overdetermined and charged with ideological content.
Marx, for example, rejects the term "individual" as part of the fiction

created by capitalist ideology—the myth of the free, unified, whole, determining agent. For Marx, true individuality cannot exist in the alienated and alienating state under capitalism since conditions alienate and smother people under the weight of material circumstances and capitalist ideology. Subjectivity or real individualism is possible, in theory, but only after the overthrow of the system and the (re-)installation of socialism/communism. Until then, false consciousness reigns.

Althusser rejects the notion of false consciousness because, he argues, ideology has material existence and constructs subjects for particular social formations. Ideology is a kind of glue that holds societies together and thus is inescapable and constitutive of subjects. As subjects are interpellated by/for an ideology through the functioning of ideological state apparatuses, subjects become bearers of the relations that make up social formations. But "subject" too is ambiguous. On the one side, the term connotes activity and control, agency, and to that degree is equal to individual; on the other, certainly as Foucault uses the term, it connotes "sub-jected," dominated by rules or forces beyond its control and thus approximates object (see Paul Smith 1988, xxxiii–xxv). Some have argued that Althusser's formulation is mechanistic and leaves little room for resistance or agency, but what is valuable in Althusser's formulation is the role of interpellation and subject construction through ideological operations.

For Jacques Lacan, ideology is part of the Symbolic—but only part, for the Symbolic is never reducible to the ideological. Lacan differentiates the subject from someone. The subject is created in the realm of the signifier and thus can be considered an attribute of a real being. While for Freud, the unconscious was a "mechanistic place where repressed memories and attitudes were relegated to a memory bank of ideational thing-representations attached to instinctual drives" (Ragland-Sullivan 1991, 98), for Lacan, there is no originary unconscious; rather everything in the unconscious gets there through symbolization. The unconscious destabilizes the conscious drive toward constancy since it overdetermines everything. Lacan locates the unconscious between "consciousness and perception, between Desire and language . . . and it shows up sporadically in dreams and daily discourse" (100). The unconscious lies at the edge of where the subject and the Symbolic cojoin. From my perspective, what this topology gains us is a space for agency and resistance since through constant mediation and interference of the unconscious, the Symbolic—and thus ideology—cannot be totally imposed, mechanistically, on a person.

Each aspect of a particular culture has, to some degree, its own structure and, with it, the potential to subject a person. Whether we refer to gender, language, law, economics, politics, family relations, dress code, diet, literature or whatever, each of these can exert an influence on a person. Given that, I shall speak of subject positions that each person can adopt. The person continually negotiates her or his relations to the world from within and among a number of possible subject positions; with the mediation of the unconscious, individual attitudes within any given subject position may demonstrate considerable or little variance. The person, considered thus, is indeed a process, not a product; split, not unitary. She or he is interpellated by language and ideology yet capable of resistance, subject to drives, yet constrained by cultural and historical givens all at the same time. I contend that in the creation of the main characters, the authors imitate, to the degree possible in a three-act play, these divisions; thus, while the characters never achieve the complexity of real people, they do advance significantly beyond the stage of development Parker could grant them. As they negotiate their relations to the dramatic world from a number of subject positions, they alternately fall in line with and push against the imperatives and impulses that configure them.

Ellie Ragland-Sullivan (1991) merges thoughts about the self with an exploration of the relations between men and women; and since all of these plays deal with both the self and its sexual relations, among many other topics, I now briefly (and admittedly, flatly) summarize Ragland-Sullivan's thoughts. She separates the masculine position (not equal to any given male or female) from the feminine position (again, not coterminous with any given female or male) as they relate to knowledge and to the "dividing effect created by learning difference as gender difference" (71). Since such learning is through language and culture, she asserts that Lacan has rewritten Freud's family romance "away from the family qua family . . . [and toward] cultural constructs and language conventions" (69–70). The phallic signifier is what "delineates difference from sameness, order from chaos, law from nature" (50). Men and women alike "inscribe themselves under the phallic signifier which structures identity on the basis of differential identifications . . . masculine and feminine traits characterize both sexes, ensuring that there be no pure feminine and masculine essence" (51). Gender identifications are necessary, nonetheless, to provide the (illusory) basis for one's being, to allow subjects to cohere. If the masculine position is allied mythically with law, logic, reason, the visible, the provable, the feminine position is cast in terms of enigma, "shadows, desire, and dreams" (73). The feminine, then, links with metonomy, the masculine with metaphor. "Men and women," she writes, "are duped into believing strange and persistent myths: that man is 'it' (the bearer of knowledge as truth) and Woman has 'it' (truth that yields itself up) as a beyond in knowledge" (72–73). Thus while man speaks believing he is whole, believing that he knows, woman "speaks because she is not-all, because she knows, even if she denies this knowledge, that something is missing in knowledge *qua* knowledge. She knows there is no totality, not even of the feminine or masculine. She speaks on and through her body, in a voice irreducible to grammar, and from a body that never ceases to pose questions about desire, whether she be nubile, pregnant, a sex bomb, or old and withered" (77); whether she be, I would add, Angela or Celestina.

Relations between men and women are not only problematical but must be constantly negotiated if they are to work at all. Most theories of comedy, focusing as they do on the conventional marriages in the final scene, seem to posit marriage as the solution to all problems. In his study of Shakespeare, Terry Eagleton (1986) suggests as much positing his idealized view of marriage:

> Marriage is not an arbitrary force which coercively hems in desire, but reveals its very inward structure—what desire, if only it had known, had wanted all the time. When you discover your appropriate marriage partner you can look back, rewrite your autobiography and recognize that all your previously coveted objects were in fact treacherous, displaced parodies of the real thing, shadows of true substance. This, broadly speaking, is the moment of the end of the comedies. Marriage is natural, in the sense of being the outward sign or social role which expresses your authentic inward being, as opposed to those deceitful idioms that belie it. It is the true language of the erotic self, the point at which the spontaneity of individual feeling and the stability of public institutions harmoniously interlock. . . . As such, marriage is the organic society in miniature (20–21).[2]

2. This is an interesting passage in light of Eagleton's other writings, even in light of other things he says in this book. Here he posits a kind of Platonic vision of the beloved, who contrasts with the "shadows," marriage as a true language, and institutional stability. There is an essentializing going on here that contrasts with what he elsewhere teaches us, about the nature and truth value of language, the instability of institutions, the "naturalness" of culture and cultural practices, and the "end of histo-

Such a perfect dovetailing between man and woman might possibly occur if each partner could totally fuse herself or himself with the received, prescribed roles a society lays down for what is male and what female. Such a marriage Ragland-Sullivan (1991) terms "the charade of the happy couple . . . the social bond *par excellence*" (58). In such a union both the normative woman and man would "bow to patriarchal mythology in accepting to live by the masquerade of a master discourse: 'I am what I am' [*soy quien soy*]; / 'A man is a man'; / 'A woman is a woman.'" (58). Total acceptance leaves no room for friction or resistance.

There are plays from this period, like *El premio del bien hablar* and *El astrólogo fingido,* wherein such fusing of self and role approximates totalization. At the end of *Examen de maridos,* to mention another example, Inés accepts the men's explanations of all of the problems she has encountered and "caused," gives one of them her hand, and declares "La vida os debo" (I owe you my life) (2987), thereby reaffirming the traditional hierarchical relation. At the beginning of the play, she likewise accepted her father's and society's law that, given who and what she is, who and what she must be, she must marry. Her maid explains, "forzoso es, / señora, tomar estado; / que en su casa has sucedido, / y una mujer principal / parece en la corte mal / sin padres y sin marido" (It is necessary, madam, to marry; you are the heir to your house, and a principal lady without parents or husband looks bad in the court) (3–8). Both the Marqués and Conde Carlos reaffirm their masculine roles since, in the end, they prize male values over all and since each sees in the other what he wants, and wants others, to see in himself. So esteemed are these values and their mutually dependent and reinforcing roles that Carlos declares of his mirror image, the Marqués, "que el mundo todo ha de ver / que nadie se ha de atrever / a quien tal amigo tiene" (the whole world must see that no one can challenge whoever has such a friend) (2415–17). As the play ends, the Marqués draws both his friend and his future wife together to express the hierarchical relation: "Sois mi amigo verdadero, / y vos mi esposa querida" (You are my true friend, and you my beloved wife) (3001–2). You, Carlos, are another like me;

---

ry"—"rewrite your autobiography," etc. This portrayal of marriage stops all change like the curtain that falls at the end of plays, prohibiting speculation about the characters' future, perhaps for fear of falling into the Lady Macbeth's–children routine. What if one has no choice about the marriage partner? What if one never finds the "appropriate" one? What if what is appropriate today is not appropriate ten years hence? Once married, do people never change? Or do they always change at the same rate and in the same ways? Is there a "true language" even of the erotic self? Can desire end?

you, Inés, are the other I possess. You, Carlos, are truth; you, Inés, are the end/goal of sexual desire.

In several of the comedies from this period, the woman's view of the man seems to be expansive while the man's view of the woman tends to the reductive. Angela, in *La dama duende*, rejects Beatriz's characterization of Manuel as an obtuse male (252a); whereas Manuel spends all his time trying to pigeonhole the protean Angela (see 249a, 254a, 260a, 264b). In the play, from Manuel's perspective, Angela is the source of and answer to enigma and chaos. On the other hand, Angela tries continually to show Manuel that she is not just this or that, but rather all he can imagine and more. At the end of the play, however, despite Angela's valiant attempts, Manuel just cannot seem to grasp all of her qualities; he accepts marriage to her based not so much on who and what she may be as on what and who he must be in the social, cultural circumstances in which he finds himself. In other plays, for the female leads, the rank or financial condition of the man she loves matters less than the other more personal qualities she has come to discover in him; thus she often rejects her father's advice on marriage. For several of the men, however, the woman is little more than her *dote* (dowry). In *El hombre pobre todo es trazas,* Diego sees Clara precisely in those terms, "Doña Clara, / que éste es el nombre feliz / de la dama del dinero" (Clara, this is the happy name of the lady with money) (205b). At the beginning of *La celosa de sí misma,* Melchor too views Magdalena as a rich purse. The woman's role in such a view is to enrich the man and their family. Fray Luis de León spells out his thoughts about a woman's role in *La perfecta casada* (The perfect wife):

> . . . Pues dice agora el Espíritu Santo que la primera parte y la primera obra con que la mujer casada se perfecciona, es con hacer a su marido confiado y seguro que, teniéndola a ella para tener su casa abastecida y rica no tiene necesidad de correr la mar, ni de ir a la guerra, ni de dar sus dineros a logro, ni de enredarse en tratos viles e injustos, sino que con labrar él sus heredades, cogiendo su fruto, y con tenerla a ella por guarda y por beneficiadora de lo cogido." (34)

> (. . . Since the Holy Spirit now says that the first responsibility and the first job with which the married woman can make herself perfect is to make her husband confident and safe since, having her to maintain his home well provisioned and rich, he has no need to venture over the sea, nor go to war, nor lend

money, nor involve himself in vile or unjust deals; rather, he need only plow his own fields, reap its fruit, and have her as guardian and beneficiary of what he reaps.)

Women should bring their gifts to the marriage and work to increase those gifts:

> A los demás títulos que, siendo esta doctrina de Dios, habemos dado a la buena mujer, añadimos agora éste: que sea adelantadora de su hacienda. . . . Y así decir que compró heredamiento y que plantó viña del sudor de su mano es avisarle que es no sólo bastecer su casa, sino también adelantar su proveído, sino hacer también que se acrecienten en número los bienes.

> (To the other titles, this being God's doctrine, that we must give to the good woman, we now add this one: that she be the promoter of his fortune. . . . And so when we say that he bought an estate and planted vineyards with the sweat of his hands is to advise her . . . not only to provision his house but also to improve what he provided, and also to increase his goods.)

Luis de León, however, seriously circumscribed woman:

> Y pues no las dotó Dios ni del ingenio que piden los negocios mayores, ni de fuerzas las que son menester para la guerra y el campo, cuídanse con lo que son y conténtese con lo que es de su parte, y entiendan en su casa y anden en ella, pues las hizo Dios para ella sola. Los chinos, en naciendo, les tuercen a las niñas los pies, porque cuando sean mujeres no los tengan para salir fuera, y porque, para andar en su casa, aquéllos torcidos les bastan. Como son los hombres para lo público, así las mujeres para el encerramiento; y como es de los hombres el hablar y el salir a la luz, así dellas el encerrarse y encubrirse. (130)

> (Since God did not endow women with the skills for business nor the strength for war or for working the fields, let them take good care of what they are and content themselves with their role, and concern themselves with their home and take care of it since God made them for it alone. The Chinese, when girls are born, wrap their feet so that when they are women, they may not use them to go out, and because, to get about in the house, those deformed feet are good enough. As men are made

for public affairs, women are for staying in the home; and as it is for men to speak and to venture out, so for women is seclusion and concealment.)

Luis de León writes prescriptively because the world around him, even then, was changing; he admits that such women as he describes are increasingly hard to find, "Es dificultosa hallarla y son pocas las tales" (It is difficult to find her and there are few like that) (24). In many of these plays, the woman's actions, as she critically examines and works within her circumstances, might have made the Salamancan professor wonder what had happened.

I look briefly first at how some of the women, then how some of the men, find space for resistance within which to renegotiate the self. I shall begin with *La celosa de sí misma,* a play already discussed in Chapter 1, to which I refer my reader for filling out the plot. Magdalena is subject to a number of conditions that provoke splits in her character. She is the daughter of a *perulero,* Alonso, who served as a government official abroad, made a lot of money, tired of his work, returned to Madrid, and now seeks to marry his daughter to the noble but poor son of an old friend from León. Jerónimo, Alonso's son, explains to Sebastián:

> Tengo un padre perulero,
> Que de gobiernos cansado,
> Treguas ofrece al cuidado,
> Y empleo a su dinero.
> Ciento y cincuenta mil pesos
> Trae aquí con que casar
> Una hija, en quien lograr
> Intereses y sucesos
> Que en Indias le hicieron rico.
> (129a)

(My father is recently returned from Peru tired of governorships, seeking respite from responsibility, and proper use for his money. He brings one hundred and fifty thousand pesos here with which to marry off his daughter in whom to further the investments and events that made him rich in the Indies.)

He seeks to marry her to Melchor, rather than to a local noble, because "maridos cortesanos / Son traviesos y livianos" (courtly husbands are dissolute and fickle) (129b).

Since Alonso is wealthy, he can defend the arranged marriage as different from the normal arranged marriage in which fathers "sell" their daughters for gold. Simultaneously, he praises himself as a virtuous man:

> No quiero yo más hacienda
> Que la heredada virtud
> Que miro en su juventud.
> El padre avariento venda
> Al oro la libertad
> De sus hijas; que el valor
> De tu esposo Don Melchor,
> Y la ley de mi amistad,
> Juzga por más oportuna
> La sangre que la riqueza.
> (134b)

(I want no more wealth than the inherited virtue that I see in his [Melchor's] youth. Let the avaricious father sell his daughters' freedom for gold; for the worth of your husband Melchor and the law of friendship judges blood more valuable than wealth.)

However, Magdalena's role in the exchange differs little from her sisters': she is a commodity to be sold or bartered, if not for gross material wealth, then for less tangible though no less important social gain. Magdalena's marriage to Melchor represents, in part, for Alonso an effort to recoup what he lost by his financially beneficial tour in the Indies, namely, reputation.

Indianos were assumed to be rich, stingy, guardians of their hard-won wealth, and generally suffered from a poor reputation. People like Melchor, on the other hand, coming as he does from León, or las Montañas, were seen as noble by definition. Lope states in *El premio del bien hablar*, "Para noble nacimiento, / Hay en España tres partes: / Galicia, Vizcaya, Asturias, / O las Montañas se llamen" (For a noble birth, there are three places in Spain: Galicia, Biscay, Asturias, or the Mountains as they call them) (1251a). In *Don Quijote* we read, "Hidalgo como el rey, porque era montañés" (as noble as the king because he was from the mountains) (2:48). Herrero García (1963) adds that people believed that there, in the mountains of León, "no había llegado la mezcla de sangre judía o mora; allí se conservaba, juntamente con la fe antigua, la sangre antigua y la vida impertur-

bada de los antiguos godos" (the mixing of Jewish or Moorish blood
never got there: there they preserved, along with the ancient faith,
the ancient blood and unperturbed life of the ancient Goths) (228).
But their other characteristic is their poverty:

> La nobleza de las Montañas fue ganada por armas y conser-
> vada con servicios hechos a los reyes; y no se han de manchar
> con hacer oficios bajos; que allá, con lo poco que tienen, se sus-
> tentan, pasando lo peor que pueden, conservando las leyes de
> hidalguía, que es andar rotos y descosidos con guantes y calzas
> atacadas (Herrero García 1963, 232–33).

> (The nobility of the Mountains was earned by arms and pre-
> served by service to the kings; they must not stain themselves
> by doing lowly jobs; for there, with what little they have, they
> maintain themselves, getting by as best they can, preserving
> the laws of nobility, that is to say they go about ragged and
> unstitched with their gloves and hose sewn together poorly.)

In *Por el sótano y el torno*, Mari Ramírez states, "Heredé / limpieza de
la montaña / y pobreza juntamente" (I inherited purity of the mountains and poverty together) (572a). In *La celosa de sí misma*, Melchor
complains of having to marry for money. When Ventura quizzes him
about the *tapada* (veiled woman) he has fallen in love with, Melchor
defends his choice of the unseen woman over Magdalena. When Ventura asks what he will do if the *tapada* (veiled woman) turns out to be
poor, Melchor responds, "Llevarémela a León, / Y con ella en quieta
vida, / Al yugo de amor atado, / Daré dueño a mi familia, / Señora a
mi herencia corta, / Y a mi padre nuera y hija" (I will take her with
me to León, and with her in a quiet life, harnessed to love's yoke; I
will give a mistress to my family, a mistress to my small inheritance,
and a daughter-in-law and daughter to my father), to which the servant snorts, "¡Buena vejez le acomodas!" (You are preparing a won-
derful old age for him!) (136b).

Magdalena approaches marriage to Melchor with trepidation
(133c). She complains of her father's procedures and of her involun-
tary role in the arrangements. In addition her doubts and hesitation
have been increased by meeting the attractive and gallant man who
approached her in church that very morning. She can only hope, she
says, that Melchor can approximate the qualities she saw in the
stranger. When Quinones offers the possibility that Melchor could be
even better, Magdalena scoffs, "¿Cómo será eso posible? / ¡Tan cortés

urbanidad! / ¡Tanta liberalidad, / Y sazón tan apacible . . . !" (How can
that be possible? What urbane courteousness! What generosity and
gentle maturity!) and then tellingly adds, "No era digna della yo" (I
was not worthy of it) (134a).

Magdalena seems to have a low opinion of herself as the play opens.
She offers herself as the nervous but passive participant in the exchange, as bartered merchandise, as dutiful daughter subject to her
father's will; perhaps, since her father is a *perulero,* she feels somehow unworthy. When Sebastián and his sister, Angela, enter, Magdalena, perhaps as part of an effusive greeting to the upstairs neighbors who have never entered her quarters, perhaps not, once more
stresses her lower status now in relation to the lovely Angela, "Casa
en que tal dueño mora, / Es digna de estimar, / Y mas el ofrecimiento
/ Con que esta merced me hacéis / Cuando en mí, señora, veis / Tan
corto merecimiento" (A house wherein such an owner resides is worthy of praise, and even more the offer you make me with the favor
you do me when in me, madam, you see such little merit) (134a).
Then when the beautiful Angela expresses her thoughts on marriage,
"¡Jesús! Delante de un cura / . . . / . . . ¿ha de haber / tan atrevida
mujer, / Que le diga a un hombre: sí? / . . . / ¡Jesús! Quien hace tal
cosa / O es muy libre y animosa, / O no tiene mucho seso" (Jesus!
Before a priest . . . can there a woman so bold as to say yes to a man?
Jesus! Whoever would do such a thing is either very brash or brave or
is not very bright) (134b), Magdalena's worries at such a tension-
filled moment in her life could not but increase as her self-esteem
falls even more.

When Magdalena sees that Melchor is the stranger she saw in
church, Quinoñes is certain that her mistress must be thrilled, "¿Hay
suerte como la tuya? / ¡Que el primer hombre que quieres / Sea tu
esposo! ¡Dichosa eres!" (Is there anyone as lucky as you? That the first
man you love will be your husband! How lucky you are!) (135a). But
instead of ecstasy, Magdalena experiences very mixed emotions. She
loves him, she says, for "Su gentileza, valor, / Talle, liberalidad, /
Discreción, gracia y amor" (his elegance, worth, shape, generosity,
discretion, grace, and love) (135b), all of which she observed as *tapada*
(veiled woman); but other thoughts bother her. While she might seek
such qualities in a suitor, marriage is a very serious matter, thus she
wonders:

> . . .¿con qué seguridad
> Rendiré mi voluntad
> A quien, con tan fácil fe,
> La primer mujer que ve

Triunfa de su voluntad?
Hombre que a darme la mano
Viene aquí desde León,
Y es tan mudable y liviano.
Que a la primera ocasión,
Liberal y cortesano,
A un manto rinde despojos
Y a una mano el alma ofrece,
¿No quieres que me dé enojos?
Quien así se desvanece,
Y sin penetrar sus ojos
Lo que, por no ver, ignora,
Se suspende y enamora,
Exagera y sutiliza . . .
¿Qué satisfacción daré
A quien por dueño le espera?
¿O quién me asegurará
De voluntad tan lijera,
Que, desposado, no hará
Lo mismo con cuantas mire,
Y yo con él mal casada,
Quejas al alma retire,
Llore mi hacienda gastada,
Y sus mudanzas suspire?
                                    (135c)

(with what security will I surrender my will to whom, so easily
lets the first woman he sees triumph over his will? A man who
comes here from León to give me his hand and is so fickle and
inconstant that at the first opportunity, generous and fawning,
gives all he has to a cloak and offers his soul to a hand,
shouldn't that make me angry? Who is so crazy, without even
seeing what he doesn't know, as to admire and love, praise and
glorify? . . . How can I excuse that in the person I expect to be
my husband? Or who can assure me that since he has such a
flighty will that after he is married, he will not do the same
thing with all the women he sees, and I, poorly married to him,
will quietly complain to my self, will weep for my lost fortune,
and will sigh over his inconstancy?)

In this lengthy quote, Magdalena presents a number of important
concerns. First, even though Melchor is from León, he appears as
fickle and faithless as any man from Madrid she might have met.

Second, given the foregoing, if she marries him, she may regret her choice since he may simply take her money and spend it on other women. Third, Melchor has fallen in love with a woman he literally cannot see. His inability, or refusal, to look beyond the surface bodes ill for her future. Thus she decides to test him.

Magdalena is a split character working at cross-purposes. At the church, she tells Melchor that she knows all about Magdalena. She refuses to let him see her face because she knows "Que vuestro deseo me pinta / Mas bella de lo que soy, / Y temo perder la estima / En que estoy, imaginada, / Cuando no la iguale, vista" (That your desire paints me prettier than I am, and I fear losing the esteem in which, as imagined, I am, when seen, I do not live up to it) (137b). In this insightful passage, Magdalena understands completely the power of desire, Melchor's blindness, and the dominion of the fantasy ideal. As she says, were she simply to show him that she is the *tapada* (veiled lady), in no way could she live up to the image Melchor has painted in his own mind. Thus, as *tapada,* she demands that he abandon the arranged marriage and leave Magdalena's house (137c). At this point the invention of the "Countess of Chirinola" enters. When Melchor hears her addressed so, he astonishedly asks, "¿Condesa, mi bien? (Countess, my love?), to which she responds "Creed, / . . . / Lo que os esté bien en eso." (Believe . . . what is best for you about that) (138c). Her open response permits Melchor to add yet one more level to his fantasy creation, thereby alienating him even further from Magdalena.

Once at home, Magdalena has a long conversation with Quinoñes detailing the splits and divisions in herself and in her circumstances:

> Esto pasa: yo, Quinoñes,
> Soy amada aborrecida,
> Desdeñada y pretendida:
> ¡Mira mis contradicciones!
> Cubierta, doy ocasiones
> A su pasión amorosa;
> Vista soy fea y odiosa
> Enamoro y desobligo;
> Y compitiendo conmigo,
> De mí misma estoy celosa . . .
> Porque me adora, le adoro;
> Y porque no, le aborrezco. . .
> Yo le querré eternamente,
> Y eternamente también

Se vengará mi desdén
De lo que en el suyo siento.
(140a/b)

(This is what is happening, Quiñones, I am a hated beloved, disdained and sought after: look at my contradictions! When covered, I arouse his loving passion; when seen, I am ugly and hateful. I cause love and alienation; and competing with myself, I am jealous of myself . . . because he adores me, I adore him; because he does not, I hate him. . . . I will love him eternally and eternally also will my disdain avenge itself for what I feel in his [disdain].)

Happy and angry, loved and spurned, Magdalena has yet to decide how to coordinate her two identities.

What begins to bring them together is the appearance of another person, Angela, disguised as the Countess. At the church once more, Melchor meets who he thinks is his Countess. When she shows him an eye, Ventura says that that is not the eye he saw yesterday. Melchor, however, insists that this is the eye he adores. Magdalena then enters to discover that her competitor knows all. This is so because Quiñones, seduced by Sebastián's offer of money to help him and his sister marry whom they desire—he loves Magdalena and she, Melchor—has told Angela everything. Magdalena's thoughts, now that she has another competitor, split even more, "Que en tres dividirme ves, / Y aunque una sola en tres soy, / Amada en cuanto una, estoy / Celosa de todas tres" (because you see me divide myself in three, and even though I am only one, I am three, loved as one; I am jealous of all three) (146b).

Now moved to take further action, Magdalena, as Countess, invites Melchor to meet her at night at her friend's, Magdalena's, balcony. There she tells him that she really must return to Italy to marry a cousin, and that, as her last request, she wants him to marry Magdalena. Melchor reluctantly agrees only to have the Countess turn on him and accuse him of fickleness.

As he attempts to recoup lost ground by calling Magdalena names, Magdalena appears, invited by the Countess, to hear his oaths. Magdalena, in turn, reinforces the lesson the Countess began, "Quien habla mal en ausencia / De mujeres principales, / . . . / . . . bien será que pierda / Como el crédito conmigo, / El amor de la Condesa" (who slanders absent principal women . . . it is right for him to lose credit with me and the Countess's love) (148a). She then slams the windows shut, leaving Melchor even more deflated than he was when he ear-lier thought he had lost both women.

All the men arrive and threaten Melchor who swears he is there to speak to the Countess. At that moment, Angela steps forth to say that she is the Countess only to be countered by Magdalena, Quiñones, and Santillana. But what is most important in this clarification scene and the conventional marriages that follow—Melchor-Magdalena, Jerónimo-Angela, Ventura-Quiñones—is how Magdalena now char-acterizes and presents herself to Melchor.

Primaj Halkhoree (1989) states that in the final scene, the Count-ess must be eliminated so that Melchor can marry Magdalena, since first, the Countess never existed and second, she stands as an impedi-ment to the marriage (92–93). But that is not correct. The Countess does exist as the embodiment of Melchor's fantasy ideal and thus can never be totally eliminated. No one knows this better than Mag-dalena who, at every turn, runs up against this fantasy. Magdalena, instead of trying to do away with the Countess, incorporates her into her new self. She tells Melchor, along with the united cast, "yo soy la Condesa / (si en el título fingida, / En la sustancia de veras)" (I am the Countess [though in the title feigned, true in substance]) (148c). Her final comment, then, overthrows Melchor's, and Halkhoree's, attempt to fix *a* position, *a* role for Magdalena and thereby undercuts the po-larities both Melchor and Halkhoree see.

If we compare *La celosa de sí misma* with Alarcón's *Examen de maridos* and Moreto's later *El desdén con el desdén,* we can see the degree to which Tirso's play inverts the others. In *Examen,* Inés is set up in a powerful position to test the men who would be her husband. The men, in turn, repress their jealousy and their conflictive and combative nature so as to compete chivalrously for her hand. Compli-cating the matter is Blanca's jealous machinations that would force Inés to marry the man she does not love and therby deprive the men of the choices they would make. However, by following Inés's rules, the men are led to value male friendship above all so that in the end, both women's plans are overturned in favor of the imposition of iden-tificatory unity, patriarchal rule, and the reification of patriarchal values. Since both women engage in "prohibited behavior," they must be tamed. The phallus, to use the Lacanian term, must be wrested from their control and returned to the men, as the women become apologists for the phallocentric system they had momentarily dis-turbed.

Moreto's play takes Alarcón's a step further. In Alarcón's play, the powerful woman began by accepting her father's advice that she marry as a given. In Moreto's *Desdén,* Diana rejects marriage from the outset. As an "antinatural," powerful woman, she refuses to submit to patriarchal law by refusing to take her role as commodity in the marital system of exchange. The smooth progress of the aristocratic society then comes to a screeching halt since Diana rejects the linchpin marriage. She retires to the company of women and takes refuge in anti-male myths. None of the men can figure out how to control her; thus money, time, and energy are wasted in fruitless festivals. Finally, a trickster figure tells his master how, in time, to overthrow the "unnatural" woman by reflecting back her disdain. Eventually all the men participate in the game by courting Diana's maidens and ignoring her completely. She begins to feel neglected by the entire community and soon humbly repents. Then and only then can the sacred marriage occur by which difference and "right order" are restored. Those two plays, as Barbara Freedman (1991) notes about *The Taming of the Shrew,* turn "woman into an apologist for the phallocentric system which oppresses her. . . . [The plays offer] as a corrective to a blatantly diseased aristocratic society the scapegoating of woman as solution; the rebellious woman becomes the cause rather than the symptom of class struggle. Since comedies about the illness of society still masquerade as comedies about the illness of women, it appears that we have not yet escaped the scene of shrew taming" (134). In the Spanish plays, men take on roles that go against their desires only so as to reverse the field on the women. In *La celosa de sí misma,* Tirso changes the perspective and focuses on the problems caused by the men and their concepts as he posits woman as she who knows and teaches. In *Desdén* and *Examen,* difference must be silenced; in *Celosa,* difference is proclaimed by and incorporated into the female lead.

Tirso recognizes gender roles as arbitrary but necessary and continually shows the price women must pay for participation in the system they inhabit. What rattles, however, is the limited, culturally specific, narrow roles in which men cast them. Woman exists as a fantasy, as a theatrical construct, Tirso shows; as *La celosa de sí misma,* along with other plays, ends, marriage occurs, thereby insisting on woman's prescribed role in the exchange system as the basis for civilization. Nonetheless, what this play and others by Tirso illustrate is the woman's conscious, painful awareness of how man tries to fit them with a unitary mask. While the mask can never be destroyed, Magdalena's performance (which stands in counterpoint to the narrative thrust of the play) works to show Melchor and the audience that any one definition of her is wholly inadequate to her protean being.

In that sense in this play, if we adopt the distinction between theater and drama, theater works dialectically against drama.

In Chapter 3 I wrote of the suture. That notion could now be extended here to encompass theater itself. To a large degree an actress, a living human being, is "sutured" into a role in a play. That role is a constraining form whose overarching structure, shape, and direction is controlled first by an author and then a director. The overlaps between the actress's self and the character she represents may be many or few. While the actress cannot control what happens to the character she plays, still in all she does have a certain, admittedly limited, freedom—through voice, inflection, tone, gesture, movement, makeup, and so forth—to affect how the character will be seen or understood. "Theater," Barbara Freedman (1991) remarks, "is always placing the living body's energies in tension with a constraining form, it is always recording the cost of entry into the symbolic" (142). The actress's energies, however, can work with or against the prescribed role; she can help the audience "view from another angle the looks that inscribe us, and so look back" (142).

The Madrid society depicted as *La celosa de sí misma* opens has become a stale repetition of prescribed roles and values. Both Melchor and Magdalena stand ready to fulfill the roles their fathers have agreed they will play. The fathers, in turn, are playing out their roles as guarantors of the future based on the past. Sebastián too has his future already decided, "Un hábito he pretendido, / Que ya medio conseguido" (I have sought a knighthood, now half obtained) (129b); he has "seis mil ducados de renta" (six thousand ducats in income) and a marriageable sister to oversee. Likewise Jerónimo sees himself as a continuation of his father's successes, living in Madrid with the expectation of inheriting half his substantial wealth. Luis, Melchor's cousin, has just gained his *mayorazgo* (primogeniture inheritance) through the legal system and, in comparison to Melchor, is rich. Though Luis loves Magdalena, he will not compete with his cousin for her hand because of their family ties, because of the advantage Melchor's arranged marriage represents for the poorer relative, and because Luis's wealth would put him in an unfair position, "Vos sois pobre; vuestra dama / Tiene sesenta mil pesos, /. . . / Yo soy rico, y vuestro deudo: / No he de competir con vos" (You are poor; your lady has sixty thousand pesos. . . . I am rich, and your relative: I will not compete against you) (133b).

There seems no place in this world of fixed roles, paternal and filial duties, honor, family ties, of money's power, wherein operates the smooth passing down from father to son of wealth and position through the fulfilling of pre-scribed tasks, for anything like true desire, self-development, or recognition of the multiplicity of the self and the other to exist. Desire exists, of course, but it is often seen as illicit: Magdalena's fears of Melchor's pre- and postnuptial wanderings, Luis's repressions, or Angela's and Sebastián's transformation of desire into violence.

The play shows the tensions underlying the seemingly smooth functioning of this repetitive social machine. Money is one of the oils that keeps the machine humming along. Money will surely improve Melchor's future as it rewires the broken connection between his social position and economic standing. Likewise, the arranged marriage and the social benefit it offers will help Alonso erase any smirch deriving from his enrichment abroad since through his buying power he can acquire an untouchable patent by marrying Magdalena into the Leonese family. Both Luis and Sebastián believe that money will give them an advantage over the insolvent Melchor. When Angela remarks to her brother, "Don Melchor es muy galán" (Melchor is very gallant), he responds, "Pero más lo es el dinero" (but money is more so) (139a). Yet money's power has a nasty side too. Melchor feels that the lure of Alonso's money has deprived him of his right to choose (128b/c): money, or the lack of same, places him in an inferior position. Money can also threaten the justice system that should guarantee society's fairness and exemplify Madrid as the king's home:

> Tiene en sus calles
> Todos los vicios Madrid.
> Haz cuenta que es una tienda
> De toda mercaduría.
> Siendo así, ¡bueno sería
> Que aquí el interés no venda
> Testigos falsos!
>   (139b)

(Madrid holds all vices in its streets. Understand that it is a store filled with all kinds of merchandise. Since that is true, it would be amazing if money could not buy false witnesses!)

The split between the accepted links of appearance and reality are strongly underscored.

Likewise characters are split, as is clear in the secondary plot in Angela's movement from her anti-marriage to pro-marriage stance; Melchor insists on the differences between the *tapada* (veiled woman)/Countess and Magdalena, perceiving each as separate and opposite from the other. Yet despite the Countess's insistence that she and Magdalena are very similar, from Melchor's perspective, one is the nearly absolute negation of the other. Magdalena's task is bring Melchor to a more flexible view, to teach him that no single description is sufficient: she must reframe him by reframing herself; she must renegotiate her self.

Central to her project are the two roles she plays. Often in Tirso's theater, women must take on two or more roles to bring about a solution to their problems and, of course, those role shifts are a fine mechanism for producing humor. Also, frequently the new roles they take involve a shift on the social scale. Violante, in *La villana de Vallecas,* becomes a *panadera* (breadseller), thus allowing her the freedom to criticize, mock, or burlesque aristocratic male behavior, social customs, and distinctions, and Madrid's upperclass women, as in her *avechucha* (ugly bird) speech quoted earlier. In other plays, women become men, to the horror of the moralists, as in the rollicking *Don Gil de las calzas verdes* or in *La huerta de Juan Fernández,* thereby allowing them to play off gender difference and male roles. Such androgyny underscores disguise's power to set up and call into question categories of identity through overlaid and relativized roles and expose them to dialogic review (see Lloyd Davis 1975, 129–66). In those plays, however, the women take on the new roles rather easily, almost unself-consciously. What sets *La celosa de sí misma* apart from those other plays is precisely the consideration of some of the possible ramifications on the woman for having to adopt those roles; Magdalena often speaks of the pain produced by her divided self. To show Melchor who she is, she must become who she is not. She must work at cross-purposes so as to bring about her desire. She must play unitary roles, the roles he has cast her in, in order to show the insufficiency of his casting and the multiplicity of her self. She encourages Melchor to believe in his fantasies, "Creed, / . . . / Lo que os esté bien en eso" (Believe . . . what's best for you about that) (138b) so as to eventually disrupt those beliefs, to reframe and displace them.

But if we look only at this split in Magdalena, we do not get very far because she merely repeats the duality already imposed by Melchor and by the society in which she lives: woman as angel or devil, castrated or castrator, natural or antinatural, or woman as the mysterious Other. If we keep her in those roles, we can only see her as the superior Countess or the controlled and inferior daughter. Thereby, she seems to swing between either loving or hating Melchor and once more replicates the positions he has always given her. In such a reading, he still holds the controlling position: he loves her as the Countess and hates her as Magdalena. For some, the mere inversion of the relationship (woman superior, man inferior), wherein as Countess she controls Melchor may be enough. But this love/hate, controlling/controlled duality simply reproduces what Ellie Ragland-Sullivan (1991) calls "a Sisyphean ritual whose repetition becomes its own *raison d'être*" (55). Such a ritual involves (gender) power politics that would place woman alternately in superior and inferior roles.

If woman or man is reduced to a role, an identity, or a class, a power politics is invoked that forces the man or woman to become one with the cultural norm. Such a position can be occupied by a man or a woman "who seeks to identify with difference where difference delineates the one who knows, the possessor of the law" (Ragland-Sullivan 1991, 54). Such men or women accept the patriarchal order's division of the world and live by its master tropes: this is what a man is, this is what a woman is, "soy quien soy." Culture imposes gender difference from birth; thus gender identity is an enforced ideology and always political.

Melchor, as the play opens, says that he knows who and what he is. He knows that he is to play out his role in the arranged marriage because Magdalena will bring to their union the financial security he and his father lack. Yet he feels that he has no active role in the determination of his life's partner; thus when he sees the Countess, he infuses her with all those aspects he finds lacking in Magdalena and fulfilling to his self-concept. With the Countess he would have not only wealth and prestige, but an idealized beauty, a fantasy that he and his cultural norms have created together. Thus to marry her is to be true to himself while marrying Magdalena would be false since there is something missing in her and in him. Melchor believes in his metaphors, sees them as offering a unity: Magdalena is this, the Countess is that. Metaphor tries to reduce the multiple to the singular, whereas plurality and not singularity is the characteristic of every woman and man.

Magdalena knows that she is "Magdalena" and that she is the "Countess" as well, but she also knows that she is not just "Magdalena" nor the "Countess." If Magdalena knows, then we can posit yet another position for her, a position inside and outside of the roles Melchor and Alonso prescribe for her. That other role, however, is not that of synthesis within the thesis-antithesis-synthesis triad; rather, it is more negotiator or mediator among the roles she is capable of playing—"Magdalena," "Countess," true lover, wife, trickster, avenger, and so on—within the cultural confines in which she operates. Love is important to Magdalena, but love is not enough if it is accompanied by her immanent reduction, for "to stake all on love or on *an* interpretation is to opt for imaginarized symbolic answers that close out knowledge of the human masquerade going on before our eyes" (Ragland-Sullivan 1991, 74).

At the end of the play, Melchor says that he now recognizes the hand (the fetishized part-object) as belonging to both the Countess and to Magdalena. He then says, "en ella sella mis labios." One way of reading his statement would, of course, be formulaic: he recognizes his misrecognition and begs her pardon. Another way would be to hope that Melchor has learned the lesson Magdalena has been trying to teach him; thus "sella mis labios" might indicate that he recognizes her multiplicity and will cease his essentializing metaphorization—she is this, she is that—and quietly but knowingly accept the plurality she is and thus the plurality he must also be. He will accept mix and contradiction; he will attempt to forgo the inherited ideological roles he projects upon her, and upon himself. He will, in a word, seal his lips, since he realizes that no eternal hierarchical or symmetrical relation between himself and her can be finally spoken.

Magdalena's self-theatricalization, her framing and reframing herself, then, works on the side of the performative, of the theater as opposed to drama, on the side of the semiotic, to resist the tyranny of the role(s) Melchor, Alonso, Sebastián, and Jerónimo would cast her in. Though in the end she accepts the role of "wife," even there she cannot be seen as "unitary." Earlier in the play, she promised "Yo le querré eternamente, / Y eternamente también / Se vengará mi desdén / De lo que en el suyo siente" (I shall love him eternally, and eternally also will my disdain avenge itself, for what I feel in his [disdain]) (140b). That promise stands as a warning against any final attempt to impose the single mask of the humble wife over her multifaceted self.

If Magdalena creates a space for resistance to the roles others would imprison her in, so too do some men resist traditional precepts and suffer as well. In *La moza de cántaro*, Don Juan finds himself the object of the affection of the wealthy widow, Ana, despite the fact that his friend, the Conde, desires her. Juan has no interest in Ana; rather, he is embarrassed by her attentions because of his friendship with the Conde and because he has fallen in love with Isabel, the *moza de cántaro* (literally: the girl with the jug, i.e., watercarrier). In an *academia*-like reunion in Ana's house, Ana, the Conde, and then Juan recite poems they wrote, and each poem reflects something about the character (see Chapter 1). Juan declares his strong attraction to a *moza de cántaro* to whom, when he saw her filling her water jug, "rendí la vida" (I surrendered my life) (1117). Immediately both Ana and the Conde criticize him for his choice of subject matter. "¿Un caballero discreto / escribe a tan vil sujeto? / No lo creyera jamás" (A wise gentleman writes to such a vile subject? I would never believe it) (1122–24), emphatically states the piqued Ana. The only way such a subject might be acceptable, she declares, is if Juan employs the *moza* as metaphor, "Si es disfrazar vuestra dama, / como suelen los poetas, / por tratar cosas secretas / sin ofensa de su fama, / está bien; pero, si no, / bajo pensamiento ha sido" (if it is to disguise your lady, as poets often do, to treat secret things without offense to her fame, it is fine; but if not, it is an unworthy thought) (1133–38). Juan replies that he is not speaking metaphorically to which Ana rejoins that such a woman would be better for Martín, Juan's servant, than for "un caballero, un hombre / como vos" (a gentleman, a man like you) (1161–62).

José María Diez Borque (Vega, Lope de 1990), in his introduction to the play, states that in this scene, Ana "juzga a Doña María más adecuada para el amor de Martín (judges Maria more adequate for Martín's love) (vv. 1158 y sigs.); 'cosa baja' (a lowly thing) (vv. 1184–1185)" (41). The appreciation of this play depends on perspective. From the audience's perspective, as Diez Borque insists, there is no conflict, or rather, to use his words, "es un falso conflicto" (it is a false conflict) (42) because the person about whom Juan speaks is not really a peasant, but Doña María instead. He is surely correct, provided that the audience maintains throughout the play sufficient distance from the action, provided that they see ironically all that Juan says. But from Juan's perspective, a perspective shared throughout the play by Ana and by the Conde, "Doña María" does not exist; who exists is Isabel and it is she who Ana thinks more appropriate for Martín. Unable to think beyond their social prejudices, Ana and the Conde condemn in the strongest possible terms Juan's infatuation with the watercarrier because love must align with rank. Juan, on the other hand, has a different view of love:

> No es elección
> amor; diferentes son
> los efetos de su nombre.
> Es [la moza], desde el cabello al pie,
> tan bizarra y aliñosa,
> que no es tan limpia la rosa,
> por más que al alba lo esté.

Tiene un grave señorío,
en medio desta humildad,
que aumenta su honestidad
y no deshace su brío.
Finalmente, yo no vi
dama que merezca amor
con más fe, con más rigor.

(1162–75)

(Love is not free choice; different are the effects of its name. From head to toe she is gallant and refined, no rose even at dawn is as pure. In her humbleness she has a noble bearing about her that augments her honesty and does not diminish her spirit. Finally I never saw a lady who deserved more faithful, unswerving love.)

to which Ana takes more than passing umbrage for social and personal reasons. Juan, however, sees beyond appearances to Isabel's inner qualities.

Throughout the rest of the play, Juan struggles with his feelings and the social opprobrium that they create but he holds firm in his love of Isabel. "Vive Dios, que te he querido / y te quiero y te querré" (By God, I have loved you, I do love you and I will love you) (2255–56), he swears to her. In a later monolog he vows that he will not lose her no matter what, that such is her beauty and her nobility of spirit that "del cántaro por armas pienso honrarme" (I shall honor myself by taking the jug as my coat of arms) (2419–20). When in the final scene before the gathered cast he declares his love for Isabel and his intention to marry her, Ana declares him mad and the Conde says that he will kill Juan before allowing "tal bajeza" (such vileness) (2643). Then the Conde tells his servants to take Isabel away and kill her, "¡Hola, criados! ¡Echad / esta mujer hechicera / por un corredor, matadla!" (Listen, servants! Throw this witch into a hallway, kill her!) (2644–46). For the Conde, there is no other possible explanation than that Isabel is a witch for no nobleman could possibly want to marry such a lowly creature. But Juan represents another kind of nobility that has little to do with social state. Jaime Fernández (1989), in an article that parallels my own thoughts about the characters and the play, states:

La actitud de Don Juan tiene todos los rasgos de la auténtica discreción, en el sentido de conducta ética recta, porque ha sabido usar la razón y enfrenar sus sentimientos instintivos más bajos. En este punto, sin lugar a dudas, reside la verdadera grandeza del caballero. (444)

(Juan's attitude has all the marks of true discretion, in the sense of upright ethical conduct, because he has learned to use his reason and bridle his lowest instincts [in opposition to the *indiano* who tries at one point in the play to rape Isabel]. In this, undoubtedly, resides the gentleman's true greatness.)

Juan's insight and fidelity, despite censure from those of his class, finds its double reward first in Isabel's reciprocal love and then in her restoration to her true state, Doña María. The play, then, ends in orthodoxy but not before Juan has declared his unorthodox love.

Unlike *La moza de cántaro* wherein the audience knows from the outset that Doña María/Isabel is noble, in *Esto sí que es negociar*, Leonisa's familial lines are not sorted out until the very last scene. While throughout the play there are more than enough hints that she is not just the rustic she seems to be, until the *dea ex machina* end, despite her beauty, her virtue, intelligence, and wit, all believe she springs from peasant roots.

When Rogerio suddenly becomes heir to the Duke of Bretaña, when he recognizes the young man as his illegitimate son—the Duke's official marriage proved barren; thus he now wants Rogerio to inherit his holdings—Rogerio now feels compelled to turn away from his childhood sweetheart, Leonisa, and bow to his newly discovered father's wish that he marry Clemencia, the Duke's niece and Duchess of Orleans. Rogerio rejects Leonisa and though he tries to maintain neutrality if not disdain toward her in his public dealings with her, Rogerio suffers intensely. "Perdíte," he soliloquizes, "ya no es posible / en desiguales estados / dar alivio a mis cuidados / . . . / Intentar cumplir mi amor / por medio menos que honesto / ni aún pensarlo . . . / Morir, Leonisa, es mejor" (I have lost you; it is no longer possible, given the inequality of estates, to seek relief from my cares. . . . To attempt to satisfy my love by less than honest means is unthinkable . . . Leonisa, it would be better to die) (972–74, 982–84, 986). Though he might have been able to marry her when he was the son of a lower noble—his other father wants her to marry Filipo, another nobleman—now he believes that he cannot given his unexpected elevation. He is trapped between social imperatives springing from recently inherited notions of class boundaries and his long-standing affection.

Throughout the play, as Leonisa schemes to bring Rogerio to a new understanding of the true values beneath outward appearances, she and others mount a growing defense of the nobility of spirit. Leonisa begins:

> Si es el alma la que da
> valor, aquélla será,
> que es mejor, mas bien nacida.
> ¿No es más noble el alma, cielo
> de pensamientos mejores?
> ¿no son los míos mayores,
> pues encumbran más su vuelo?
> (1047–53)

(If the soul is what is truly wanting, then the one that is best is the one born best. Heavens, isn't the most noble soul the one with the best thoughts? Aren't mine greater since they soar so high?)

When Rogerio jealously argues with Filipo, who is more than willing to marry Leonisa despite her presumed class fetters, Filipo replies to Rogerio's objections with his "no mancha el mar una gota / de tinta" (a drop of ink does not discolor the sea) speech, commented on in Chapter 1. Once alone, Rogerio meditates on Filipo's comparisons:

> La imagen del roble bella
> con que Filipo me avisa
> en abono de Leonisa
> puede obligarme a querella.
> El cielo ha encerrado en ella
> discreción de más valor
> que la calidad mayor
> y es ignorante bajeza
> despreciar por la corteza
> lo que es noble en lo interior.
> (2094–2113)

(The image of the lovely oak with which Filipo admonishes me and vouches for Leonisa could oblige me to love her. Heaven has included in her discretion of great value as her greatest quality and it is vile ignorance to scorn for the bark what is noble inside.)

He then extends Filipo's examples to include the nature/nurture realm that Shakespeare exploited so well in the May festival discussion between Perdita and Polixenes (*The Winter's Tale,* IV, iv) (see Chapter 1). Rogerio has seen the truth of Filipo's logic but must still fight the pressure of traditional ways of being.

Enrique, Clemencia's spurned lover, works with Leonisa to carry out her plan—she "becomes" the Duchess Margarita—and at one point in the play, even this high-ranking man is so taken by the "rustic woman's" charms and abilities that he exclaims:

> Pero Leonisa es de modo
> que, aunque en sangre desigual,
> si ser quiere el principal,
> temo que se alce con todo.
> Perlas enseña su risa,
> cielos logra su presencia,
> ¿qué tiene que ver Clemencia
> con los ojos de Leonisa?
> Pero, ¿qué digo? ¿Estoy loco?
>   (2200–2208)

(But Leonisa is such that even though in blood she is unequal, if she wants to be first, I fear she will take the prize. Her smile shows pearls, her presence is heavenly, how can Clemencia compare with Leonisa's eyes? But, what am I saying? Am I mad?)

He questions his sanity because Enrique, as will shortly be shown, has a strong class bias, thus being attracted to Leonisa and then comparing her advantageously to Clemencia must be madness.

Rogerio must learn to see Leonisa's inner values; to do so he must learn to resist the social imperatives and inherited mind-sets within which he believes it necessary to operate when he becomes heir apparent to the dukedom. When "Margarita" appears, Rogerio thinks that she represents a way out of the quandry. So perfectly does the noble Margarita physically mirror Leonisa that he believes that by marrying the simulacrum he can solve his problems. However, as part of the plan, Enrique asks the old Duke for her hand before Rogerio can, but that does not prevent Rogerio from proposing anyway. He tells Margarita that he does not love Clemencia but that she, on the other hand, is the very picture of who he loves. He proposes, thereby declaring his willingness to act in the face of social and familial opposition.

But Rogerio's lessons are not over yet. When he speaks with Enrique about his intentions toward Margarita, the latter, following Leonisa's plan, says that he will cede to Rogerio's wishes to marry her because he, Enrique, now wants to marry a *serrana* (mountain girl), namely Leonisa. Rogerio erupts:

> ¡Pues sacaréos yo la lengua
> con que ese sí le habéis dado!
> pues, si ha de ser Margarita
> mi esposa, y a esotra imita,
> quien della está enamorado
> de mi esposa lo estará.
> (2597–2602)

(I will cut out your tongue if you have said yes to her! because if Margarita is to be my wife and she looks like this other woman, then whoever is in love with her will be in love with my wife.)

Rogerio then proposes to Leonisa. Thereafter he approaches madness as he laments his divided self and his inability to merge the two women. In the end, however, since he cannot conflate the two, he must choose and he decides for Leonisa no matter what, "(Si mi padre se indignare, / perdone, que en más estimo / ser de mi serrana esposo / que del Duque Carlos hijo)" (If my father becomes indignant, I am sorry, for I esteem more being my mountain girl's husband than Duke Carlo's son) (2820–23). Then before the united cast he explains:

> Su [de Leonisa] esposo tengo de ser
> aunque el patrimonio rico
> pierda que en Bretaña adquiero
> y otra vez viva estos riscos.
> Sé que he de perder la vida
> luego que pierda el arrimo
> que hasta agora la sustenta.
> (2874–80)

(I must be her husband even if I lose the rich patrimony I acquired in Bretaña and once more must live on these cliffs. I know that my life is lost as soon as I lose the support that has sustained it up to now.)

At that moment, the real Margarita arrives and declares Leonisa her long-lost cousin, thereby allowing Rogerio to marry with neither loss of position nor face. While throughout the play the audience has had numerous hints of Leonisa's real social status, Rogerio has not and he has been unable to make the two women—Leonisa and "Margarita"—one. He has had to anguish over his choice and over the results of that choice; he has had to chose between inner values and social appearance. Thus when he decides for Leonisa, he is willing to relinquish that which matters less, the dukedom, to have the woman he loves by his side. In the end, her "class" matters less than she.

The lesson—look beyond social prejudice—is driven home from another angle, interestingly by the two characters to whom social class seems to matter more than anything. First, Enrique criticizes Rogerio. The latter has spent most of his life in the country as the son of a local noble. Though he had the privileges of his father's rank, money, and education, and though he is respected by the locals as a good and fair man, there is a great chasm to be leapt from there to the court, from there to the heir to the throne. Thus when Enrique sees his beloved Clemencia, Duquesa de Orliens, enamored of this upstart, he not so subtly shifts his love complaint to the political register, to terms invoking tyranny and usurpation:

> ¿Y será razón
> que *tiranice un bastardo*
> mis esperanzas, Clemencia?
> ¿Es bien que, amándoos los dos,
> me venga a *usurpar* con vos
> destos *estados* la herencia
> un pobre, hijo de una sierra,
> entre rústicos criado?
> (1138–45; my emphasis)

(Is it right for a bastard to tyrannize my hopes, Clemencia? Is it right, you two being in love, for him to come and usurp, with you, the inheritance of these states, since he is a poor man, son of the mountains, raised among rustics?)

Adopting a position in many ways parallel to Rogerio's toward Leonisa when Rogerio is suddenly elevated, Enrique complains of the bastard's luck, of his lowly upbringing and rustic social environment. The equally haughty Clemencia—see her attitude toward Leonisa whom she calls *grosera, rústica, bárbara, malcriada* (gross, rustic, barbarous, ill bred) (728–852)—

in a speech that parallels Filipo's speech about Leonisa, defends the natural worth of the Duke's rural bastard:

> El oro, que idolatrado
> es en el mundo, se encierra
> en las groseras entrañas
> de un monte, una sierra fría
> diamantes produce y cría;
> plata nos dan las montañas
> más ásperas, que después
> goza del mundo imperio.
> Nació en los montes Rogerio,
> mas es diamante, oro es,
> que os hace tanta ventaja
> en presencia y discreción
> que cualquier comparación
> es con él humilde y baja.
>
> (1146–59)

(Gold, idolized in the world, is enclosed in the gross innards of a mountain, a cold mountain range produces and nurtures diamonds; the roughest mountains give us silver which then enjoys dominion over the world. Rogerio was born in the mountains, but he so far outdistances you in presence and discretion that any comparison with him is humble and low.)

Since Enrique can come to admire Leonisa and Clemencia can fall in love with the bastard and prefer him over the well-born Enrique, both of these characters stress in the secondary plot the lessons of the primary plot.

One of the things that these three plays have in common is the search for the self and the other by questioning who and what one is or would/could be in terms of the societal and cultural givens, norms, expectations, and received values. One way of looking at this questioning is through the binary division of the public and private self. Thomas A. O'Connor (1993) remarked recently that the "Spanish *comedia* as genre apparently never tired of presenting the dichotomy of personal/private self in conflict with the social/public self" (176). The range of resolutions to such questioning runs from privileging the former, as in Inés's acceptance of the role her father prescribes (*El examen de maridos*), to emphasizing the latter, for example by the overthrow of arranged marriage or the willingness to give up social status to marry by choice (*Esto sí que es necociar*). In the process of negotiating the personal and the private, desire and duty, impulse and imperative, characters often find themselves divided to the point of madness. Onstage, division can also be represented through disguise. It seems as though to become "someone else," to express other, hidden, or unknown aspects of their persona, characters change clothes.

A character's division, however, should not be viewed solely as a binarism since a binary division already preexists the character's new role. For example, Violante in *La villana de Vallecas* is already both the noble and the dishonored woman before she becomes the breadseller; Angela in *La dama duende* is already the quiet widow living humbly in her brother's house and the frustrated, attractive young woman flirting in the plaza before adopting the roles she uses to lead Manuel through the labyrinth. The new persona then creates a third term from an already binary relation thus introducing a crisis, creating a space for challenge, or "deconstructing" the original relations. If the second role questions the self-sufficiency and unitary identity of the first, then the third, standing amidst and above the two, opens a path out of the gainsaying affirmation/negation of the binary (see Garber 1993, 11). The character who changes clothes also changes personality, perspective, rank, and often, linguistic registers (Violante in *La villana de Vallecas,* Baltasar in *Desde Toledo a Madrid*). Through clothing and the changes it brings, boundaries blur between noble/non-noble, lower noble/higher noble, even between male/female. Such crossovers point to a crisis of category and also to "a *category crisis elsewhere,* an irresolvable conflict or epistemological crux that destabilizes comfortable binarity, and displaces the resulting discomfort onto a figure that already inhabits, indeed incarnates, the margin" (Garber 1993, 17; emphasis in original). That crisis elsewhere might well be what lay at the heart of the moralists' complaints about theater and its "excesses." The world was changing, older values appeared to be breaking down and with them the traditional male and female roles. A certain social mobility was questioning the traditional hierarchy, people were on the move, lawsuits multiplied, economic problems worsened—all of this shows up in the plays and the characters, some of whom adopt disguises and/or marginal positions to seek solutions to problems. Such marginal characters in these comedies include widows, servants, itinerant sales- or servicepersons, soldiers, *toqueras, panaderas, mozos de mulas, mozas de cántaro, duendes, indianos* (headress sellers, breadsellers, muleteers, water carriers, phantoms, returnees from the Indies). The creation of the other, the third, is most often represented on stage by changing costume. In the Golden Age as well as today, clothes make the person; characters know that and dress for success.

Clothing is central to the last play that I will write about, Tirso's *Desde Toledo a Madrid,* a comedy that deals with a marriage between Mayor and Luis arranged by Mayor's father, Alonso, and overthrown by collusion between Mayor and Baltasar. To carry out the overthrow, Baltasar, a Cordoban noble, dresses as Lucas Berrío, a *mozo de mulas* (muleteer).

After Baltasar kills a man at night in Toledo, he breaks into Alonso's house seeking refuge from the law, and accidentally locks himself in Mayor's room. Fearing the wrath of the owner and charges of ignominy, "Hallándome aquí encerrado, / doy sospecha a una bajeza / indigna de la nobleza / que mi sangre ha profesado" (If they were to find me enclosed here, my presence would give rise to suspicions of vileness unworthy of the nobility my blood has professed) (796b), he catches his breath and looks around the room. After an inventory and by means of the clothing and furnishings he sees, he knows that the woman who lives here is noble, but her furnishings inspire certain feelings in him, "al paso que considero / la autoridad, policía / y el adorno que viendo estoy, / crece en mí con el respeto / el recelo" (as I consider the authority, neatness, and the adornment I am seeing, along with my respect, my fear grows) (797b). He already respects her but worries about how she will react when she finds him there. Clothing and furnishings function as indices of her nobility, decency, propriety, and virtue. Everything in the room is culturally and socially readable.

Mayor enters complaining to her maid about her upcoming forced marriage. The maid leaves, Mayor sees Baltasar, and faints. When she comes to in his arms, she accuses "Don Luis" of vile impatience, fearing that he has come to her room before he has the right to do so. But when she discovers that the man is not her promised husband, her fears increase. Baltasar begins to explain his presence, Mayor seeks a candle, and in the light it gives off, Baltasar finds the visual confirmation of his earlier reading of her possessions, "¡Qué divina perfección!" (What divine perfection!) he exclaims. On seeing him, Mayor too begins to relax and then to believe his story because she notes "el talle bien nacido" (well-born form) (801b). The two feel an instant attraction for each other but Mayor believes it fruitless since she must leave on the morrow for Madrid to marry Luis. She helps Baltasar escape and adds, "Don Baltasar, / creed que me he de casar, / por vos, muy de mala gana" (Baltasar, believe that I must marry, but because of you, unwillingly) (803a).

In the second act, on the road toward Madrid, Baltasar appears dressed as a *mozo de mulas* (muleteer); when we hear him we see that in the disguise he has shifted linguistic registers. "Bonda pan y queso / para beber un trago" (there is a lot of bread and cheese, and to drink, a swallow [of wine]) (810a), he declares to his companions. Mayor feigns illness to escape the coach and ride Baltasar's, or rather Lucas Berrío's mule with him at her side. Alone for a few minutes, Mayor expresses dismay at Baltasar's clothing:

> ¿Ansí se desautoriza
> valor y sangre que ilustra
> persona de tantas partes?
> ¿No pudiera hallar la industria
> artificio más decente?
>
> (811b)

(Thus do you devalue the worth and blood that shows in a person of so many gifts? Couldn't your ingenuity find a more decent ruse?)

Baltasar counters that his disguise is the best possible idea; dressed as he is, he can accompany her nearly unnoticed by her father, Luis, and the other noble members of the retinue. He adds that were it not for the love he feels for her: "¿pareceos a vos, señora, / que osaran poner en duda / indecencias deste traje / el valor que disimulan?" (does it seem to you, my lady, that [I would allow] the indecencies of those clothes to put in doubt the value they disguise?) (811b). To insist on his true worth, he tells her that he is pursuing a lawsuit in Madrid that should make him a marquis with ten thousand more in income. He concludes that the humble apparel and identity should be seen as a sign, a profession, of his love—that a man so noble as he would become for her a *mozo de mulas* (muleteer). Mayor begins to understand:

> Prométoos que cuando os vi
> concertar cabalgaduras
> con mi padre esta mañana,
> diestro en la desenvoltura,
> interesable en el precio,
> malicioso en las preguntas
> y grosero en el lenguaje,
> que hizo el alma conjeturas
> sobre si érades de veras

lo que parecéis de burla;
mas satisfíceme luego;
que el alma no se deslumbra,
cuando quiere bien, por sombras
que verdades disimulan.

(813a)

(I swear that when I saw you with my father arranging for the mounts expert in your free and easy manner, mercenary about the price, malicious in your questions, and vulgar in your language, my soul wondered if you were in truth what you seem in jest; but now I know; the soul does not dazzle when it truly loves, rather with shadows it disguises its truths.)

Culturally conditioned to read clothing and language indexically, Mayor begins to learn another way of seeing as Baltasar begins to show her an essentialist view of the self that surpasses the accidentals. Mayor must learn to read through to the subtext of truth beyond the "anecdotal" level where the others stop, to see that which lies beneath the apparel, to discern the message. Outward appearance can trick many, but if the two are to really communicate, they both must go beyond only what they see.

Yet Baltasar uses the normal culturally conditioned means of reading to "prove" to Luis that he "is" what he appears so that Luis will not suspect Baltasar's intentions. Luis addresses Lucas/Baltasar as "mozo de mulas" (muleteer) (814a), and Lucas counters that he is a "sobrestante del ganado," a fact easily understood if only one looks at the clothing:

Los que en calzones de lienzo
monterilla con punta
al cogote y alpargatas,
a pata en invierno sudan,
son mancebos de camino,
mas los que en cabalgadura
acompañan, con espuela,
sombrero, calza de abuja,
su borceguí encima della,
manga o jubón de camuza,
capotilla de rajeta,
valona y liga que cruza,
espada y daga de ganchos;

estos tales se entitulan
sobrestantes del ganado.
(814a/b)

(Those in canvas trousers, small cap that comes to a point in
back and hemp sandals, on foot and sweaty in the summer are
walking helpers, but those who ride, with spurs, hat, sewn leg-
gings with buskins over them, long sleeves or jackets of
chamois, varicolored light-cloth capes, walloon collars and
crossed garters, sword and hooked knife, those hold the title of
stock foremen.)

Clothing, he deceptively swears to his rival, is an accurate, readable
text not only among nobles but among the working classes as well.

Lucas's marginalized identity allows him a freedom he could not
have were he dressed in Baltasar's normal attire. For one, he can put
his hands on Mayor, lifting her onto his mule. Luis objects, but Baltasar says that this is part of his job, "Paso, hidalgo, que no se usa /
quitalle el oficio a nadie: / cada cual al suyo acuda" (Easy, sir, it is not
right to deny anyone his position: everyone in his place) (814b).

That evening, Lucas spurs the mule and runs off with Mayor for a
long interview about his past, present, and future prospects (819–22).
Luis searches for them in the dark and overhears the last part of
their conversation when Mayor promises to marry Lucas:

Es desvarío
pensar que ha de cautivarme
amante a quien no me inclino,
cuando le hace ventajas
tantas el señor Berrío.
(822b)

(It is crazy to think that a lover who I am not inclined to can
hold me when Mr. Berrío offers so many advantages over him.)

Fuming, Luis decires Mayor's perfidy and barbarism, swearing to
"dar castigo / a tan bárbara elección / y al infame desatino / de tu
desigual amante" (punish such a barbarous choice and your unequal
lover's infamous folly) (822b). Mayor cools him down by playing once
more on appearance and on culturally conditioned stereotypes. Lucas,
she says, "es el tonto más sencillo / . . . que vio Toledo" (is the sim-
plest fool . . . that Toledo has ever seen) (823b), and she has decided to

play a joke on him by promising to be his wife, a misalliance so gross that everyone but a simpleton would laugh at even the thought. Alonso roars with pleasure looking forward to the diversion from the tedium of travel, but Luis squirms everytime Lucas gets near Mayor.

In the third act, Mayor promises herself publicly to Lucas during the "marriage ceremony":

BALTASAR: ¿quiere en fin, ser mi mujer?
MAYOR: ¿Pues no lo habrá de querer?
             Digo que sí.
BALTASAR: ¿Y se obliga
             a quedarlo desde aquí?
MAYOR: Mil veces sí. ¿Queréis vos
             ser mi marido?
BALTASAR: Resí.
                  (834a)

(B. Do you want to be my wife? M. Well, shouldn't I want to? I answer yes. B. And do you promise to be so from here on? M. A thousand times yes. Will you be my husband? B. Yes and yes again.)

Luis burns, "¡Vive Dios que me dan pena / estas burlas!" (By God these jests are painful to me!) (834a).

In the end, after a brief absence, Baltasar returns "muy bizarro" (841a). Alfonso recognizes the man as a fine noble but fails to see that he and Lucas are one in the same. Baltasar explains that he has returned for his bride, Mayor:

> no se altere
> ninguno: Lucas Berrío
> está aquí, si ya no quieren
> que sea Don Baltasar
> de Córdoba.
>
>   (841a)

(let no one get upset Lucas Berrío is here, if he's not also Baltasar of Cordoba.)

He must explain to the "blind" Alonso and Luis that he is both the wealthy, shrewd noble, future marquis and the humble, loving, simple Lucas. Baltasar's clothing and comportment show him to be noble to those who stop with appearance, just as Lucas's clothing first so distressed Mayor and led the men to think him a fool. Clothing shows only the outside and that appearance is legible; however, there are manifest and latent readings. In the end, Alonso reads Baltasar's clothing and statements as proof that he is a wealthy and powerful, soon to be titled, man and thus a better catch, as it were, than Luis; thus he agrees to the new marriage. For him, Lucas Berrío was little more than a ruse. For Mayor, Lucas Berrío, after the initial shock, proved to her the strength of Baltasar's love, so strong that a nobleman would disguise himself as a lowly worker only to be near her. Baltasar has taught her, at least, to read through externals.

Disguise, along with Baltasar's and Mayor's ludic performances, creates a carnivalesque atmosphere in the play, producing its humor. In the end, Baltasar changes costume, resumes his true identity, and order is restored, but both the humble and the elegant costumes are true and false. Disguise is a double-edged sword that, while neither always supportive of or antithetical to dominant values, allows some viewers to perceive order and hierarchy while others see the permeability of normal, traditional limits, the openness of apparently closed boundaries. Carnival and theater may teach some, as the moralists feared, to explore regulations, push boundaries, and not return docilely to the fold. Carnival celebrates, as some writers insist, the *temporary* liberation from prevailing truths and established order, but it and comedy may also teach just how tenuous that order is. If by simply changing clothes, one may gain a measure of freedom, then the person in disguise is a threat to traditional order. Since changing clothes is fundamental to theater, then theater, as some moralists insist, is indeed dangerous.

In this period, sumptuary laws were passed in an attempt to control appearance. In 1621, for example, prostitutes were required to wear short *mantos* to differentiate themselves from honorable women (Deleito y Piñuela 1948, 49; Rodríguez Marín 1948, 178). In 1600, laws were passed to prohibit the use of *broqueles* (bucklers) to all but royalty, priests, and knights (Sempere 1788, 99), and in 1611, pages and other servants were prohibited from using certain items (Sempere 1788, 104). The sumptuary laws also extend beyond clothing to include other abuses, such as coaches and even forms of address.

As the sumptuary laws attempted to control social legibility, thereby insisting on social order, so too did the moralists and some legislators attempt to restrict what could be shown on stage in an effort to control what could be written and "read." Clothing can be an index of stability or instability because its proper or improper use can make the wearer legible or illegible, safe or dangerous, as changing costume in *comedia* clearly shows.[3] While *Desde Toledo a Madrid* returns to orthodoxy when Baltasar appears in his noble's garb to claim Mayor, he will not let the assembled cast nor the audience forget Lucas Berrío, nor could the audience totally forget that the costume he now wears is, in fact, only one more guise worn by an actor whose "true identity" is hard to see behind the garments, and whose success is measured by how well he plays the part he is currently outfitted for. Disguise and clothing stress the "createdness" of category at the same time that it threatens, potentially, to undermine it.

If the audience understands the power of clothing through which one can "become" someone else, act differently, speak differently, be perceived and accepted differently, then that same audience might begin to reconsider the notion of category itself. It might begin to realize that category, like the clothes that emblematize it, are manmade, not God-given. If one can become someone else simply by changing clothes, then perhaps the accepted order is less permanent than hitherto believed. As Melveena McKendrick (1974) notes referring to a parallel context, "Indeed, art may have influenced reality. Most of the incidents involving [real] women in masculine dress, for example, belong to the period when their dramatic counterparts were already well-established stage characters. It is not impossible that the theatre inspired some real-life 'mujeres varoniles' to take action or at least suggested to them the form that action might take" (43). The self lives in exchange, is not forever fixed, and can look to models from literature as well as from life for new ways to conceive itself.

In the real world, clothing can work like costume and disguise in theater to emphasize, to bring to the fore the display and the fashioning—in the sense of production—of the self. Disguise re-presents

---

3. Such legibility was often difficult outside of the theater, as can be seen from the following, "Tres o cuatro días ha que prendieron aquí a un hombre, el cual por la mañana antes de amanecer se vestía unos andrajos y se fingía tullido y enfermo, y con grandes lástimas y súplicas pedía hasta cerca de la una. Luego se recogía a su aposento y comía y se vestía de seda a las mil maravillas y se peinaba. Es de buen talle, y salía como un pino de oro a pasearse" (Three or four days ago they arrested a man here who, before dawn, dressed in rags and pretended to be sick and crippled, and with loud complaints and supplications begged until nearly one P.M. Then he withdrew to his rooms and ate and dressed marvelously in silk, and combed his hair. He has a good figure, and he went out looking very handsome to stroll about) (*Cartas de algunos PP. de la Compañía de Jesús* 1862, 6:305). Also, in the *Noticias de Madrid* (1942), 1622, "Este día prendieron a un hombre estrangero, porque fingió ser del Hábito de Santiago y le traía puesto" (Today they arrested a stranger because he pretended to belong to the Knighthood of Saint James and wore its special garb) (40). How many who used disguises and were not caught, no one can know.

what Lloyd Davis (1975) has called "the ideology of characterization" (10). Costume both identifies and misidentifies. In the comedies, characters adopt disguise when they can think of no other way of solving a problem or of bringing their goals to fruition. Though in the final scenes characters remove their masks, still in all there always remains a residue, a trace of the mask, and with it, the new perspectives, mobility, and freedom it brought. The disguised characters, at the end of the play, are not what they were in the beginning. Disguise and the success it brings highlights the continual negotiation of the self. Thus the question arises as to exactly what differences there are between the character and the role(s) she or he played, and between those and the "essential self" that Mariana strove to protect and preserve. Theater and theatricality plays a central role, then, in any debate between true and false selves. Disguise can be used to question or to reaffirm social values; it can be used to highlight what was there in the character's initial makeup or it can add or reveal new and sometimes unexpected or disturbing facets of the self. What cannot be controlled, however, is how character and disguise will be received by an audience, for the characters in these plays have more than one dimension and new possibilities peek out from behind the mask.

One of the moralists' fears about theater was that it taught people in the audience how to act, speak, and present themselves differently. Theater has the potential, as Juan de Mariana believed, to exert such an effect on everyone, "de toda edad, sexo y calidad" (of every age, sex, and quality) (413a). From his perspective, that effect is corrosive, but from another perspective, it may be liberating. Theater teaches, at times, that one's role is not necessarily fixed forever and that acting cannot be confined to the stage. The fear is that if the ties that bind, if the relation between sign and meaning come asunder, if social and sexual identities can be faked, can be mutable, then society itself may come unhinged.

These comedies engage their historical moment in many different ways, of which I have sought to suggest only a few. In the last several years, students of Spanish Golden Age theater have focused on the relations between literary works and their historical cultural milieu, showing the integration of *comedia* into its culture as well as *comedia*'s ability not just "to reflect" the world, but to comment, affirm, and criticize, perhaps even to mold opinions, attitudes, and beliefs. The continuing debate over whether *comedia* was an accomplice or a tool in the dissemination of aristocratic values or whether it was a subversive agitator, smilingly undermining those same values even as it pretended to comply with them is symptomatic of redirected concerns.

As I said near the beginning of this study, these comedies were written and represented in a monarchical, imperialist, Catholic, semi-feudal, semimercantalist, proto-capitalist, heterosexual and male-dominated, sexist, racist, stratified society. Moreover, characters in the plays achieve whatever happiness they do, and find whatever solutions to problems they may within that given, overarching society. But that does not mean that the society or *comedia* was of one piece, stable, monocular, and homogeneous. The seventeenth century in Spain, and in Europe, was an age of crisis and conflict, of competing parties and ideas, and populated by many powerful heterogeneous, multifaceted, and contradictory voices. It was a period of economic, political, and social problems; international, regional, and civil wars; of migrations, agricultural difficulties; of epidemics, religious dissension, and suspicion, all in a country—Spain—only nominally unified, and wherein regional and local customs, traditions, rights, and languages varied enormously. Even the role of the king and his ministers was widely debated, though monarchy itself was rarely questioned.

To maintain the polar divisions between the complicitousness or subversiveness of *comedia,* to my mind, is too facile, too sweeping to be of great value in explaining the complex relations between the plays and their historical circumstances. For though such works as *Desde Toledo a Madrid* and *El examen de maridos* both end in marriage, they nevertheless foreground differently the role of men and women and offer us concepts, comparisons, language, and perspectives that we can use to discuss the adequacy of such roles. Though plays like *Esto sí que es negociar* and *La moza de cántaro* present characters who are really noble and only seem to be or pretend to be commoners, the plays present perspectives on social responsibility, social prejudice, and the nature of nobility from which we can explore questions of individual worth and personal choice. While the plays inevitably end in orthodoxy, the characters still in all find or make a space for agency within the strictures they inhabit and which to varying degrees inform them, and thereby create space for dialogue.

The plays explore, sometimes extoling, sometimes criticizing, the ideas and values of their society. The characters live in a network of values and relationships that control and depress, liberate and excite them at the same time, and it is those relationships and structures, with their joys and sorrows, that made their lives meaningful to them and to their audience. In part, what makes these comedies funny and appealing is how the characters bend the rules, how they cleverly cope with the strictures they live in to get what they want. That they end up where society would have wanted them anyway was, no doubt, comforting and satisfying to many. What horrified others was the path the characters blazed to get there, and whether one foregrounds the path or the destination could provoke radically different reactions. What an audience might take away from the theater, then, would depend on each person's perspective, a perspective that neither the dramatist nor the censor could totally control. And that inability to control the interplay of perspectives among the plays, their contexts, and the audience was what made comedy, to many people's minds, open and dangerous.

Appendix

The following is a list of the plays considered in this volume and their dates (culled from various sources).

Amar sin saber a quién (Lope de Vega)
   1620–22, Morley and Bruerton

Amor, pleito y desafío (Lope de Vega)
   1621, Morley and Bruerton

El astrólogo fingido (Calderón de la Barca)
   1624–25, Valbuena Briones

¡Ay verdades que en amor . . . ! (Lope de Vega)
   1625, Morley and Bruerton

Los balcones de Madrid (Tirso de Molina)
   1622–24, Cazottes

Casa con dos puertas mala es de guardar (Calderón de la Barca)
   1629, Valbuena Briones

La celosa de sí misma (Tirso de Molina)
   1621, Wade; 1622–23, Kennedy

La dama duende (Calderón de la Barca)
   1625, Greer; 1629, Valbuena Briones, Greer

Desde Toledo a Madrid (Tirso de Molina)
1625, Kennedy

En Madrid y en una casa (Tirso de Molina)
1625–26, Kennedy

Esto sí que es negociar (Tirso de Molina)
1623–25, Kennedy

El examen de maridos (Juan Ruiz de Alarcón)
1623–25, King

El hombre pobre todo es trazas (Calderón de la Barca)
1628, Valbuena Briones

La huerta de Juan Fernández (Tirso de Molina)
1626, Kennedy, Pallares

La moza de cántaro (Lope de Vega)
1625, Kennedy; before 1627, Morley and Bruerton

Por el sótano y el torno (Tirso de Molina)
After 1623, Kennedy

Por la puente Juana (Lope de Vega)
1624–25, Morley and Bruerton

El premio del bien hablar (Lope de Vega)
1624–25, Morley and Bruerton

La toquera vizcaína (Juan Pérez de Montalván)
1628–29, J. Parker

La villana de Vallecas (Tirso de Molina)
1620, Kennedy

Select Bibliography

Albrecht, Jane. 1994. *Irony and Theatricality in Tirso de Molina*. Ottawa: Dovehouse Editions (Ottawa Hispanic Studies, 16).

Actas de las Cortes de Castilla. 1913. Vol. 36. Madrid: Sucesores de Rivadeneyra.

Agheana, Ion Tudor. 1972. *The Situational Drama of Tirso de Molina*. Madrid: Playor.

Alcalá-Zamora, José N. 1989. *La vida cotidiana en la España de Velázquez*. Madrid: Ediciones Temas de Hoy.

Alcalá-Zamora y Torres, Niceto. 1949. *El derecho y sus colindancias en el teatro de Don Juan Ruiz de Alarcón*. Mexico City: Imprenta Universitaria.

Althusser, Louis. 1972. *Lenin and Philosophy and Other Essays*. New York: Monthly Review Press.

Altman, Ida. 1989. *Emigrants and Society: Extremadura and America in the Sixteenth Century*. Berkeley and Los Angeles: University of California Press.

Alvar Ezquerra, Alfredo. 1989. *El nacimiento de una capital europea: Madrid entre 1561 y 1606*. Madrid: Turner Libros, Ayuntamiento de Madrid.

Arjona, J. Homero. 1937. "El disfraz varoniol en Lope de Vega." *Bulletin Hispanique* 39:120–45.

Arquero Soria, Francisco. 1992. *La Virgen de Atocha*. Vol. 8 of *Temas Madrileños*. Madrid: Instituto de Estudios Madrileños.

Arrellano, Ignacio. 1984. "El sabio y melancólico Rogerio: interpretación de un personaje de Tirso." *Criticón* 25:5–18.

———. 1988. "Introducción a "Don Gil de las calzas verdes." In *Tirso de Molina. Marta la piadosa, Don Gil de las calzas verdes*, 40–68. Barcelona: PPU.

Asensio, Jaime. 1981. "Tirso, Vargas y Juan Fernández." In *Homenaje a Tirso,* 119–31. Madrid: Revista "Estudios."

Ashcom, B. B. 1960. "Concerning 'La mujer en hábito de hombre' in the *Comedia.*" *Hispanic Review* 28:43–62.

Astrana Marín, Luis. 1935. *Vida azarosa de Lope de Vega.* Barcelona: Juventud.

Azorín, Francisco. 1991. *Leyendas y anécdotas del viejo Madrid.* Madrid: Avapiés. Original edition, 1983.

Barish, Jonas. 1981. *The Antitheatrical Prejudice.* Berkeley and Los Angeles: University of California Press, 1981.

Barnes, Trevor J., and James S. Duncan, eds. 1992. *Writing Worlds: Discourse, Text, and Metaphor in the Representation of Landscape.* London: Routledge.

Barrell, John. 1972. *The Idea of Landscape and the Sense of Place, 1730–1840: An Approach to the Poetry of John Clare.* Cambridge: Cambridge University Press.

Barthes, Roland. 1986. "Semiology and the Urban." In *The City and the Sign: An Introduction to Urban Semiotics,* edited by M. Gottdiener and Alexandros Ph. Lagopoulos, 87–98. New York: Columbia University Press.

Belsey, Catherine. 1980. *Critical Practice.* London: Methuen.

———. 1985. "Disrupting Sexual Difference: Meaning and Gender in the Comedies." In *Alternative Shakespeares,* edited by John Drakakis, 166–90. London: Methuen.

Bennassar, Bartolomé. 1973. "Etre noble en Espagne. Contribution à l'étude des comportements de longue durée." In *Mélanges en l'honneur de Fernand Braudel.* 95–106. Toulouse: Edoard Privat.

———. 1979. *The Spanish Character.* Berkeley and Los Angeles: University of California Press.

———. 1983. *La España del Siglo de Oro.* Translated by Pablo Bordonava. Barcelona: Editorial Crítica.

Benstock, Shari. 1991. *Textualizing the Feminine: On the Limits of Genre.* Norman: University of Oklahoma Press.

Benveniste, Emile. 1971. *Problems in General Linguistics.* Miami: University of Miami Press.

Bergmann, Emilie. 1991. "The Exclusion of the Feminine in the Cultural Discourse of the Golden Age: Juan Luis Vives and Fray Luis de León." In *Religion, Body and Gender in Early Modern Spain* edited by Alain Saint-Saens, 124–36. San Francisco: Mellen Research University Press.

Blanco Aguinaga, Carlos, Julio Rodrígues Puértolas, and Iris M. Zavala. 1981. *Historia social de la literatura española.* Vol. 1. Madrid: Castalia.

Blue, William R. 1986. "Echoing Desire, Mirroring Disdain: Moreto's *El desdén con el desdén.*" *Bulletin of the Comediantes* 38, no. 1:137–46.

Borch-Jacobsen, Mikkel. 1991. *Lacan the Absolute Master.* Translated by Douglas Brick. Stanford: Stanford University Press.

Braudel, Fernand. 1974. "The Mediterranean Economy in the Sixteenth Century." In *Essays in European Economic History, 1500–1800,* edited by Peter Earl, 1–44. Oxford: Clarendon.

———. 1982. *Civilization and Capitalism, 15th–18th Century.* Vol. 2, *The Wheels of Commerce.* Translated by Sian Reynolds. New York: Harper and Row. French original, 1967.

Bravo-Villasante, Carmen. 1955. *La mujer vestida de hombre en el teatro español (siglos XVI–XVII).* Madrid: Revista de Occidente.

Bristol, Michael D. 1989. *Carnival and Theater: Plebian Culture and the Structure of Authority in Renaissance England.* London: Methuen, Routledge. Original edition, 1985.

Brown, Jonathan. 1978. *Images and Ideas in Seventeenth-Century Spanish Painting.* Princeton: Princeton University Press.

Buezo, Catalina. 1992. *El carnaval y otras procesiones burlescas del viejo Madrid.* Madrid: Avapiés.

Butler, Martin. 1987. *Theatre and Crisis, 1632–1642.* Cambridge: Cambridge University Press. Original edition, 1984.

Calderón de la Barca, Pedro. 1973. *Obras completas I, II,* ed. Angel Valbuena Briones. Madrid: Aguilar.

Callahan, William J. 1980. *La Santa y Real Hermandad del Refugio y Piedad de Madrid, 1618–1832.* Madrid: Instituto de Estudios Madrileños.

Campos, Juana G., and Anas Barella. 1975. *Diccionario de refranes.* Madrid: Anejos del Boletín de la Real Academia Española.

Caro Baroja, Julio. 1965. *El carnaval, analísis histórico-cultural.* Madrid: Taurus.

Cartas de algunos PP. de la Compañía de Jesús. 1862. Edited by Pascual de Gayangos y Arce. Memorial Histórico Español, 13–19. Madrid: Imprenta Nacional.

Castañeda, James A. 1974. *Agustín Moreto.* New York: Twayne.

Cervantes, Miguel de. 1958. *Don Quijote de la Mancha I, II,* ed. Martín de Riquer. Barcelona: Juventud.

Chueca, Fernando. 1951. *El semblante de Madrid.* Madrid: Revista de Occidente.

Cipolla, C. M., J. H. Elliott, and P. Vilar, eds. 1979. *La decadencia económica de los imperios.* Madrid: Alianza Editorial. Original edition, 1973.

Cixous, Hélène. 1974. "The Character of Character." *New Literary History* 5:383–402.

———. 1983. "The Laugh of Medusa." In *The Signs Reader: Women, Gender and Scholarship,* 279–97. Chicago: Chicago University Press.

Cohen, Walter. 1985. *Drama of a Nation: Public Theatre in Renaissance England and Spain.* Ithaca: Cornell University Press.

Colección de documentos inéditos para la historia de España, 69. 1883. Madrid: Miguel Ginesta. Original edition, 1881.

Corral, Helia M. 1981. "Elementos populares, puntos sobresalientes y comentarios sobre *La moza de cántaro* de Lope de Vega." In *Lope de Vega y los orígenes del teatro español,* 449–60. Madrid: Edi-6.

Correa Calderón, E., ed. 1950. *Costumbristas españoles.* Madrid: Aguilar.

Cosgrove, Denis E. 1984. *Social Formation and Symbolic Landscape.* London: Croom Helm.

Cosgrove, Denis E., and Stephen Daniels, eds. 1988. *The Iconography of Landscape.* Cambridge: Cambridge University Press.

Cotarelo y Mori, Emilio. 1904. *Bibliografía de las controversias sobre la licitud del teatro en España*. Madrid: Est. tip. de la "Revista de Archivos, Bibliotecas y Museos."

Covarrubias, Sebastián de. 1943. *Tesoro de la lengua Castellana o Española*. Barcelona: S.A. Horta. Original edition 1611; reprint 1674.

Cruz, Anne J. 1989. "Sexual Enclosure, Textual Escape: The *Pícara* as Prostitute in the Spanish Female Picaresque Novel." *Seeking the Woman in Late Medieval and Renaissance Writings*, edited by Sheila Fischer and Janet E. Halley, 135–59. Knoxville: University of Tennessee Press.

Cruz, Anne J., and Mary Elizabeth Perry, eds. 1992. *Culture and Control in Counter-Reformation Spain*. Minneapolis: University of Minnesota Press.

Darst, David H. 1974. *The Comic Art of Tirso de Molina*. Estudios de Hispanófila, 28. Chapel Hill: University of North Carolina Department of Romance Languages.

Davis, Lloyd. 1975. *Guise and Disguise: Rhetoric and Characterization in the English Renaissance*. Toronto: University of Toronto Press.

Davis, Natalie Zemon. 1975. *Society and Culture in Early Modern France*. Stanford: Stanford University Press.

De Armas, Frederick. 1976. *The Invisible Mistress: Aspects of Feminism and Fantasy in the Golden Age*. Charlottesville, Va.: Biblioteca Siglo de Oro.

———. 1986a. "'*En Madrid y en una casa*': un palimpsesto de amantes invisibles." In *IX Congreso de la Asociación Internacional de Hispanistas*, edited by Sebastian Neumeister, 341–51. Berlin: Vervuert.

———. 1986b. *The Return of Astrea: An Astral-Imperial Myth in Calderón*. Lexington: University Press of Kentucky.

De la Villa, Julián. 1956. *Historia del Hospital General*. Madrid: Sección de Cultura.

De Lauretis, Teresa. 1984. *Alice Doesn't: Feminism, Semiotics, Cinema*. Bloomington: Indiana University Press.

Del Corral, José. 1966. *La fecha de los dibujos del plano de Texeira*. Madrid: Anales del Instituto de Estudios Madrileños.

———. 1976. "Las casas a la malicia." Ciclo de Conferencias 6. Madrid: Ayuntamiento de Madrid, Instituto de Estudios Madrileños.

———. 1982. *Las composiciones de aposento y las casas a la malicia*. Madrid: Instituto de Estudios Madrileños.

———. 1987. *El Madrid de los Austrias*. Madrid: Avapiés. Original edition, 1983.

———. 1990. *Los misterios de Madrid en el Siglo de Oro*. Madrid: Avapiés.

Deleito y Piñuela, José. 1942. *Sólo Madrid es corte*. Madrid: Espasa-Calpe.

———. 1943. *. . . También se divierte el pueblo*. Madrid: Espasa-Calpe.

———. 1946. *La mujer, la casa y la moda (en la España del Rey Poeta)*. Madrid: Espasa-Calpe.

———. 1947. *El declinar de la monarquía española*. Madrid: Espasa-Calpe.

———. 1948. *La mala vida en la España de Felipe IV*. Madrid: Espasa-Calpe.

———. 1952. *La vida religiosa bajo el cuarto Felipe*. Madrid: Espasa-Calpe.

———. 1988. *El rey se divierte*. Madrid: Alianza Editorial.

Derrida, Jacques. 1976. *Of Grammatology*. Translated by Gayatri Chakravorty Spivak. Baltimore: Johns Hopkins University Press.

Díaz Plaja, Fernando. 1983. "Un día madrileño en tiempos del Emperador." *Anales del Instituto de Estudios Madrileños* 20, special issue.

Díez Borque, José María. 1976. *Sociología de la comedia española del siglo XVII.* Madrid: Cátedra.

———. 1977. *Estructura social del Madrid de Lope de Vega. Ciclo de conferencias sobre Madrid en el siglo XVII.* Madrid: Ayuntamiento de Madrid, Instituto de Estudios Madrileños.

———. 1978. *Sociedad y teatro en la España de Lope de Vega.* Barcelona: Bosch.

———. 1990. *La vida española en el Siglo de Oro según los extranjeros.* Barcelona: Ediciones del Serbal.

Dollimore, Jonathan. 1984. *Radical Tragedy: Religion, Ideology and Power in the Drama of Shakespeare and His Contemporaries.* Chicago: Chicago University Press.

Domínguez Ortiz, Antonio. 1960. *Política y hacienda de felipe IV.* Madrid: Ediciones Pegaso.

———. 1963. *La sociedad española en el siglo XVII.* Madrid: Consejo Superior de Investigaciones Científicas.

———. 1984a. *Crisis y decadencia de la España de los Austrias.* Barcelona: Ediciones Ariel. Original edition, 1969.

———. 1984b. *Política fiscal y cambio social en la España del siglo XVII.* Madrid: Instituto de Estudios Fiscales.

———. 1991. "La nobleza cortesana en el antiguo régimen." In *Visión histórica de Madrid (Siglos XVI al XX).* Madrid: Real Sociedad Económica Matritense de Amigos del País.

Drakakis, John, ed. 1985. *Alternative Shakespeares.* London: Methuen.

Dramáticos contemporáneos a Lope de Vega, vol. 2. 1924. Ed. Ramón de Mesonero Romanos. Madrid: Librería de los sucesores de Hernando.

Durán, María Angeles, ed. 1981. *Actas de las primeras jornadas de investigación interdisciplinaria. Nuevas perspectivas sobre la mujer.* Madrid: Universidad Autónoma de Madrid.

———, ed. 1984a. *Actas de las segundas jornadas de investigación interdisciplinaria. La mujer en la historia de España (siglos xvi-xx).* Madrid: Universidad Autónoma de Madrid.

———. 1984b. "Lectura económica de Fray Luis de León." In *Nuevas perspectivas sobre la mujer,* 257–73. Madrid: Seminario de Estudios de la mujer de la Universidad Autónoma de Madrid.

Eagleton, Terry. 1983. *Literary Theory: An Introduction.* Oxford: Basil Blackwell.

———. 1986. *William Shakespeare.* Oxford: Basil Blackwell.

Earle, Peter, ed. 1974. *Essays in European Economic History, 1500–1800.* Oxford: Clarendon.

Egido López, Teofanes. 1973. *Sátiras políticas de la España moderna.* Madrid: Alianza Editorial.

Elliott, J. H. 1977. "Self-Perception and Decline in Early Seventeenth-Century Spain." *Past and Present* 74:41–61.

———. 1982a. "Introspección colectiva y decadencia en España a principios del siglo xvii." In *Poder y sociedad en la España de los Austrias,* edited by J. H. Elliott, 198–223. Barcelona: Editorial Crítica.

———, ed. 1982b. *Poder y sociedad en la España de los Austrias.* Barcelona: Editorial Crítica.

———. 1986. *The Count-Duke of Olivares: The Statesman in an Age of Decline.* New Haven: Yale University Press.

Elliott, J. H., and José de la Peña, eds. 1978. *Memoriales y cartas del Conde Duque de Olivares.* 2 vols. Madrid: Ediciones Alfaguara.

Erickson, Peter B. 1991. "Sexual Politics and the Social Structure in *As You Like It*." In *Shakespeare's Comedies,* edited by Gary Waller, 156–67. New York: Longman.

Escohotado, Antonio. 1991. *El espíritu de la comedia.* Barcelona: Anagrama.

Espadas Burgos, Manuel. 1977. *Abastecimiento y alimentación de Madrid en el Siglo XVII. Ciclo de Conferencias sobre Madrid en el Siglo XVII,* vol. 13. Madrid: Ayuntamiento de Madrid, Instituto de Estudios Madrileños.

Evans, Malcolm. 1986. *Signifying Nothing: Truth's True Contents in Shakespeare's Text.* Athens: University of Georgia Press.

Evans, Peter W. 1978. "Language and Structure in *La villana de Vallecas*." *Forum for Modern Language Studies* 14:32–41.

Ferguson, Margaret, Maureen Quilligan, and Nancy Vickers, eds. 1986. *Rewriting The Renaissance: The Discourses of Sexual Difference in Early Modern Europe.* Chicago: University of Chicago Press.

Fernández, Jaime, S.J. 1989. "Esencia del amor y valoración de la persona en 'La moza de cántaro' de Lope de Vega." In *Actas del IX Congreso de la Asociación de Hispanistas,* edited by Sebastián Neumeister, 441–48. Frankfurt: Vervuert.

Fernández Utrera, María Soledad. 1993. "'Juegos de lenguaje' en *La dama duende*." *Bulletin of the Comediantes* 45:13–28.

Fisher, Sheila, and Janet E. Halley, eds. 1989. *Seeking the Woman in Late Medieval and Renaissance Writings: Essays in Feminist Contextual Criticism.* Knoxville: University of Tennessee Press.

Foucault, Michel. 1979. *Discipline and Punish: The Birth of the Prison.* New York: Vintage Books.

———. 1980. "Questions on Geography." Translated by Colin Gordon et al. In *Power and Knowledge: Selected Interviews and Other Writings, 1972–1977,* edited by Colin Gordon, 63–77. New York: Pantheon Books.

Fox, Dian. 1991. *Refiguring the Hero: From Peasant to Noble in Lope de Vega and Calderón.* University Park: Pennsylvania State University Press.

Fraser, Nancy. 1989. *Unruly Practices: Power, Discourse, and Gender in Contemporary Social Theory.* Minneapolis: University of Minnesota Press.

Freedman, Barbara. 1991. *Staging the Gaze: Postmodernism, Psychoanalysis, and Shakespearean Comedy.* Ithaca: Cornell University Press.

Freedman, Richard, and Seumas Miller. 1992. *Re-thinking Theory.* Cambridge: Cambridge University Press.

Frege, Gottlob. 1985. *The Foundations of Arithmetic: A Logicomathematical Enquiry into the Concept of Number.* 2d rev. ed. Translated by J. L. Austin. London: Basil Blackwell.

Frye, Northrop. 1957. *Anatomy of Criticism.* Princeton: Princeton University Press.

Gallego, Julián. 1972. *Visión y símbolos en la pintura española del siglo de oro*. Madrid: Aguilar.

Garber, Marjorie B. 1981. *Coming of Age in Shakespeare*. London: Methuen.

———. 1993. *Vested Interests: Cross-Dressing and Cultural Anxiety*. New York: HarperPerennial.

García de la Concha, Víctor, and Jean Canavaggio, et al., eds. 1990. *Teatro del Siglo de Oro: Homenaje a Alberto Navarro González*. Kassel: Edition Reichenberger.

Garzón Pareja, Manuel. 1984. *Historia de la hacienda de España*. Madrid: Instituto de Estudios Fiscales.

Girard, René. 1965. *Deceit, Desire, and the Novel: Self and Other in Literary Structure*. Translated by Yvonne Freccero. Baltimore: Johns Hopkins University Press.

Godzich, Wlad, and Nicholas Spadaccini, eds. 1986. *Literature Among Discourses: The Spanish Golden Age*. Minneapolis: University of Minnesota Press.

Goldberg, Jonathan. 1985. "Shakespearean Inscriptions: The Voicing of Power." In *Shakespeare and the Question of Theory*, edited by Patricia Parker and Geoffrey Hartman, 116–37. New York: Methuen.

Gottdiener, M. 1986. "Culture, Ideology, and the Sign of the City." In *The City and the Sign*, edited by M. Gottdiener and Alexandros Ph. Lagopoulos, 202–18. New York: Columbia University Press.

Gottdiener, M., and Alexandros Ph. Lagopoulos, eds. 1986a. *The City and the Sign: An Introduction to Urban Semiotics*. New York: Columbia University Press.

———. 1986b. Introduction to *The City and the Sign*, 1–22. New York: Columbia University Press.

Graullera, Vicente. 1985. "Mujer, amor y moralidad en la Valencia de los siglos xvi y xvii." In *Amours légitimes, Amours illégitimes*, edited by Agustín Redondo, 109–19. Paris: Centre de Recherches sur l'Espagne des xvi et xvii Siècles.

Greer, Margaret. Unpublished. "The (Self) Representation of Control in *La dama duende*."

———. 1992. *The Play of Power: Mythological Court Dramas of Calderón de la Barca*. Princeton: Princeton University Press.

Gurewitch, Morton. 1975. *Comedy: The Irrational Vision*. Ithaca: Cornell University Press.

Halkhoree, Primaj. 1968. "Satire and Symbolism in the Structure of Tirso de Molina's *Por el sótano y el torno*." *Forum for Modern Language Studies* 4:374–86.

———. 1989. *Social and Literary Satire in the Comedies of Tirso de Molina*. *Ottawa Hispanic Studies* 5. Ottawa: Dovehouse.

Hamilton, Earl J. 1934. *American Treasure and the Price Revolution in Spain, 1501–1650*. Harvard Economic Studies 43. Cambridge: Harvard University Press.

———. 1947. *War and Prices in Spain 1651–1800*. Cambridge: Harvard University Press.

Heath, Stephen. 1977–78. "Notes on Suture." *Screen* 18, no. 4:48–76.

Heiple, Daniel. 1982. "Tirso's *Esto sí que es negociar* and the Marriage Negotiations of 1623." *Bulletin of the Comediantes* 34, no. 2:189–99.

Herrero García, Miguel. 1963. *Madrid en el teatro*. Madrid: Instituto de Estudios Madrileños.

———. 1966. *Ideas de los Españoles del siglo XVII*. Madrid: Gredos.

Hidalgo Monteagudo, Ramón, Rosalía Ramos Guarido, and Fidel Revilla González. 1990. *Madrid literario. Recorridos Didácticos por Madrid.* Madrid: Ediciones La Librería.

Hogan, Patrick Holm, and Lalita Pandit, eds. 1990. *Criticism and Lacan.* Athens: University of Georgia Press.

Hormigón, Juan Antonio, ed. 1983. *V Jornadas de Teatro Clásico Español.* Madrid: Técnicas Gráficas Forma.

Howard, Jean E. 1987. "Renaissance Antitheatricality and the Politics of Gender and Rank in *Much Ado About Nothing.*" In *Shakespeare Reproduced: The Text in History and Ideology,* edited by Jean E. Howard and Marion F. O'Connor, 163–87. New York: Methuen.

———. 1994. *The Stage and Social Struggle in Early Modern England.* London: Routledge.

Howard, Jean E., and Marion F. O'Connor, eds. 1987. *Shakespeare Reproduced: The Text in History and Ideology.* New York: Methuen.

Huston, J. Dennis. 1981. *Shakespeare's Comedies of Play.* New York: Columbia University Press.

Ibáñez Losada, Isabel. 1977. *"El siglo xvii, hablando en plata."* Ciclo de Conferencias sobre Madrid en el siglo xvii. Madrid: Ayuntamiento de Madrid, Instituto de Estudios Madrileños.

Jago, Charles. 1982. "La 'crisis de la aristocracia' en la Castilla del Siglo XVII." In *Poder y sociedad en la España de los Austrias,* edited by J. H. Elliott, 248–86. Barcelona: Editorial Crítica.

Jardine, Lisa. 1993. *Still Harping on Daughters: Women and Drama in the Age of Shakespeare.* 2d ed. New York: Columbia University Press. Original edition, 1989.

Jenkins, Ronald Scott. 1994. *Subversive Laughter: The Liberating Power of Comedy.* New York: Free Press.

Jones, C. A. 1971. "Some Ways of Looking at Spanish Golden Age Comedy." In *Homenaje a William L. Fichter,* edited by A. David Kossoff and José Amor y Vásquez, 329–39. Madrid: Castalia.

Jones, Harold G., and Vern G. Williamsen. 1991. "Dos refundiciones tirsianas: 'Amor no teme peligros' y 'Los balcones de Madrid.'" In *Homenaje a Tirso,* 133–55. Madrid: Revista "Estudios."

Jones, R. O., ed. 1973. *Studies in Spanish Literature of the Golden Age Presented to Edward M. Wilson.* London: Tamesis.

Kagan, Richard L. 1981. *Lawsuits and Litigants in Castile, 1500–1700.* Chapel Hill: University of North Carolina Press.

Kahn, Coppélia. 1991. "The Cuckoo's Note: Male Friendship and Cuckoldry in *The Merchant of Venice.*" In *Shakespeare's Comedies,* edited by Gary Waller, 128–37. New York: Longman.

Kamen, Henry. 1983. *Spain, 1469–1714.* London: Longman.

Kennedy, Ruth Lee. 1942. "On the Date of Five Plays by Tirso de Molina." *Hispanic Review* 10:183–214.

————. 1943. "Studies for the Chronology of Tirso's Theater." *Hispanic Review* 11:17–46.

————. 1971. "Tirso's *Desde Toledo a Madrid:* Its Date and Place of Composition." In *Homenaje a Tirso,* edited by David A. Kossoff and José Amor y Vásquez, 357–66. Madrid: Castalia.

————. 1974. *Studies in Tirso I.* North Carolina Studies in the Romance Languages and Literatures 3. Chapel Hill: University of North Carolina Department of Romance Languages.

Kern, Edith. 1980. *The Absolute Comic.* New York: Columbia University Press.

King, Willard. 1989. *Juan Ruiz de Alarcón, letrado y dramaturgo. Su mundo mexicano y español.* México: El Colegio de México.

Kossoff, A. David, and José Amor y Vásquez, eds. 1971. *Homenaje a William L. Fichter.* Madrid: Castalia.

LaBelle, Jenijoy. 1988. *Herself Beheld: The Literature of the Looking Glass.* Ithaca: Cornell University Press.

Lacan, Jacques. 1977. *Ecrits. A Selection.* Translated by Alan Sheridan. New York: Norton.

————. 1981. *The Four Fundamental Concepts of Psycho-Analysis.* Translated by Alan Sheridan. New York: Norton.

Langer, Susanne Katherina. 1953. *Feeling and Form: A Theory of Art.* New York: Scribner.

Larquié, Claude. 1976. "Barrios y parroquias urbanas: el ejemplo de Madrid en el siglo xvii." *Anales del Instituto de Estudios Madrileños* 12: 33–63.

————. 1985. "Amours légitimes et amours illégitimes à Madrid au XVIIe siècle." In *Amours Légitimes, Amours Illégitimes en Espagne (XVI–XVII siècles),* edited by Augustin Redondo, 69–91. Paris: Centre de Recherche sur l'Espagne des XVI et XVII Siècles.

Larson, Catherine. 1991. *Language and the Comedia: Theory and Practice.* London: Associated University Presses.

Le Flem, Jean-Paul, Joseph Pérez, et al., eds. 1987. *La frustración de un imperio, 1476–1714. Historia de España.* Barcelona: Labor.

Ledrut, Raymond. 1986a. "The Images of the City." In *The City and the Sign,* edited by M. Gottdiener and Aleandros Ph. Lagopoulos, 219–40. New York: Columbia University Press.

————. 1986b. "Speech and the Silence of the City." In *The City and the Sign,* edited by M. Gottdiener and Alexandros Ph. Lagopoulos, 114–34. New York: Columbia University Press.

Lee, Jonathan Scott. 1990. *Jacques Lacan.* Amherst: University of Massachusetts Press.

Legatt, Alexander. 1974. *Shakespeare's Comedy of Love.* London: Methuen.

Lentricchia, Frank. 1980. *After the New Criticism.* Chicago: University of Chicago Press.

León Pinelo, Antonio Rodríguez de. 1931a. *Anales de Madrid.* Vol. 1 of 2 vols. Edited by Ricardo Martorell Téllez Girón. Madrid: Ediciones Maestre.

————. 1931b. *Anales de Madrid de León Pinelo, reinado de Felipe III, años 1598–1621.* Vol. 2 of 2 vols. Madrid: Estanislao Maestre.

Leventen, Carol. 1991. "Patrimony and Patriarchy in *The Merchant of Venice.*" In *The Matter of Difference: Materialist Feminist Criticism of*

Shakespeare, edited by Valerie Wayne, 59–79. Ithaca: Cornell University Press.

Lindenbaum, Peter. 1986. *Changing Landscapes: Anti-Pastoral Sentiment in the English Renaissance.* Athens: University of Georgia Press.

López Jaen, Juan. 1970. *Las murallas de Madrid.* Ciclo de Conferencias sobre monumentos madrileños. Vol. 1. Madrid: Ayuntamiento de Madrid, Instituto de Estudios Madrileños.

Lublinskaya, A. D. 1983. *La crisis del siglo xvii y la sociedad del absolutismo.* Barcelona: Editorial Crítica. Original edition, 1979.

MacCary, W. Thomas. 1985. *Friends and Lovers: The Phenomenology of Desire in Shakespearean Comedy.* New York: Columbia University Press.

———. 1991. *"The Comedy of Errors:* A Different Kind of Comedy." In *Shakespeare's Comedies,* edited by Gary Waller, 30–38. New York: Longman.

MacCurdy, Raymond R., ed. 1971. *Spanish Drama of the Golden Age: Twelve Plays.* New York: Appleton-Century-Crofts.

Malcolmson, Christina. 1991. "'What You Will': Social Mobility and Gender in *Twelfth Night.*" In *The Matter of Difference: Materialist Feminist Criticism of Shakespeare,* edited by Valerie Wayne, 29–57. Ithaca: Cornell University Press.

Malvezzi, Virgilio. 1968. *Historia de los primeros años del reinado de Felipe IV.* London: Tamesis.

Mandel, Adrienne Schizzano. 1985. "La *dama* juega al *duende:* pretexto, geno-texto y feno-texto." *Bulletin of the Comediantes,* 29:41–54.

Marañón, Gregorio. 1972. *El Conde-Duque de Olivares (la pasión de mandar).* 6th ed. Madrid: Espasa-Calpe.

Maravall, José Antonio. 1973. "La imagen de la sociedad expensiva [sic] en la conciencia castellana del siglo xvi." In *Mélanges en l'honneur de Fernand Braudel,* 369–88. Toulouse: Edoard Privat.

Marcus, Leah. 1989. *The Politics of Mirth: Jonson, Herrick, Milton, Marvell and the Defense of Old Holiday Pastimes.* Chicago: University of Chicago Press. Original edition 1986.

Mariana, P. Juan de. 1872. *Obras del Padre Juan de Mariana.* Vol. 31 of *Biblioteca de Autores Españoles.* Madrid: M. Rivadeneyra.

Mariscal, George. 1991. *Contrary Subjects: Quevedo, Cervantes, and Seventeenth-Century Spanish Culture.* Ithaca: Cornell University Press.

Martinengo, Alessandro. 1983. *La astrología en la obra de Quevedo.* Madrid: Editorial Alhambra.

Martínez Kleiser, Luis. 1926. *Guía de Madrid para el año 1656.* Madrid: Imprenta Municipal.

McFadden, George. 1982. *Discovering the Comic.* Princeton: Princeton University Press.

McKendrick, Melveena. 1974. *Woman and Society in the Spanish Drama of the Golden Age: A Study of the "Mujer Varonil."* London: Cambridge University Press.

Mebane, John S. 1989. *Renaissance Magic and the Return of the Golden Age.* Lincoln: University of Nebraska Press.

Menton, Seymore, ed. 1961. *Veinte cuentos españoles del siglo veinte.* New York: Appleton-Century-Crofts.

Mesonero Romanos, Ramón. 1990. *El antiguo Madrid, paseos histórico-anecdóticos por las calles y casas de esta villa.* Madrid: Asociación de Libreros.

Michaels, Walter Benn. 1987. *The Gold Standard and the Logic of Naturalism.* Berkeley and Los Angeles: University of California Press.

Middleton, Thomas. 1976. "The Urban and Architectural Environment of the *Corrales* of Madrid: The Corral de la Cruz in 1600." PhD. dissertation, University of California, Los Angeles.

———. 1982. *"El urbanismo madrileño y la fundación del corral de la Cruz."* In *V Jornadas de Teatro Clásico Español,* edited by Juan Antonio Hormigón. Almagro: Técnicas Gráficas Forma.

Miller, Jacques-Alain. 1977–78. "Suture (elements of the logic of the signifier)." *Screen* 18:24–34.

Molina Campuzano, Miguel. 1960. *Planos de madrid de los siglos xvii y xviii.* Madrid: Instituto de Estudios de Administración Local.

Montero Alonso, José. 1977. *Las comediantas.* Ciclo de Conferencias sobre Madrid en el siglo xvii. Madrid: Ayuntamiento de Madrid, Instituto de Estudios madrileños.

Montrose, Louis A. 1991. "Sport by Sport O'erthrown: *Love's Labor's Lost* and the Politics of Play." In *Shakespeare's Comedies,* edited by Gary Waller, 52–72. New York: Longman.

Neely, Carol Thomas. 1985. *Broken Nuptials in Shakespeare's Plays.* New Haven: Yale University Press.

———. 1991. "Broken Nuptials: *Much Ado About Nothing.*" In *Shakespeare's Comedies,* edited by Gary Waller, 139–54. New York: Longman.

Newman, Karen. 1985. *Shakespeare's Rhetoric of Comic Character: Dramatic Convention in Classical and Renaissance Comedy.* New York: Methuen.

———. 1991. "Renaissance Family Politics and Shakespeare's *The Taming of the Shrew.*" In *Shakespeare's Comedies,* edited by Gary Waller, 41–55. New York: Longman.

Niño Azcona, Lorenzo. 1955. *Biografía de la Parroquia de Santa Cruz de Madrid.* Madrid: Juan Bravo.

Nomland, John V. 1946. "A Laughter Analysis of Three *Comedias* of Tirso de Molina." *Modern Language Forum,* 31:25–40.

Nougué, André. 1956. "Le Théme de l'aberration des sens dans le théâtre de Tirso de Molina: Une source posible." *Bulletin Hispanique* 58:23–35.

Noticias de Madrid 1621–1627. 1942. Edited by Angel González Palencia. Madrid: Ayuntamiento de Madrid.

O'Callaghan, Joseph F. 1975. *A History of Medieval Spain.* Ithaca: Cornell University Press.

O'Connor, Thomas A. 1993. *"Infantas, Conformidad,* and the Marriages of State: Observations on the *Loa* to Calderón's *La púrpura de la rosa."* *Bulletin of Hispanic Studies,* 70.1, 175–85.

Olson, Elder. 1968. *The Theory of Comedy.* Bloomington: Indiana University Press.

Oppenheimer, Max. 1948. "The *Burla* in Calderón's *El astrólogo fingido."* *Philological Quarterly* 27, no. 3:241–63.

Oriel, Charles. 1991. "Deceptive Perceptions: The Metaphysics of Tirso's *Cautela contra cautela."* *Romance Languages Annual,* 2, 510–14.

Parker, Alexander A. 1957. *The Approach to the Spanish Drama of the Golden Age.* London: Hispanic and Luso Brazilian Councils.

———. 1959. "The Approach to the Spanish Drama of the Golden Age." *Tulane Drama Review* 4:42–59.

Parker, Barbara L. 1987. *A Precious Seeing: Love and Reason in Shakespeare's Plays.* New York: New York University Press.

Parker, Geoffrey. 1980. *Europe in Crisis, 1598–1648.* Ithaca: Cornell University Press.

Parker, Jack H. 1975. *Juan Pérez de Montalván.* Twayne World Authors Series 352. Boston: G. K. Hall.

Parker, Patricia, and Geoffrey Hartman, eds. 1985. *Shakespeare and the Question of Theory.* New York: Methuen.

Parr, James, ed. 1972. *Critical Essays on the Life and Works of Juan Ruiz de Alarcón.* Madrid: Editorial Dos Continents.

———. 1991. *After Its Kind: Approaches to the Comedia.* Kassel: Reichenberger.

Pellicer, Casiano. 1804. *Tratado histórico sobre el origen y progresos de la comedia y del historicismo en España.* 2 vols. Madrid: Administración del Real Arbitrio de beneficiencia.

Penning-Roswell, Edmund, and David Lowenthal, eds. 1986. *Landscape Meanings and Values.* London: Allen and Unwin.

Pérez de Montalván, Juan. 1881. *La toquera vizcaína. Dramáticos contemporáneos de Lope de Vega.* Edited by Ramón de Mesonero Romanos. Biblioteca de Autores Españoles. Madrid: M. Rivadeneyra.

Pérez Firmat, Gustavo. 1991. "Rum, Rump, and Rumba: Cuban Contexts for *The Mambo Kings Play Songs of Love.*" *Dispositio* 16:61–69.

———. 1994. *Life on the Hyphen: The Cuban-American Way.* Austin: University of Texas Press.

Pérez, Louis C. 1981. "*La moza de cántaro,* obra perfecta." In *Lope de Vega y los orígenes del teatro español,* 441–48. Madrid: Edi-6.

Pérez Moreda, Vicente. 1980. *Las crisis de mortalidad en la España interior, Siglos XVI-XIX.* Madrid: Siglo Veinte Editores.

Pérez Pastor, Cristóbal. 1901. *Nuevos datos acerca del histrionismo español en los siglos XVI y XVII.* Madrid: La Revista Española.

Perry, Mary Elizabeth. 1980. *Crime and Society in Early Modern Seville.* Hanover, N.H.: University Press of New England.

———. 1990. *Gender and Disorder in Early Modern Seville.* Princeton: Princeton University Press.

Peyton, Myron. 1945. "Some Baroque Aspects of Tirso de Molina." *Romantic Review* 36:43–69.

Philip IV, King of Spain. *A Proclamation for Reformation, Published and Commanded. . . .* 1623. London: Nathaniell Butler, Nicholas Bourne, Thomas Archer.

Pitt, Angela. 1981. *Shakespeare's Women.* Totowa, N.J.: Barnes and Noble.

Poesse, Walter. 1972. *Juan Ruiz de Alarcón.* New York: Twayne.

Profeti, Maria Grazia. 1970. *Montalbán: un commediografo dell'eta di Lope.* Instituto Di Letteratura Spagnola E Ispano-Americana 19. Pisa: Universita di Pisa.

Ragland-Sullivan, Ellie. 1987. *Jacques Lacan and the Philosophy of Psychoanalysis.* Urbana: University of Illinois Press.

————. 1991. "The Sexual Masquerade: A Lacanian Theory of Sexual Difference." In *Lacan and the Subject of Language,* edited by Ellie Ragland-Sullivan and Mark Bracher, 49–80. New York: Routledge.

Ragland-Sullivan, Ellie, and Mark Bracher, eds. 1991. *Lacan and the Subject of Language.* New York: Routledge.

Ranold, Margaret Loftus. 1987. *Shakespeare and His Social Context.* New York: AMS Press.

Read, Malcolm K. 1990. *Visions in Exile: The Body in Spanish Literature and Linguistics, 1500–1800. Purdue University Monographs in Romance Languages* 30. Amsterdam, Philadelphia.

————. 1992. *Language, Text, Subject.* West Lafayette: Purdue University Press.

Redondo, Augustin, ed. 1985. *Amours Légitimes, Amours Illégitimes en Espagne (XVI-XVII siècles).* Paris: Centre de Recherche sur l'Espagne des XVI et XVII Siècles.

————, ed. 1987. *Autour des Parentés en Espagne aux XVI et XVII Siècles: Histoire, Mythe et Littérature.* Paris: Publications de la Sorbonne.

Remiro de Navarra, Baptista, and José Esteban, eds. 1987. *Los peligros de Madrid.* Madrid: Clásicos El Arbol.

Rennert, Hugo Albert. 1909. *The Spanish Stage in the Time of Lope de Vega.* New York: Hispanic Society of America.

Ringrose, Davis R. 1983. *Madrid and the Spanish Economy, 1560–1850.* Berkeley and Los Angeles: University of California Press.

Rire et société dans le théâtre espagnol du Siècle d'Or. 1981. Groupe d'Etudes sur le théâtre espagnol (Centre National de la Recherche Scientifique). Paris: CNRS.

Rodríguez Marín, Francisco, ed. 1948. *Cervantes: Novelas ejemplares I.* Madrid: Espasa-Calpe.

Ruiz de Alarcón, Juan. 1971. *El examen de maridos. Spanish Drama of the Golden Age.* Edited by Raymond R. MacCurdy, 333–77. New York: Appleton-Century-Crofts.

Ruiz Martín, Felipe. 1973. "Demanda y oferta bancarias (1450–1600)." In *Mélanges en l'honneur de Fernand Braudel,* 521–36. Toulouse: Edoard Privat.

Ruiz Ramón, Francisco. 1988. *Historia del teatro español (Desde sus orígenes hasta 1900).* Madrid: Cátedra.

Rull, Enrique. 1990. "Calderón: Razón y desengaño en el género comedia." In *Teatro del Siglo de Oro: Homenaje a Alberto Navarro González,* edited by Víctor García de la Concha, Jean Canavaggio and et al., 536–76. Kassel: Edition Reichenberger.

Sage, Jack W. 1973. "The Context of Comedy: Lope de Vega's *El perro del hortelano* and Related Plays." In *Studies in Spanish Literature of the Golden Age Presented to E. M. Wilson,* edited by R. O. Jones, 247–66. London: Tamesis.

Saint-Saens, Alain, ed. 1991. *Religion, Body and Gender in Early Modern Spain.* San Francisco, Calif.: Mellen Research University Press.

Saínz de Robles, Federico Carlos. 1977. *El teatro en el Madrid del siglo xvii.* Ciclo de Conferencias sobre Madrid en el siglo xvii. Madrid: Ayuntamiento de Madrid, Instituto de Estudios Madrileños.

Sampelayo, Juan H. 1977. *Los días madrileños del siglo xvii.* Ciclo de conferencias sobre Madrid en el siglo xvii. Madrid: Ayuntamiento de Madrid, Instituto de Estudios Madrileños.

Sánchez, Francisco J., and Nicholas Spadaccini. 1992. "Baroque Culture and Individual Consciousness." *Indiana Journal of Hispanic Literatures* 1:63–81.

Sempere y Guarinos, Juan. 1788. *Historia del luxo y de las leyes suntuarias de España.* Madrid: Imprenta Real.

Sepúlveda, Ricardo. 1888. *Madrid viejo.* Madrid: Librería de Fernando Fé.

———. 1898. *Antiguallas.* Madrid: Librería de Fernando Fé.

Sexton, Joyce H. 1978. *The Slandered Woman in Shakespeare.* Victoria, Canada: English Literary Studies Monograph Series.

Shakespeare, William. 1958. *A Midsummer Night's Dream.* The Folger Library General Reader's Shakespeare Series. New York: Washington Square Press.

———. 1959. *As You Like It.* The Folger Library General Reader's Shakespeare Series. New York: Washington Square Press.

———. 1974. *The Winter's Tale.* In *The Riverside Shakespeare,* edited by G. Blakemore Evans, 1564–1605. Boston: Houghton Mifflin.

Shergold, N. D. 1967. *A History of the Spanish Stage from Medieval Times Until the End of the Seventeenth Century.* Oxford: Clarendon.

Shumway, David R. 1989. *Michel Foucault.* Charlottesville: University Press of Virginia.

Sieber, Claudia. 1986. "The Invention of a Capital: Philip II and the First Reform of Madrid (Spain)." PhD. dissertation, The Johns Hopkins University.

Simón Díaz, José. "El arte en las mansiones nobiliarias madrileñas de 1626." *Goya: Revista de Arte* 154:200–205.

———. 1980a. "Autos sacramentales y comedias palaciegas y de colegio en el Madrid de 1626 según un copero pontificio." *Segismundo* 4:85–102.

———. 1980b. "Dos privados frente a frente: El Cardenal F. Berberini y el Conde-Duque de Olivares (Madrid, 1626)." *Revista de la Biblioteca Archivo y Museo* 7 and 8:7–53.

———. 1980c. *Encuentros del Cardenal F. Berberini con Lope de Vega y con el Príncipe de Esquilache en Madrid, 1626.* Madrid: Academia de Arte e Historia de San Dámaso.

———. 1980–81. "Los monasterios de las Descalzas Reales y de La Encarnación en el año 1626." *Villa de Madrid* 66:31–37.

———. 1990. "Calderón de la Barca en una guía literaria de Madrid." In *Teatro del Siglo de Oro: Homenaje a Alberto Navarro González,* edited by Víctor García de la Concha, Jean Canavaggio, et al., 617–28. Kassel: Edition Reichenberger.

Smith, Paul. 1988. *Discerning the Subject. Theory and History of Literature* 55. Minneapolis: University of Minnesota Press.

Smith, Paul Julian. 1988. *Writing in the Margin.* Oxford: Clarendon.

————. 1989. *The Body Hispanic: Gender and Sexuality in Spanish and Spanish American Literature*. New York: Oxford University Press.

Soons, Alan. 1982. *Juan de Mariana*. Boston: G. K. Hall.

Soulier, Didier. 1992. *Calderón et le grand théâtre du monde*. Paris: Presses Universitaires de France.

Stallybrass, Peter. 1991. "The World Turned Upside Down: Inversion, Gender and the State." In *The Matter of Difference*, edited by Valerie Wayne, 201–20. Ithaca: Cornell University Press.

Stoll, Anita K., and Dawn L. Smith, eds. 1991. *The Perception of Women in Spanish Theater of the Golden Age*. Lewisburg: Bucknell University Press.

Stone, Lawrence. 1965. *The Crisis of the Aristocracy: 1558–1641*. Oxford: Clarendon.

Stradling, R. A. 1988. *Philip IV and the Government of Spain, 1621–1665*. Cambridge: Cambridge University Press.

Stroud, Matthew. 1987. "Social-Comic Anagnorisis in *La dama duende*." *Bulletin of the Comediantes* 45:96–102.

Suárez de Figueroa, Christóval. 1913. *El pasagero*. Ed. Francisco Rodríguez Marín. Madrid: Renacimiento.

Sullivan, Henry W. 1976. *Tirso de Molina and the Drama of the Counter-Reformation*. Amsterdam: Rodopi.

————. 1991. "*Homo sapiens* or *Homo desiderans:* The Role of Desire in Human Evolution." In *Lacan and the Subject of Language*, edited by Ellie Ragland-Sullivan and Mark Bracher, 36–48. New York: Routledge.

ter Horst, Robert. 1981. "The Origin and Meaning of Comedy in Calderón." In *Studies in Honor of Everett W. Hesse*, edited by William C. McCrary and José A. Madrigal, 143–54. Lincoln: Society of Spanish and Spanish-American Studies.

————. 1982. *Calderón: The Secular Plays*. Lexington: University Press of Kentucky.

Thomas, Brook. 1987. *Cross-examination of Law and Literature*. Cambridge: Cambridge University Press.

Thomas, Keith. 1971. *Religion and the Decline of Magic*. London: Weidenfield and Nicholson.

Tirsiana: Actas del Coloquio sobre Tirso de Molina. Edited by Berta Pallares y John Kuhlmann Madsen. Madrid: Castalia.

Tirso de Molina. 1913. *Cigarrales de Toledo*. Edited by Víctor Saíd Armesto. Madrid: Biblioteca Renacimiento.

————. 1944. *Comedias escogidas de Tirso de Molina*. Edited by Juan Eugenio Hartzenbusch. BAE 5. Madrid: Ediciones Atlas.

————. 1958. *Obras dramáticas completas*. Vol. 3. Edited by Blanca de los Ríos. Madrid: Aguilar.

————. 1982a. *Los Balcones de Madrid*. Edited by Gisèle Cazottes. Madrid: Ayuntamiento de Madrid.

————. 1982b. *La huerta de Juan Fernández*. Edited by Berta Pallares. Madrid: Castalia.

————. 1985. *Esto sí que es negociar*. Edited by Víctor García Ruiz. Pamplona: Ediciones Universidad de Navarra.

————. *Don Gil de las calzas verdes.* 1991. Ed. and trans. Gordon Minter. Warminster: Aris and Phillips.

Tomás y Valiente, Francisco. 1969. *El derecho penal de la monarquía absoluta (siglos XVI–XVII–XVIII).* Madrid: Editorial Tecnos.

Tovar Martín, Virginia. 1983. *Arquitectura madrileña del siglo XVII (datos para un estudio).* Madrid: Instituto de Estudios Madrileños.

Traub, Valerie. 1991. "Desire and the Difference It Makes." In *The Matter of Difference,* edited by Valerie Wayne, 81–114. Ithaca: Cornell University Press.

Turner, James G. 1979. *The Politics of Landscape: Rural Scenery and Society in English Poetry, 1630–1660.* Cambridge: Harvard University Press.

Varey, John E. 1972. "'*Casa con dos puertas mala es de guardar*': Towards a Definition of Calderón's Comedy." *Modern Language Review* 67:83–94.

Varey, J. E., and N. D. Shergold. 1971. *Teatros y comedias en Madrid: 1600–1650, Estudio y documentos.* London: Tamesis.

Vega, Lope de. n.d. *Cartas completas.* Vols. 1 and 2. Edited by Angel Rosenblat. Buenos Aires: Emecé Editores.

————. 1873. *Amor, pleito y desafío.* Madrid: M. Rivadeneyra.

————. 1990. *La moza de cántaro.* Edited by José María Díez Borque. Madrid: Espasa-Calpe.

Victorio, Juan, ed. 1991. *Poema de Alfonso Onceno.* Madrid: Cátedra.

Vilar, Pierre. 1974. "The Age of Don Quijote." In *Essays in European Economic History, 1500–1800,* edited by Peter Earle, 100–112. Oxford: Clarendon.

Vilar Berrogain, Jean. 1973. *Literatura y economía. La figura satírica del arbitrista en el Siglo de Oro.* Translated by Francisco Bustelo García del Real. Madrid: Revista de Occidente.

Viñas y Mey, Carmelo. 1955. "Notas sobre la estructura social-demográfica del Madrid de los Austrias." *Revista de la Universidad de Madrid* 4:461–96.

Vossler, Karl. 1965. *Lecciones sobre Tirso de Molina.* Madrid: Taurus.

Wade, Gerald E. 1971. "*La celosa de sí misma* de Tirso de Molina." In *Homenaje a William F. Fichter,* edited by A. David Kossoff and José Amor y Vásquez, 755–63. Madrid: Castalia.

————. 1974. "Elements of a Philosophic Basis for the Interpretation of Spain's Golden Age Comedy." In *Estudios literarios de hispanistas norteamericanos dedicados a Helmut Hatzfeld con motivo de su 80 aniversario,* edited by Josep M. Solá-Solé, Alessandro Crisafulli, and Bruno Damiani, 323–47. Barcelona: Ediciones Hispan.

————. 1981. "The *Comedia* as Play." In *Studies in Honor of Everett W. Hesse,* edited by William C. McCrary and José A. Madrigal, 165–77. Lincoln, Neb.: Society of Spanish and Spanish-American Studies.

Waller, Gary, ed. 1991. *Shakespeare's Comedies.* New York: Longman.

Wardropper, Bruce. 1966. "Calderón's Comedy and His Serious Sense of Life." In *Hispanic Studies in Honor of Nicholson B. Adams,* edited by John B. Keller and Karl-Ludwig Selig. Chapel Hill: University of North Carolina Press.

———. 1967. "El problema de la responsabilidad en la comedia de capa y espada." In *Actas del Segundo Congreso de la Asociación Internacional de Hispanistas,* edited by J. Sánchez Romeralo and N. Paulussen, 689–94. Nijemegen.

———. 1978. "La comedia española del siglo de oro." In *Teoría de la comedia,* translated by Salvador Oliva and Manuel Espín. Barcelona: Editorial Ariel.

Wayne, Valerie, ed. 1991. *The Matter of Difference: Materialist Feminist Criticism of Shakespeare.* Ithaca: Cornell University Press.

Weimann, Robert. 1987. *Shakespeare and the Popular Tradition in the Theater.* Baltimore: Johns Hopkins University Press. Original edition, 1978.

Whigham, Frank. 1991. "Ideology and Class Conflict in *The Merchant of Venice.*" In *Shakespeare's Comedies,* edited by Gary Waller, 108–28. New York: Longman.

Williamsen, Vern. 1982. *The Minor Dramatists of Seventeenth-Century Spain.* Boston: G. K. Hall.

Williamson, Marilyn. 1986. *The Patriarchy of Shakespeare's Comedies.* Detroit: Wayne State University Press.

Wilson, Edward M. 1936. "The Four Elements in the Imagery of Calderón." *MLR* 31:34–47.

Wilson, Margaret. 1977. *Tirso de Molina.* Boston: G. K. Hall.

Yarbro-Bejarano, Yvonne. 1994. *Feminism and The Honor Plays of Lope de Vega.* West Lafayette: Purdue University Press.

Zayas y Sotomayor, María de. 1989. *Tres novelas amorosas y tres desengaños amorosos,* edited by Alicia Redondo Goicoechea. Madrid: Editorial Castalia.

Zizek, Slavoj. 1991. "The Truth Arises from Misrecognition." In *Lacan and the Subject of Language,* edited by Ellie Ragland-Sullivan and Mark Bracher, 188–212. New York: Routledge.

INDEX